MAKING LEARNING-CENTERED TEACHING WORK

MAKING LEARNING-CENTERED TEACHING WORK

Practical Strategies for Implementation

Phyllis Blumberg

STERLING, VIRGINIA

Stylus

Library of Congress Cataloging-in-Publication Data
The CIP data for this text has been applied for.

13-digit ISBN: 978-1-62036-894-7 (cloth)
13-digit ISBN: 978-1-62036-895-4 (paperback)
13-digit ISBN: 978-1-62036-896-1 (library
networkable e-edition)
13-digit ISBN: 978-1-62036-897-8 (consumer
e-edition)

Printed in the United States of America

All first editions printed on acid-free paper
that meets the American National Standards Institute
Z39-48 Standard.

Bulk Purchases

Quantity discounts are available for use in
workshops and for staff development.
Call 1-800-232-0223

First Edition, 2019

Dedicated with love to Aaron Miles Kosherick, my first grandchild, born in 2018. May he and his generation learn from learning-centered teachers.

Contents

Preface

Since learning-centered teaching is not a pedagogical fad, you may wish to implement it. Also, higher education administrative leaders and educational developers are applying greater pressure on faculty to use this approach. However, you, like many faculty, may need practical guidance on implementing learning-centered teaching. *Making Learning-Centered Teaching Work: Practical Strategies for Implementation* describes a practical system for changing teaching practices. This book is an easy-to-follow how-to guide for you to achieve learning-centered teaching; it also provides increased evidence for this approach to teaching as well as specific direction on how to begin and how to use the change process gradually to improve teaching. After reading this book, you will be able to apply learning-centered teaching in your courses without sacrificing content and rigor. You will be able to explain to students why they are using this approach and how it will foster deep and long-lasting student learning.

This book is a rethinking of the successful model and strategies I discussed in a 2009 Jossey-Bass book called *Developing Learner-Centered Teaching: A Practical Guide for Faculty*. Ever since this book was published I have been reading the growing literature on learning-centered teaching and making notes on how to improve the model. This book builds on Weimer's (2013) and Blumberg's (2009) ideas by describing a more evidence-based learning-centered teaching model that relies on the advantage of 10 years of experience. *Making Learning-Centered Teaching Work: Practical Strategies for Implementation* has three important innovations:

1. It introduces a preferred order of transitioning to learning-centered teaching.
2. It offers a refined set of components, now called actions, based on the experience of faculty using the initial Blumberg (2009) model.
3. It describes how to assess the implementation of learning-centered teaching.

Current literature on the concepts underlying the actions led to changes in the definitions or explanations. Faculty who used the rubrics provided me feedback that led to a rewording of many of the actions; the wording is clarified to make them more operational and measurable. There are also new actions that reflect current thinking. I have included published examples showing how every action has been used successfully.

Although my 2009 book suggested that the rubrics be used for self-assessment of teaching, that book did not offer guidance on how to do self-assessment. This book explains how the rubrics can be used for assessment, what data should be collected, and how to summarize the data. Furthermore, it describes how the rubrics can be used to assess the learning-centered status of individual faculty members, courses, and educational programs.

How to Use This Book

I wrote this book to help you make learning-centered teaching work for you and your students. This book can help you and your faculty colleagues in the following ways:

- Consider this book a workbook or active planning document, and write your responses to the many prompts for reflection and questions about implementation. There are numerous places where I suggest you record your ideas for implementation (many of which are also available online in a downloadable and editable format) including:
  o Questions on how you can implement ideas discussed in each box
  o Taking Stock exercises at the end of chapters 1, 2, and 8 through 12

o Worksheets on your ideas for transitioning to learning-centered teaching on each construct at the end of chapters 3 through 7

• This books also contains guidance on how to reflect on and personalize your teaching styles. The following are constructs on which to build your frameworks:

o Three actions within the Developing Responsibility for Student Learning construct: the instructor fosters the development of learning skills; encourages self-directed, lifelong learning skills; and fosters the students' use of metacognitive skills and habits of the mind.

o Three actions within the Function of Content construct: the instructor uses organizing schemes that are discipline-specific conceptual frameworks, fosters the development and use of discipline-specific methodologies, and provides practice using inquiry or ways of thinking in the discipline.

o Two actions within the Balance of Power construct: the instructor establishes safe, moral, and ethical environments and allows for some flexibility in course policies, assessment methods, learning methods, deadlines, or how students earn grades.

o Chapter 8: Table 8.1 asks you to catalogue all ideas you thought of in previous chapters.

o The exercise at the end of chapter 8 called Taking Stock: Planning where you would like to use more learning-centered actions and record your thoughts in Box 8.2

• This book can be the topic for a semester-long book group or be a resource for a faculty learning community to increase their use of learning-centered teaching in different ways. Each chapter could be discussed at a different session. Such groups of faculty can also work collaboratively to overcome institutional barriers and resistance to the implementation of learning-centered teaching.

• As faculty are being increasingly asked to document their teaching practices or how effective they are, this book describes a plan for systematically assessing the extent to which they implement learning-centered teaching. This assessment can be used for individual faculty member assessments or for groups of faculty in departments or colleges to document their implementation of learning-centered teaching.

Faculty developers can work with faculty to increase their use of learning-centered teaching in different ways. The format of this book can lead to easy-to-plan faculty development workshops where the worksheets are reflections and used as activities. This is especially useful for part-time faculty developers. Faculty developers can cite the examples in one-to-one consultations with faculty. The book can also be used as the basis for course design institutes. Faculty developers can collaborate with faculty on the assessment of teaching.

The Internet has revolutionized how we read; many people no longer read in a linear fashion, starting at the beginning of a book and reading each chapter (Carr, 2010). Instead, many people skip around and read on a topic of interest in different places in a non-linear manner; therefore, I am providing some ways to read efficiently on selected topics rather than reading complete chapters. Table P.1 shows where you can find information on specific topics.

We are also impatient readers who want to be able to read quickly. Therefore, each chapter has the following features:

• An opening box with highlights of the chapter to help you decide if you want to read this chapter
• Quick-to-read features like figures, bulleted lists, and tables
• Boxes that describe examples of successful implementation that are in the literature (each example includes reflection questions to help you adapt this example to your own type of teaching)
• Chapter summary

Readers can visit the Stylus Publishing website at https://styluspub.presswarehouse.com/browse/book/9781620368954/Making-Learning-Centered-Teaching-Work to download PDFs of Table 8.1, Box 8.2, Appendix B, and Appendix C.

TABLE P.1. Where to Find Specific Information

Topic	Where You Can Find Relevant Information
Working with specific populations or types of courses:	
• STEM	• Box 1.1, Table 1.3, Box 3.2, Box 3.5, Box 4.4, Box 5.5, Box 5.7, Box 6.6, Box 6.8, Box 7.8, the section in chapter 8 called STEM Students, Table 8.3, and Table 8.4
• Foreign language learners	• Chapter 8, Table 8.2
• Underprepared, unmotivated, or first-year college students	• All of chapters 4, Boxes 3.4, 3.7, and the section in chapter 8 called Underprepared, Unmotivated, or First-Year College Students
• Research methods/design courses	• Chapter 3 action on creating appropriate learning outcomes, chapter 5 action on teaching use of discipline-specific research skills, chapter 6 actions on formative feedback, peer and self-assessment, and authentic assessment and their associated boxes, the list embedded in the chapter 8 section called "Suggestions for Serving Specific Student Populations: STEM Students," and Table 8.4
Implementation examples	Boxes in every chapter
Helping students to succeed	Chapter 3 action on creating success-oriented teaching, Table 3.6, other success-oriented actions, and chapter 4
Helping students to engage successfully in group activities	Boxes 1.1, 3.5, 4.8, 5.4, 7.6, and 8.1
Examples of learning-centered pedagogies and techniques	Appendix A lists where learning-centered pedagogies and techniques are discussed Table A.1 lists learning-centered techniques or teaching/learning practices that transcend disciplines. Table A.2 lists learning-centered techniques or teaching/learning practices that use online or electronic educational technologies.
Explanation of five constructs and their supporting actions	Chapter 3 through 7
Explanation and rationale for this model of learning-centered teaching	Chapter 2

(Continues)

TABLE P.1. (Continued)

Topic	*Where You Can Find Relevant Information*
Rubrics measuring the extent of implementation of these actions along these four levels	Appendix B
Contrast between learning-centered and instructor-centered teaching approaches	Tables in chapter 3 through 7 titled "Summary of Construct and Actions Contrasting Instructor-Centered Approaches With Learning-Centered Approaches"
Four levels showing incremental changes from instructor-centered to learning-centered teaching approaches, which levels also make suggestions for your aspirations	Tables in chapter 3 through 7 titled "Instructor Characteristics for the Use of Specific Action on the Four-Level Continuum from Instructor-Centered to Learning-Centered Approaches"
Assessment of implementation of learning-centered teaching	Chapters 10 through 12
Individual assessment of learning-centered teaching	Chapter 11
Program assessment of implementation of learning-centered teaching	Chapter 12
Developing personal goals for increasing your use of learning-centered teaching	Chapters 11 and 12 discussions on how you can establish goals, and Table 11.1 listing of some goals for you to consider
How to change teaching behaviors using evidence-based, popular behavior change and assessment models	Chapters 9, 11, and 12

Acknowledgments

Writing teachers always remind students and aspiring writers to write to a specific audience. All faculty in higher education are my primary audience, along with graduate students preparing to become faculty and secondary education teachers. I created an audience of faculty to review my ideas and chapters by asking for volunteers to read parts of my manuscript. The volunteers came from all disciplines and ranged from first-year faculty and adjunct faculty with practitioner careers to full professors, senior administrators, and faculty developers. They were exactly the audience for this book and provided me with very valuable insights into how it could be clarified and improved. I read their feedback and revised accordingly. I want to acknowledge and thank the following faculty who reviewed chapters of this book: Brooklyn Cobb, Sarah Corcoran, Marcia Hospedales, Barbara Kellar, Robert Martin, Alison Mostrom, Nick Owens, Ester Sesmero, Kymber Taylor, Sister Janet Thiel, Pete Watkins, and Kalina White.

I owe all of the following people my deep gratitude for helping me complete this book me in many different ways: Sabrina Ahmadzai, my very talented undergraduate research assistant who completed various tasks including developing the reference list, working on the index, and creating a complex figure; Ellen Goldman, a professional colleague and friend, who graciously allowed me to publish her creative stair model in chapter 3, which I have shared widely with faculty over the years; Donna Ryan, another professional colleague and friend who helped with formatting the tables and figures; Ella Singer, my sister, who most carefully proofread my manuscript; Kymber Taylor, another professional colleague and friend, who managed the data analysis and suggested ways to communicate the data effectively and simply; and Sister Janet Thiel, an assessment expert, who made many suggestions to improve the assessments chapters. Finally, I want to thank my colleagues and friends at Stylus—David Brightman, Alexandra Hartnett, and John von Knorring, who moved the book forward in timely manner and crafted the title that really conveys what the book is aiming to do. Kathleen Dyson created the beautiful cover and tree/leaf illustrations used throughout this book from my vague ideas.

PART ONE

USING LEARNING-CENTERED TEACHING APPROACHES

CHAPTER 1

Introduction

Chapter Highlights

Learning-centered teaching is an evidence-based best educational practice that focuses on

- what students are learning,
- how they are learning, and
- the application of learning.

Use of this pedagogy yields increased deep and meaningful learning and greater retention of students. Therefore, educators in higher education are increasingly accepting and implementing learning-centered teaching.

Would you like to improve your teaching by employing learning-centered practices? Perhaps you already use some learning-centered practices but would like to use more of them. Because the academy no longer considers learning-centered teaching a pedagogical fad, you may want or feel obligated to try using it in a systematic way. However, you may need practical guidance on how to modify your teaching. If so, keep reading this book because it is an effective, easy-to-follow how-to teaching guide for full-time and part-time, new and experienced faculty members. This book will provide specific, practical guidance on how to begin or continue and how to use the change process to improve your teaching by adopting learning-centered teaching strategies and techniques. Learning-centered teaching enhances your ability to help your students master content with rigor. Plus, you will be able to explain to your students why you are using this approach and how it will foster deep and long-lasting student learning. You will be able to describe how and why you teach in a systematic way on your performance evaluations and teaching dossier.

Effective Teaching Is Vital

Educating students has always been a primary function of higher education (Schuster & Finkelstein, 2008). Even though many doctoral students, particularly in the liberal arts, anticipate careers in higher education, they spend very little time in graduate school learning how to teach (Austin & McDaniels, 2006). Most graduate students study at research-intensive universities and focus on their research, especially toward the end of their graduate careers, but they will get jobs where teaching will occupy most of their time (Austin & McDaniels, 2006). Consequently, many academics are not well prepared for their jobs. In addition, although faculty frequently update the content of their courses, they rarely modify their teaching methods.

Many faculty continue to teach as they were taught, even if these methods are not effective (Bok, 2015).

Historically, educators assumed that if they taught, students would learn. Now, academics need to assess and demonstrate that students do learn (Haras, Taylor, Sorcinelli, & von Hoene, 2017; Kuh, Kinzie, Schuh, & Whitt, 2010). Unfortunately, the data are disappointing (Arum & Roksa, 2011). Although many students learn well enough to pass their courses, they do not retain the information and they cannot apply it to solving problems later (Doyle, 2011; Felder & Brent, 2016; Weimer, 2013). Does the blame lie with poorly motivated, underprepared students or with the instructors? According to increasing evidence, the traditional model of lecture-based education in higher education is not effective (Weimer, 2013). Instructor-centered teaching allows the students to be passive while the instructor does most of the heavy lifting and learning through delivering lectures often accompanied by detailed presentation slides and teacher-created study guides or notes. Students are bored in class, and many do not even bother to attend (Pascarella & Terenzini, 2005). Instead of teaching using ineffective instructor-centered teaching methods, all instructors can use effective, evidence-based teaching approaches. Evidence-based teaching integrates professional expertise with the best available evidence from systematic research both in simulated and real learning situations (Felder & Brent, 2016; Weimer, 2013).

In addition, only about 60% of the students who start bachelor's degree programs complete them within 6 years (McFarland et al., 2017). The graduation rates vary widely depending on the type of institution (open enrollment to highly selective) and the demographic characteristics of the students. Given this less than satisfactory retention rate, higher education administrators, with pressure from state and federal governments, are pressuring instructors to teach more effectively and to support students so they can succeed. Given the new burdens to demonstrate teaching effectiveness and helping students to succeed, instructors might be confused as to what they should do.

Instructors need to change their teaching practices based on evidence that what they should do works. Empirical research indicates that using learning-centered teaching, an evidence-based teaching approach, leads to better results (Bok, 2015; Weimer, 2013). The American Council on Education (ACE) is a coordinating agency representing the presidents of accredited higher education institutions. According to their review of the extensive literature, effective teaching leads to a range of improved student outcomes. ACE characterizes effective teaching as using active learning, students collaborating rather than competing, frequent assessment of learning, and focusing on fostering student success in the beginning of their careers (American Council on Education, 2018; Haras et al., 2017). Learning-centered teaching employs all these characteristics.

The literature on teaching in higher education often contrasts learning-centered teaching with traditional approaches, usually referred to as instructor-centered teaching. Table 1.1 shows contrasts between these two teaching approaches.

A Note About Terminology

I am deliberately using the term *learning* rather than *learner* that I used in my previous book on this topic (Blumberg, 2009). This is an intentional and purposeful shift because *learner-centered* focuses on the person or the student. *Learning* emphasizes the learning process, which I believe is a more important focus. Learning-centered teaching is more congruent with the content of the book, which gives you concrete ways to help students learn better. Some people use student-centered learning, but this customer satisfaction phrase might give the wrong impression that students can expect to get a good grade even without working for it.

Learning-Centered Teaching Is Essential for Deep Student Learning

Learning-centered teaching focuses on what and how students are learning. Instructors are not the center of focus in learning-centered teaching. Instead, learning-centered instructors create safe, respectful, and inclusive environments that facilitate student learning. Their teaching features student-to-student interactions where students actively create meaning with the content and then integrate this new content with real-world applications. The responsibility rests with the students to be actively engaged in the creation of their own meaning and knowledge. As a result, students acquire deep and lasting learning that they can use later (Weimer, 2013). This increased learning occurs

TABLE 1.1. Contrasts Between Learning-Centered Teaching and Instructor-Centered Teaching

Concept	*Learning-Centered Teaching*	*Instructor-Centered Teaching*
Focus	Student	Teacher
Role of student	Actively engaged in meaningful social interactions about the content	Passively reading or listening to a lecture
Role of instructor	Fostering student learning	Disseminating information
Responsibility for learning	Students assuming increasing responsibility for learning	Shouldering most of the responsibility for student learning
Function of learning	Developing deep and lasting understanding	Acquiring correct facts
Demonstration of learning	Confirming own meaning, understanding of content	Documenting that material was memorized
Function of assessments	Providing feedback to promote greater learning	Assigning grades
Impact of education	Students able to use what has been learned later and in new situations	Rote learning leads to much not being retained

because this approach is congruent with research on learning from the epistemology of learning, psychology, and the cognitive sciences (Alexander & Murphy, 1998; Bransford, Brown, & Cocking, 2000; Ramsden, 2003). I will discuss this research in the next chapter.

Learning-centered teaching is not a single teaching method, but rather emphasizes a variety of techniques and pedagogies that encourage instructors to create an environment that facilitates student learning. I will discuss many examples throughout this book. Further, academics have successfully used learning-centered teaching in all levels of higher education, from developmental education through medical school, and in all types of courses, including agriculture, engineering, business, and all disciplines of the liberal arts (Piskadlo, 2016).

Research indicates that learning-centered teaching fosters the following positive student outcomes:

- Improved critical thinking skills (Kuh et al., 2010)
- Increased motivation to learn (Cornelius-White, 2007; Kuh et al., 2010; Piskadlo, 2016)
- Deep learning that can be applied to new situations and personal growth (Doyle,

2008; Harris & Cullen, 2010; Pascarella & Terenzini, 2005; Weimer, 2013)
- Greater satisfaction with the overall college experience and a greater sense of being connected to their institution and their learning (Laird, Shoup, Kuh, & Schwarz, 2008; Piskadlo, 2016)
- Student persistence and retention to graduation (Pascarella & Terenzini, 2005; Piskadlo, 2016; Tinto, 2010)

International Call to Use Learning-Centered Teaching

Since the end of the twentieth century, the call to adopt a learning-centered paradigm is increasing (Barr & Tagg, 1995; Weimer, 2013). Because of the focus on learning, many policymakers and administrators are advocating for increased use of learning-centered teaching throughout higher education (Harris & Cullen, 2010; Huba & Freed, 2000). Accreditation agencies, professional associations, and government departments of education around the world are exerting pressure on administrators and faculty for its adoption (Haras et al., 2017; Sursock & Smidt, 2010). Because of these international movements, UNESCO is pressing for learning-centered teaching visions and educational models (Arceo, 2016).

United States

According to a recent authoritative proposal coming from ACE, teaching excellence now equates with learning-centered teaching (Haras et al., 2017). The authors of the ACE report hypothesize that when more faculty have the skills to teach using learning-centered teaching, the quality of instruction in higher education will improve. The rest of this book shows how faculty can acquire and use these skills. Consequently, higher education administrative leaders and educational developers are applying greater pressure on faculty now to use learning-centered teaching than 10 years ago (Haras et al., 2017). Some academic administrators are trying to persuade their faculty to use learning-centered teaching by relying on the strength of over 20 years of research evidence (Bok, 2015; Doyle, 2011; Weimer, 2013). Table 1.2 shows various well-regarded professional associations and U.S. government agencies that have endorsed learning-centered teaching because its use leads to significantly improved learning that lasts and improves retention to graduation (Elder, 2014; Verst, 2010).

Europe

The ministers of departments of education in 29 European countries agreed to the Bologna Declaration of 1999, which endorsed learning-centered teaching. This declaration set standards for higher education including calling for lifelong learning, active learning, use of formative assessment, documentation that students meet learning outcomes, and flexibility in paths toward a degree. Learning-centered teaching is an empowering mechanism to provide all students access to quality education. This approach also provides a good solution for sustainability of higher education (Arceo, 2016; Pereira, 2016; Sursock & Smidt, 2010). Arceo (2016) believes that so much evidence-based research and theory supports learning-centered teaching that it should propel an educational reform imperative to innovate curricula and change teaching practices.

Asia

Learning-centered teaching is gaining widespread acceptance in Asia. For example, the Thai National Education Act mandates that educators at all levels from primary school to higher education apply learning-centered teaching approaches (Naruemon, 2013).

TABLE 1.2. Partial List of Professional Associations and Government Agencies That Have Endorsed Learning-Centered Teaching

Professional Associations or Organizations	*U.S. Government Agencies*
The American Educational Research Association (AERA)	The National Science Foundation (NSF)
The American Psychological Association (APA)	The U.S. Armed Forces
The Association of American Colleges and Universities (AAC&U)	
The American Association for Higher Education (AAHE)	
The Carnegie Foundation for the Advancement of Teaching	
The Educause Learning Initiative (ELI)	
The National Research Council (NRC)	
The Professional and Organizational Development Network in Higher Education (podnetwork)	

From Verst, 2010.

Dilemma: Why Do Academics Not Fully Embrace Learning-Centered Teaching?

Learning-centered teaching is not yet the dominant teaching approach as many faculty continue to use instructor-centered teaching (Bok, 2015; Pascarella & Terenzini, 2005; Weimer, 2013). In fact, even after over 20 years, adoption is haphazard or sporadic at best (Harris & Cullen, 2010). Because individual faculty may adopt learning-centered teaching but do not implement it consistently in educational programs or entire colleges, peer faculty and students still consider learning-centered teaching a novel way to teach and learn. Even though many institutions claim they support learning-centered teaching, public announcements or internal desire do not reflect true teaching practices (Piskadlo, 2016).

Given the supporting research-based evidence, calls for adoption from ministers of education, top-level administrators, leaders in higher education thinking, and professional organizations, the question remains: Why have academics not universally accepted learning-centered teaching? This is perplexing to me, as it seems like the best way to teach. When I gave my first lecture to over 250 bored students many years ago, I knew something was wrong with that instructional model. I had done all the hard work and probably learned more than the students did. I began looking for another teaching method where the students would engage and learn more. I became a learning-centered teacher in the mid-1980s even before the phrase came into use. I enjoyed teaching far more and felt more connected to my students. More recently, the overwhelming literature support made learning-centered teaching seem like the obvious choice. I was surprised that the evidence-driven scientists and health professional faculty I work with at my specialized science school did not embrace learning-centered teaching upon hearing the evidence for it. Therefore, I reflected and read more to understand the lack of widespread use. I believe there are varied reasons for resisting adoption of learning-centered teaching. The following list explains why faculty, students, and the current educational system and policies prevent the large-scale adoption of learning-centered teaching (Ellis, 2013; Piskadlo, 2016). Notice how similar the lists of barriers are for faculty and students.

Faculty barriers

- Change is risky and difficult.
- Learning-centered teaching is threatening to instructors because faculty fear they will lose control of their classes and their student evaluations might go down.
- Learning-centered teaching takes more time for out-of-class preparation and giving students feedback. Faculty already feel overburdened.
- Understanding of how to implement learning-centered teaching is lacking.
- Myths about learning-centered teaching are pervasive.

Student barriers

- Learning-centered teaching is threatening to students.
- Students fear not doing well in the new learning mode.
- There is resistance to change.
- Learning-centered teaching takes more time.

Institutional barriers

- Assessment processes and methods often favor instructor-centered approaches.
- Pressure to publish takes away time devoted to investing in effective teaching methods.

I think one common reason why instructors do not adopt learning-centered teaching is that they do not know how to do so efficiently. Chapter 9 will discuss overcoming faculty, student, and institutional barriers. The rest of this book will provide practical help to implement learning-centered teaching. Instructors may lack concrete knowledge of how it can work in their own discipline or the type of courses they teach. Chapter 8, on increasing your use of learning-centered teaching, will discuss specific suggestions on how to adopt learning-centered teaching to varied teaching situations. The literature on learning-centered teaching contains examples of total transformation of courses or rethinking of philosophy and practice of teaching. You can also make incremental changes to your teaching without a total transformation. The two examples given later in this chapter illustrate incremental changes and a total transformation.

You do not need to be especially creative or innovative; you can just adopt what others have done successfully. To assist you in personalizing your implementation of learning-centered teaching, this book contains many examples of how instructors around the world use learning-centered teaching in vastly different teaching situations. I chose published examples coming from books, articles, and dissertations that are available online, allowing you to read the more complete reports for more information. Many examples generalize to many different types of courses. Appendix A lists learning-centered pedagogies and techniques and references where they are discussed. This appendix lists many practices that transcend disciplines that you can use in many different types of courses as well those that are especially useful for science, technology, engineering, and mathematics (STEM) and foreign language learners. It also lists learning-centered practices that use online or electronic educational technologies. The variety and richness of these examples, presented in boxes throughout the book, should deepen your understanding of how to implement learning-centered teaching and expand your repertoire of possible practices. You could just read the examples that are relevant to your courses if you want to make some immediate changes.

Although I intentionally describe a wide array of disciplines, I oversampled examples coming from STEM courses. This overrepresentation occurs because many instructors believe that learning-centered teaching cannot be used in the lower levels of STEM courses (Felder & Brent, 2016; Weimer, 2013) although many students have trouble with traditional, lecture-based STEM courses (Chen, 2013). However, much research exists in teaching STEM during the beginning courses and this research gives successful examples of learning-centered teaching implementation. Table 1.3 shows STEM examples of learning-centered teaching practices discussed in this book.

Following the description of examples of implementation of learning-centered teaching, I provide personal reflection questions on applicability for your use. I strongly recommend that you record your reflections and ideas for change. There will be so many possible ideas for change that you will not be able to remember all of the good ideas you think about as you read this book. In chapter 8 on using learning-centered teaching, you will have an opportunity to review all of your ideas and suggestions and consolidate them into a realistic plan.

Debunking Common Myths and Fostering Truths About Learning-Centered Teaching

The following common ideas about learning-centered teaching are myths:

1. Learning-centered teaching cannot be used or does not work with
   a. beginning level students;
   b. unmotivated or underprepared students;
   c. content-rich disciplines such as the sciences, or
   d. large enrollment courses.
2. Learning-centered courses cover less material.
3. Learning-centered teaching results in lower student ratings as an instructor.
4. Learning-centered teaching promotes grade inflation.

Effective learning-centered teaching promotes and achieves increased student learning, which leads to more students earning higher grades. However, this is not grade inflation because the students earned the higher grades by demonstrating mastery of content. Instead of promoting grade inflation, learning-centered teaching actually promotes grade improvement (Mostrom & Blumberg, 2012).

Boxes 1.1 and 1.2 describe real examples that provide evidence that these ideas are not true. Box 1.1 discusses two learning-centered teaching biology courses and illustrates how you can incorporate several learning-centered practices within traditional courses and significantly improve student learning. Box 1.2 illustrates how you can engage and excite students in detailed factual material.

In contrast to the previous example, Lange and Simkins (2013) dramatically changed the day-to-day activities of a class in which the students might perceive the content as dry. This example also illustrates how some of these common ideas are myths.

These examples should help you believe these ideas are not true. The instructors mentioned in these two boxes observed many positive outcomes of learning-centered teaching and convinced them that they should not only continue teaching that way but also disseminate their findings to others.

TABLE 1.3. STEM Learning-Centered Teaching Practices Discussed in This Book

Instructional or Pedagogical Technique	Used To	Brief Description	Where Discussed in the Book
Authentic assessment	Conduct real-world projects	Students develop projects or designs that practitioner wants Practitioners and instructors grade assignments	Box 6.8
Concept map	Summarize material, identify relationships	Students represent hierarchical relations to integrate content	Box 3.8
Groups of students developing hypotheses and reading relevant literature	Appreciate value of research	Students conduct literature reviews	Box 1.1
Peer feedback	Learn importance of peer review in research or design	Instructor provides criteria, students critique peer research reports	Boxes 6.6 and 7.8
Peer tutoring	Supplement in-class learning at all levels, but especially with beginning courses	Peer and near-peers help students to learn	Box 1.1
Problem-based learning (PBL)	Help solve real-world problems	Student discussions lead to collaborative student learning	Box 3.5
Process-oriented guided inquiry learning (POGIL)	Problem-solve in sciences	Students work through structured worksheet	Box 1.1
Scaffolding	Assist students to go beyond their zone of proximal development	Instructors assist students to learn, gradually removing learning supports	Box 4.4
Small groups work on problem-solving or projects or tasks	Solve problems, answer questions, complete tasks	Students use explicit directions on their tasks in small group work, individually accountable for their work	Boxes 1.1, 3.5, 4.8, 5.4, 7.6, and 8.1
Student-centered activities for large enrollment undergraduate programs (SCALE-UP)	Supplement learning in all levels of classes (although designed for large enrollment classes, works well with smaller classes also)	Students come prepared to solve problems in small groups and can ask for assistance when needed; no lectures by instructors	Box 3.2
Thinking and problem-solving like a scientist	Encourage learning in beginning research methods course	Students discuss parts of research articles, then conduct easy research projects	Box 5.7
Use scientific method to evaluate research	Understand research literature	Students use template to identify and summarize information in research articles	Box 5.5

BOX 1.1.
Learning-Centered, Large Enrollment STEM Courses

Tracey Kuit and Karen Fildes (2014) developed biology courses to foster lifelong learning. The courses were general biology and undergraduate biochemistry with enrollments of over 400 students. To promote science lifelong learning, these instructors created supportive environments and gave students tasks they designed to increase motivation to succeed and skill development. In addition to lectures and traditional labs, the course incorporated three different types of learning experiences:

1. Near-peer (students who previously did well in the course) assisted study sessions where students working in small groups discussed the content that was in the textbook and lectures. The near-peer tutors modeled how to study along with focusing on the key concepts. These study sessions promoted self-directed learning and student accountability. Students received regular formative feedback from their peers and the tutor. There was a correlation between attending these session and final grades.
2. Three inquiry-based learning laboratories known in STEM as POGIL (process-oriented guided inquiry learning [Moog, n.d.]) with 80 students per lab. Students engaging with the POGIL process use structured problems or question sets to solve problems and analyze data to make conclusions. In these biology labs, small groups of students answered questions on a worksheet that focused on the learning process and how they could seek information to help them solve problems. These worksheets facilitated the discussion of key theoretical concepts while getting feedback from lab assistants. Students felt these labs helped them to do better on the final exam.
3. Group research project that students worked on throughout the semester. Collaborative groups of four students researched literature on application of concepts discussed in lectures. Students often chose topics that related to their major. Students had to present their summaries of the research to the class. Students and the instructor evaluated the presentations using grading criteria that the students had in advance. Students reported enthusiasm for the project as it motivated them to learn and enhanced their communication skills. Because of the project students felt more connected to each other.

Personal Reflection for Your Own Use

The case study described learning-centered teaching in biology courses, but the techniques have applicability well beyond STEM courses.

How can you incorporate near-peer assisted study sessions? They might replace recitations or be optional sessions coordinated with the tutoring center.

How can you change a few of your labs to include POGIL type activities? You may not have to develop the worksheets, as instructors have developed them in anatomy and physiology, biochemistry, biology, chemistry, computer science, engineering, math, nursing, and psychology (Moog, n.d.).

How can you incorporate student research to apply the concepts you teach? How would you integrate such research into class or online activities?

How can you incorporate peer assessments into your courses?

BOX 1.2.
Flipping a Course Led to More and Deeper Learning

David Lange and Betty Simkins (2013) wanted to foster undergraduate students' analysis, evaluation, and application in an employee benefit and retirement planning course. Previously, the instructors lectured on the material covered in the required readings and they felt that it focused on knowledge acquisition. With the new learning-centered approach, in advance of class, students were required to read chapters in a resource book intended for financial service professionals that covered 59 specific benefit or retirement plans. Each chapter addressed a different plan and discussed information in a stepwise manner, indicating its advantages and disadvantages, design features, tax implications, and how to install the plan. Rather than covering the content in the same way as in the book, the instructors assigned tasks to small groups of students for each class. They had to use the assigned reading for these tasks. The groups had to list two points that they found interesting and identified two questions about the plan for which they would like further information. On a rotating basis, students had to moderate their small group discussions to monitor even participation. The instructors collated the student lists of the interesting points. As a class, the students had to decide the most important points. Thus, they actively engaged with the content and defended their arguments through analysis. Next the students had to find answers to the questions they raised by searching industry databases, reports, or government studies to find the answers to their questions. These class activities and discussions counted for 40% of the final grade.

The authors noted the following features:

- Instead of just memorizing the factual content, the students asked challenging questions and argued over the details of plans.
- More content was covered, and in more depth through student discussions.
- The average score on the end-of-course student evaluations was 4.9 out of 5, which was higher than the previous lecture format on the same content.
- The students and the instructor found the content more interesting and the course more challenging than previously.
- The instructors felt they had to be more prepared as their students raised very challenging questions. Previously the students rarely asked higher level questions.
- Attendance averaged greater than 95%, with only 1 student missing more than 6% of the classes.
- Adopting learning-centered teaching was not as large of a pedagogical change as the instructors thought it might be. The key was flipping the course so that students covered the content outside of class through reading. The desire to focus on higher level learning such as synthesis and evaluation over factual knowledge motivated the change to learning-centered teaching.

Personal Reflection for Your Own Use

How can you motivate students to engage in dry or factual material in a way similar to what these instructors did?

How can you use the technique of students identifying the most interesting points and then creating a summary or synopsis of the most important points?

How can you use the technique of students researching information they want to learn?

Alternatively, the following common ideas about learning-centered teaching are truths (Doyle, 2011; Weimer, 2013):

- Instructors spend more time preparing for their teaching.
- Students spend more time engaged in the content of the course.
- Students acquire knowledge that is deep and long-lasting.
- Initially students may resent the extra work and criticize the instructor for not teaching, but most students come to realize that they are learning more.
- Transformation to learning-centered teaching can be incremental.
- Learning-centered practices can be incorporated into traditional courses.
- All levels of courses and all disciplines can adopt learning-centered teaching.
- Learning-centered teaching can occur outside of formal courses or out of the academy. For example, Paquette and Trudel (2018) developed guidelines for athletic coaches to use more learning-centered teaching. Federe and Leishman (2014) have suggestions for learning-centered teaching for military personnel who need to speak foreign languages when they are stationed abroad.

Students who have experienced learning-centered teaching

- are more engaged with their education and learning;
- acquire deep and lasting learning;
- possess learning skills to help them acquire new information and become lifelong learners; and

- can apply knowledge to new situations and to solve problems.

Chapter Summary

Figure 1.1 summarizes the most salient points of this chapter.

Taking Stock: How Would You Like to Implement Learning-Centered Teaching?

Why do you want to use or increase your use of learning-centered teaching?

How aligned is your philosophy of teaching and learning with learning-centered teaching?
What, if anything, would you need to adjust in your philosophy of teaching and learning before you can transform your teaching?

In what course(s) would you like to focus on using more learning-centered teaching?

What resistance do you think you will encounter?

- In yourself?

- With your peers?

- With your administrators?

FIGURE 1.1. **Mind map of main concepts of learning-centered teaching discussed in chapter 1.**

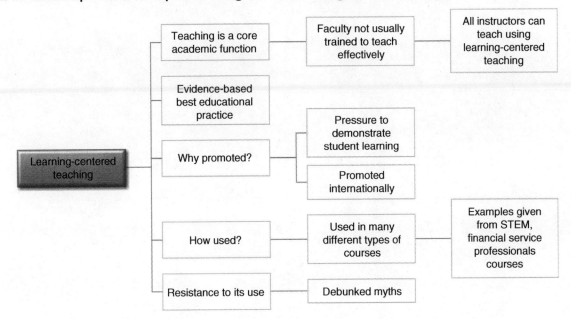

CHAPTER 2

Overview of the Model of Learning-Centered Teaching

Chapter Highlights

This chapter discusses a model of learning-centered teaching based on Weimer's (2013) work. This model has five constructs, and each construct is defined by six essential actions. Four increasing learning-centered levels help you begin to or increase your use of learning-centered teaching for each of these actions. This model is grounded in what we know about learning coming from current research and theory from constructivism, psychology, and the cognitive sciences. Figure 2.1 graphically depicts these concepts.

FIGURE 2.1. Three highlights of the learning-centered teaching model.

1. **Model of Learning-Centered Teaching Using Weimer's Five Constructs and Essential Actions That Define Each Construct**

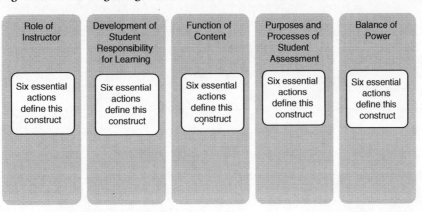

(Continues)

Figure 2.1. (Continued)

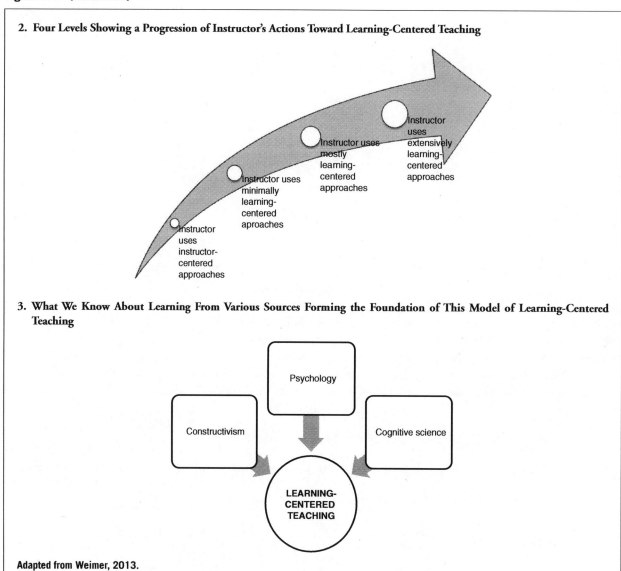

2. **Four Levels Showing a Progression of Instructor's Actions Toward Learning-Centered Teaching**

3. **What We Know About Learning From Various Sources Forming the Foundation of This Model of Learning-Centered Teaching**

Adapted from Weimer, 2013.

Understanding Weimer's Learning-Centered Teaching Model

Weimer's (2002, 2013) learner-centered teaching is the foundation of this model. Weimer's hugely successful books (Weimer, 2002, 2013) describe the following key changes in practice to implement learner-centered teaching: (a) the role of the teacher, (b) the balance of power, (c) the function of content, (d) the responsibility for learning, and (e) the purposes and processes of evaluation. The model I describe is closely tied to

Weimer's five practices, but I have reimagined the key changes to practices as constructs of learning-centered teaching. I have named and ordered those reimagined constructs as the following:

1. Role of Instructor
2. Development of Student Responsibility for Learning
3. Function of Content
4. Purposes and Processes of Student Assessment
5. Balance of Power

FIGURE 2.2. Learning-centered teaching is an integrated approach composed of five constructs.

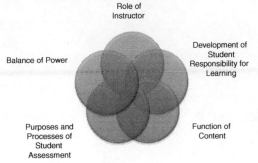

Although this model divides learning-centered teaching into five constructs, it is really an integrated framework, as shown in Figure 2.2. When you use all the constructs, your teaching should lead to deep and long-lasting student learning. This model builds on my earlier learner-centered book (Blumberg, 2009); however, it describes a more evidence-based learning-centered teaching model that relies on the advantage of 10 years of experience. Since then, many faculty members around the world have been using this approach.

Although Weimer discussed these five changes to practice, she did not operationally define them. I do that by specifically identifying six essential actions within each larger construct. Table 2.1 lists the five constructs of the learning-centered teaching approach and the essential actions associated with each construct. I discuss each construct in more detail in the next five chapters. Two of these actions, creating an inclusive environment within the Role of Instructor construct and creating a safe and moral environment within the Balance of Power construct, are crucial for students. Without them, students may not be able to succeed and may not stay in college, regardless of what else we do. Yet until recently these actions did not receive much, if any, attention.

To help you begin to or increase use of learning-centered teaching for each of these actions, I describe the following increasing learning-centered levels: (a) instructor-centered, (b) minimally learning-centered, (c) mostly learning-centered, and (d) extensively learning-centered. Each level lists instructor characteristics to help you transition to more learning-centered teaching. Because teaching is so varied, most levels contain more than one descriptor characteristic. Generally, the instructor-centered approach does not foster or may impede student learning.

Moving toward a learning-centered approach promotes greater student learning. Figure 2.3 shows how the model progresses from instructor-centered to learning-centered teaching.

As an example, Table 2.2 contains the list of instructor characteristics for the essential action of creating an inclusive environment, referred to previously, on the four-level continuum from instructor-centered to learning-centered approaches. You will find a similar table for each action within the five constructs. As you read the chapters on the constructs, you can determine which level best describes your current practice on each action by referring to these tables. Because each level lists more than one characteristic, you may be at different levels within the same action. If you desire to change your practice on each action, you can move incrementally through these four levels or you can skip a level or two, depending on your comfort level.

Readers have told me that this model appears to be confusing at first because of its complexity. However, I consistently use the same format. Think of this description as going from the forest view down as shown in illustration (Illustration 2.1). The model in its totality is the forest. The trees are the five constructs. The six actions that define the constructs are the branches of the trees. The leaves on the branches are compound leaves composed of four leaflets, like fingers on a hand, representing the four levels characterizing each action. Table 2.2 describes one such action and the four levels that characterize this action. Scientists' current evidence-based understanding of learning forms the roots of these trees (National Academies of Sciences, Engineering, and Medicine, 2018).

Although this model describes separate actions within each construct, the real goal is to have an integrated learning-centered approach to teaching. With learning-centered teaching, the sum is greater than the addition of the separate parts. However, the separate actions suggest good ways to begin the process toward integrated learning-centered teaching. You can see this as a progression of going from implementation of separate actions to many actions to an integrated learning-centered approach to all your teaching. Once you use many learning-centered techniques, you begin a total transformation of your teaching. The case studies at the beginning of the chapters on the five constructs discuss examples of integrated learning-centered teaching, even though one construct may be emphasized. Reading the authors' full reports will give you a

TABLE 2.1. The Five Constructs of the Learning-Centered Teaching Approach and the Essential Actions Associated With Each Construct

Construct	Essential Actions Associated With Each Construct
Role of Instructor	• Develops learning outcomes • Uses appropriate teaching/learning methods • Aligns objectives, teaching/learning methods, and outcomes • Creates a supportive and success-oriented environment • Creates an inclusive environment • States teaching/learning methods explicitly
Development of Student Responsibility for Learning	• Sets expectations for students to take responsibility for learning • Provides scaffolding learning support, then allows for greater student independence as the course proceeds • Develops student learning skills • Develops student self-directed, lifelong learning skills • Fosters student reflection and critical review • Fosters use of metacognitive skills, habits of mind
Function of Content	• Uses organizing scheme • Promotes meaningful student engagement with the content • Fosters development of discipline-specific methodologies • Helps students understand why they learn content • Fosters thinking in discipline • Helps students acquire in-depth conceptual understanding that facilitates future learning
Purposes and Processes of Student Assessment	• Integrates assessment and learning • Uses fair, objective, and consistent assessment policies and standards • Provides students with formative feedback • Uses student peer and self-assessment • Allows students ability to learn from mistakes • Uses authentic assessment
Balance of Power	• Establishes safe, moral, and ethical environment that empowers all students • Provides syllabus that demonstrates that students and instructors share power • Allows for some flexibility in policies and practices • Provides varied student opportunities to learn • Empowers student learning through appropriate freedom of expression • Responds to student feedback

FIGURE 2.3. Summary of each construct and how the actions transition to greater use of learning-centered teaching along four levels.

Five Constructs (Each Construct Has Six Separate Actions)			
1. Role of Instructor			
2. Development of Student Responsibility for Learning			
3. Function of Content			
4. Purposes and Processes of Student Assessment			
5. Balance of Power			

	Position Within Four Levels Showing a Progression Toward Learning-Centered Teaching Characterizes Each Action			
	Progression Toward Learning-Centered Teaching →			
	Instructor-Centered	→		Learning-Centered
Instructor-centered				
Minimally learning-centered	x			
Mostly learning-centered	x	x	x	
Extensively learning-centered	x	x	x	x

TABLE 2.2. List of Instructor Characteristics for Creating an Inclusive Environment on the Four-Level Continuum from Instructor-Centered to Learning-Centered Approaches

Levels	*Action: Creation of an Inclusive Environment, With Instructor Characteristics at Each Level*
Instructor-centered	Instructor: • Receives feedback that the class's or institution's environment is not inclusive of all diverse and different backgrounds **AND** • Does not make changes to be more inclusive
Minimally learning-centered	Instructor: • Does not focus on creating an inclusive learning environment **OR** • Teaches without regard to diversity or differences in background
Mostly learning-centered	Instructor: • Intentionally and consistently includes examples that relate to diversity and differences in background **AND** • Intentionally considers diversity while promoting inclusion when requiring students to work in groups or to interact with each other
Extensively learning-centered	Instructor: • Creates an inclusive environment that responds to and benefits from differences to foster the development and learning of all students, characterized by mutual reciprocity and respect **AND** • Promotes discussion of diversity and differences in background and abilities in an inclusive and supportive environment

ILLUSTRATION 2.1. Forest and Tree Representation of the Learning-Centered Teaching Model.

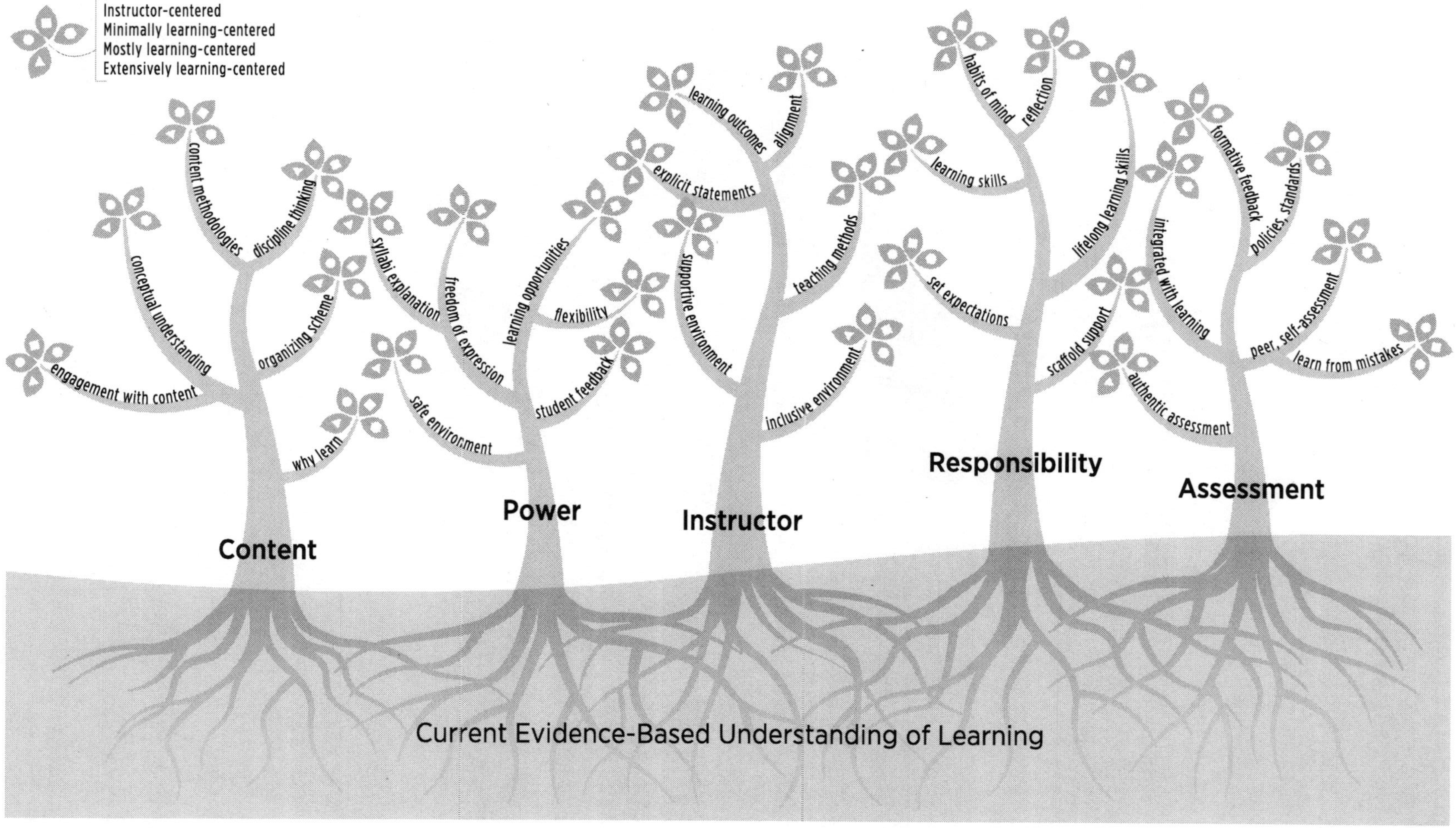

Instructor-centered
Minimally learning-centered
Mostly learning-centered
Extensively learning-centered

Assessment

learn from mistakes
peer, self-assessment
policies, standards
formative feedback
integrated with learning
authentic assessment
lifelong learning skills
scaffold support

Responsibility

reflection
habits of mind
learning skills
set expectations

Instructor

alignment
learning outcomes
explicit statements
teaching methods
inclusive environment
supportive environment

Power

flexibility
student feedback
learning opportunities
freedom of expression
safe environment

Content

syllabi explanation
organizing scheme
why learn
discipline thinking
content methodologies
conceptual understanding
engagement with content

Current Evidence-Based Understanding of Learning

FIGURE 2.4. Implementation progression of learning-centered teaching constructs.

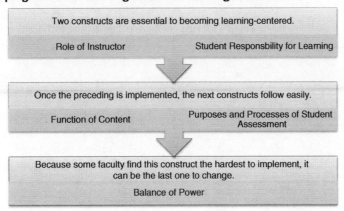

better understanding of how you might be able to fully transform your teaching. The boxes throughout the chapters illuminate the learning-centered use of a specific action; that is a good way to start or increase your use of learning-centered teaching. As you can observe from the variety of examples given, the ways to implement learning-centered teaching are quite diverse to fit the myriad teaching situations that exist.

Figure 2.4 proposes a suggested progression of implementing the constructs of learning-centered teaching. This progression is based on the experience of many faculty. The Role of Instructor construct is the first one that you should implement. Once you examine your teaching conceptions and expand your pedagogical understanding, you can be a more effective learning-centered teacher. The Development of Student Responsibility for Learning construct should also occur at the beginning of your transition to more learning-centered teaching. You need to prepare students to take responsibility for their learning by helping them develop skills that will help them to succeed with your new approaches to teaching and learning. After considering how you teach through the Role of Instructor construct and prepare your students to take responsibility for their learning, then you can transition the Function of Content and Purposes and Processes of Student Assessment to be more learning-centered. The Balance of Power construct can be your last one to implement. I found that faculty have the most resistance to this construct and it may be the most controversial. With these considerations in mind, I described Balance of Power such that you can help students to become more engaged and motivated learners without it being threatening to you.

How What We Know About Learning Supports This Learning-Centered Teaching Model

Current thinking about learning comes from constructivism, psychology, and cognitive science and is the foundation of this model of learning-centered teaching. Each field of study has a solid research base illuminating how people learn (National Academies of Sciences, Engineering, and Medicine, 2018). Therefore, this model of learning-centered teaching has an evidence-based grounding.

Constructivism

The philosophical foundation of this model of learning-centered teaching is constructivism, an epistemology of learning (Schunk, 2016). *Constructivism* means that people construct knowledge and meaning about the world from their experiences. The individual must be actively engaged; other people only assist the individual in this knowledge construction. Jean Piaget, Jerome Bruner, and Lev Vygotsky are the classical constructivists that you may have learned about in psychology. Today, where so much information is immediately available, we must change how we educate students from being consumers of information to developers of knowledge. Educators need to help students acquire the ability to continuously learn and create knowledge on their own throughout their lives (Arceo, 2016). Without continuous learning, people cannot succeed in this rapidly changing world. Vygotsky's *zone of proximal development* is the difference between the level of performance students can reach working independently and the higher level of achievement they can reach with the guidance of instructors (Schunk, 2016; Vygotsky, 1978). Learning-centered instructors can extend this zone of proximal development far more than instructor-centered teachers. Basic assumptions of constructivism include the following:

- Students are active learners.
- Learners construct understanding through interactions with people and the environment.
- Learning is a process of making sense of the world or content.
- Knowledge is individually constructed by the learner based on their beliefs and experiences.
- Instructors create environments where students are actively involved with challenging problems to solve.
- Early on instructors give more assistance and, as students learn, instructors allow students more independence, a concept called *scaffolding*.
- Instructors foster the development of students' self-regulated or self-directed learning (Fox, 2001; Schunk, 2016).

Amy Verst (2010) mapped the constructs of learning-centered teaching onto constructivism. This grounding in a well-established philosophical approach to learning fosters practical methods for teaching and learning. Box 2.1 shows Verst's mapping of learning-centered teaching constructs onto constructivist values to illustrate the implementation of these constructs.

Psychological Foundations of Learning-Centered Teaching

The American Psychological Association (1997) developed 14 learner-centered principles. These principles are classified into 4 major psychological factors. Although they were intended to guide school reform and redesign for K–12 educators, I aligned 77% of the actions in my model of learning-centered teaching to these APA principles into the model shown in Table 2.3.

The implication of these learner-centered psychological principles should lead to shifts in focus in education, as shown in Table 2.4.

A meta-analysis of effective online learning practices aligns with learning-centered teaching (U.S. Department of Education, Office of Policy, Evaluation, and Policy Development, 2010). Box 2.2 discusses how

Barbara McCombs (2015) applies these psychological principles to online learning.

Instructors often complain that students are not motivated. Psychologists recommend motivating students by

- ensuring students feel included and welcomed;
- fostering students to have control over their learning;
- building confidence and self-efficacy; and
- providing frequent formative or self-assessments.

Cognitive Science

Cognitive science uses an information processing model that is analogous to computers. Information is any type of stimulus that begins as sensory input. Current information processing models represent three types of memory, as shown in Figure 2.5. Information is held in sensory memory only long enough for it to be processed further, actually a few milliseconds. The majority of the information is constantly lost, which is fine because much of it is irrelevant to learning. Instructors can assist students to attend to the right information. If the information transfers to working memory, then it is processed or thought about. Various parts of the brain process different types of sensory information. Regardless of which part of the brain is involved, working memory is limited both in duration and capacity. What we refer to as *learning* probably occurs in working memory because it is here that the information is encoded by making this information meaningful. Factors such as elaboration, rehearsal, and organization of information foster better encoding. Information that is well encoded can be formed into schemas. Schemas consolidate large amounts of information into meaningful structures or patterns. Instructors can be influential in promoting information encoding. Meaningful information is integrated with what is already known in long-term memory. If the information in working memory is not meaningful or processed enough, it is lost.

All processed information is stored in long-term memory. Knowledge is stored in long-term memory as declarative (which includes facts, theories, and attitudes); procedural (knowledge of how to perform cognitive activities); or conditional (when to employ the other two types of knowledge and why doing so is important). If the learner cannot access stored

BOX 2.1.
Verst's Mapping of the Learning-Centered Teaching Constructs Onto Constructivist Values

Learning-Centered Teaching Construct	Constructivist Values	How Can You Apply This Value to Your Teaching?
Role of Instructor	• Instructors are guides, not primarily lecturers, even in content-driven courses. • Instructors motivate and empower students to acquire quality learning. • Instructors allow students to learn from their peers.	
Development of Student Responsibility for Learning	• Learning is a process to develop learning skills and make students ready to learn. • Students take charge of their learning with the assistance of instructors. • Students need to be self-aware and self-regulated.	
Function of Content	• Students are not empty containers to be filled by instructors. • Content must be real and relevant. • Knowledge is individually constructed.	
Purposes and Processes of Student Assessment	• All assessments also function as learning tools. • Learning should be frequently assessed. • Students need to self-assess their strengths and weaknesses.	
Balance of Power	• Courses are a collaboration between students and instructors, both with equal importance. • Students and instructors share governance and the power of classrooms. • Instructors incorporate student input throughout the course.	

Based on Verst, 2010.

knowledge, people assume it has probably been forgotten. To use information, it must be retrieved back to working memory. Retrieval depends on the manner and specificity with which it was encoded (Schunk, 2016). Once the information is back in working memory, it can be reorganized and can gain further associations. Unlike computer memories, human memories can be renewed and are constantly changing (Carr, 2010). Instructors should help students to learn, study, and recall information through metacognitive strategies that include actively processing information through answering questions or employing visual organizers (Hoy & Hoy, 2009). The figures given in this book are examples of visual organizers.

Consistent Format for the Next Five Chapters

The next five chapters describe each construct separately. The order is the suggested order that faculty should adopt to transition their teaching. The focus here is on improving teaching to be more learning

TABLE 2.3. Correspondence Between the APA Learner-Centered Principles and the Learning-Centered Teaching Model

APA Factor	APA Principle Number, Name of Principle, and Brief Description	Learning-Centered Teaching Action and Construct in Model That Uses This Principle
Cognitive and metacognitive factors	1. *Nature of the learning process.* Students construct meaning of information.	Promotes meaningful student engagement with the content and helps students acquire in-depth conceptual understanding; both are in the Function of Content construct
	2. *Goals of learning process* are the coherent representation of knowledge.	Develops learning outcomes in the Role of Instructor construct
	3. *Construction of knowledge* links new information with existing knowledge.	Uses organizing scheme in the Function of Content construct
	4. *Strategic thinking* uses thinking and reasoning strategies.	Fosters thinking in discipline in the Function of Content construct Fosters student reflection and critical review in the Development of Student Responsibility for Learning construct
	5. *Thinking about thinking* uses higher order strategies, metacognition.	Fosters use of metacognitive skills and habits of mind in the Development of Student Responsibility for Learning construct
	6. *Context of learning* is influenced by environmental factors, instructional practices.	Aligns objectives, teaching/learning methods, and outcomes; creates supportive and success-oriented environment; and creates an inclusive environment, all in the Role of Instructor construct
Motivational and affective factors	7. *Motivational and emotional influenes on learning.* Motivation to learn is influenced by emotional state, interests.	Creates supportive and success-oriented environment as well as inclusive environment, both in the Role of Instructor construct Establishes safe and moral environment in the Balance of Power construct
	8. *Intrinsic motivation* to learn is stimulated by tasks that provide for personal choice and control.	Allows for some flexibility, provides varied students opportunities to learn, and empowers students learning through appropriate freedom of expression, all in the Balance of Power construct
	9. *Effects of motivation on effort.* Deep learning requires extended effort.	Sets expectations for students to take responsibility for learning in the Development of Student Responsibility for Learning construct Helps students acquire in-depth conceptual understanding in the Function of Content construct

(Continues)

TABLE 2.3. (Continued)

APA Factor	APA Principle Number, Name of Principle, and Brief Description	Learning-Centered Teaching Action and Construct in Model That Uses This Principle
Developmental and social factors	10. *Developmental influences on learning.* There is a need to consider developmental level of learner.	Develops student learning skills and develops student self-directed, lifelong learning skills, both in the Development of Student Responsibility for Learning construct But this not a focus of this model as it intended for college students. The APA developed these principles for K–12 educators
	11. *Social influences on learning* include interactions and relationships with others.	Uses peer and self-assessment in the Purposes and Processes of Student Assessment construct Uses appropriate teaching/learning methods in the Role of Instructor construct Provides varied students opportunities to learn in the Balance of Power construct
Individual differences factors	12. *Individual differences in learning* are a function of prior experiences and heredity.	Scaffolds learning support and then allows for greater student independence as the course proceeds in the Development of Student Responsibility for Learning construct Allows for some flexibility and provides varied students opportunities to learn, both in the Balance of Power construct
	13. *Learning and diversity.* Learning is more effective when diversity is considered.	Creates inclusive environment in the Role of Instructor construct
	14. *Standards and assessments.* Assessment is an integral part of learning process.	Integrates assessment and learning; uses fair, objective and consistent policies and standards; and allows students the ability to learn from mistakes, all in the Purposes and Processes of Student Assessment construct

Personal Reflection for Your Own Use

How can you apply these psychological principles to your teaching?

centered and not on assessing teaching. Each of the next five chapters will include the following features:

- a case study that shows how an instructor implemented some of the actions in this construct;

- a table comparing instructor-centered approaches with learning-centered teaching approaches on each action;
- an easy-to-implement learning-centered teaching technique or practice with reflection questions on how you can adopt or adapt this technique or practice;

TABLE 2.4. Shifts in Focus of Education as a Result of Learning-Centered Teaching

Focus Shift From	Focus Shift To
Thinking about what we teach →	How we teach
Thinking about what the teacher does →	Thinking about student learning, learning processes
Teacher alone chooses content →	Allowing students to have some choice in their learning
Teacher defines product of learning →	and how they demonstrate it
Content to be learned →	Recognizing characteristics of students as unique learners

BOX 2.2.
Application of Psychological Principles to Online Learning

Applying the APA's learner-centered psychological principles are even more important in online environments because there is more potential for isolation and disengagement. A review of online learning literature led McCombs (2015) to identify several essential characteristics of effective online learning-centered teaching: students must feel supported and connected to others and with the content. Students perceive instructors as learning-centered when their online instruction is individualized. Individualized instruction adapts to the students' learning needs. If technology is used appropriately, students can experience more personalized learning. Online instructors particularly need to address how to motivate students, how to foster positive relationships, and how to provide formative feedback. The same strategies that motivate face-to-face students also motivate online students. Students even in massive open online courses (MOOCs) feel motivated when they choose topics for assignments that are relevant to their own learning needs. Social media can effectively connect students and students to the instructor and to the content, thus allowing learning to occur in a social environment. Students can develop positive relationships with peers and instructors whom they have never met through frequent interactions about course work and personal interests. Although it may not be as easy as face-to-face courses, students should collaborate on complex real-world problems; this can be done through using Google tools or various collaboration platforms.

Online instructors must balance support for the learner while recognizing the need to be rigorous. Rigor means maintaining high standards for all students. Challenging and varied assignments can achieve this balance. Students can be supported while maintaining rigor by scaffolding students with more assistance early on and more independence as the course proceeds. Other scaffolding strategies involve using teamwork, promoting a culture of success, fostering positive relationships among students and with the instructor, and frequent student self-assessments, which also help to balance rigor and support.

Personal Reflection for Your Own Use

How can you incorporate individualized learning in an online or partially online course?

How can you support students online?

How can you foster connectedness online?

FIGURE 2.5. **Information processing model.**

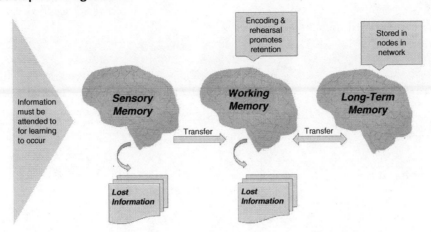

- a table that summarizes the actions of the construct and how instructors can become more learning-centered;
- a separate discussion of each action within each construct containing a published example of how instructors implemented this action in a learning-centered way;
- four levels showing a progression toward learning-centered teaching that characterizes each action; and
- a worksheet on how you can transition to more learning-centered teaching within this construct.

Chapter Summary

Figure 2.6 summarizes the main concepts of this chapter.

Taking Stock: Where Would You Like to Implement Learning-Centered Teaching?

To make these concepts more concrete, choose a course you would like to transform throughout the next five chapters. Choose a course in which you are very comfortable with the content and that you will be teaching

FIGURE 2.6. **Map of the main concepts of this model of learning-centered teaching, as discussed in chapter 2.**

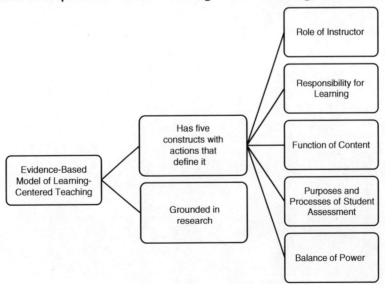

again. You can choose any level course and any type of course. Perhaps you might choose a course where you have been disappointed with students' learning or their ability to use the content.

Course name and number

Course demographics

Special considerations for the course

What is working well but could be improved with more learning-centered teaching approaches?

What aspects of the course are challenging to you or the students now? This may be content, student achievement, course management, or other factor.

What aspects of the course do you want to make more learning-centered?

learning outcomes

alignment

explicit statements

teaching methods

supportive environment

inclusive environment

Instructor

Current Evidence-Based Understanding of Learning

CHAPTER 3

Role of Instructor

Chapter Highlights

As a learning-centered instructor your role becomes more a facilitator of student learning and less a disseminator of information. You perform the following core actions that facilitate student learning:

- Use challenging, reasonable, and measurable learning outcomes that foster the acquisition of appropriate knowledge, skills, or values.
- Employ teaching/learning methods and educational technologies that promote the achievement of student learning outcomes.
- Align the three essential components of a course (learning outcomes, teaching/learning methods, and assessment measures) in terms of intellectual skill expected of the students.
- Create a supportive and success-oriented environment for learning and accomplishment for all students.
- Make learning inclusive by acknowledging and accepting diversity and differences in background.
- State teaching/learning methods explicitly.

Given the plethora of sources today, students can find information easily. Thus, your role is to help students learn and use information. You should begin your transformation toward increased learning-centered teaching with your role as an instructor because what you do is essential to student learning. Table 3.1 contrasts instructor-centered approaches with learning-centered teaching on each of the six actions that define the Role of Instructor. Each column represents a separate action of this construct. I will explain each action and provide a published example of its use. To assist you in transforming your teaching to be learning-centered, I define instructor characteristics at four levels going from instructor-centered

to learning-centered for each action in separate tables. Figure 3.1 summarizes the Role of Instructor construct and how the actions transition to greater use of learning-centered teaching along four levels.

First, I suggest an easy-to-implement learning-centered technique in Box 3.1 and describe a case study of a comprehensive template for learning-centered courses that uses many aspects of the Role of Instructor construct in Box 3.2. If you are interested in reading more about this project see the Pedagogy in Action website developed in collaboration with the Association of American Colleges & Universities' STEM reform center (Beichner & Isern, 2017).

TABLE 3.1. Summary of the Role of Instructor Construct and Actions Contrasting Instructor-Centered Approaches With Learning-Centered Approaches

Each column represents a separate action of the Role of Instructor construct. Read down to see use of learning-centered teaching.

← *Core Actions of the Role of Instructor* →

Approach	Learning Outcomes Foster Acquisition of Appropriate Knowledge, Skills, or Values	Teaching/Learning Methods That Promote the Achievement of Student Learning Outcomes	Course Aligned for Objectives, Teaching/Learning Methods, Assessment	Supportive Environment for Learning Through Specific Success Techniques	Inclusive Environment by Acknowledging Diversity and Background Differences	Explicit About Teaching/Learning Methods Chosen to Promote Learning
Instructor-Centered	Are vague or inappropriate	Teaching/learning methods or educational technologies conflicting with learning outcomes	Not aligned	Actions, attitude, or instructional methods not creating a supportive environment for all	Not inclusive of all diverse and different backgrounds	Does not mention anything about teaching and learning methods to students
Learning-Centered	Creation of and reference to measurable learning outcomes that foster the acquisition of knowledge, skills, or values	Intentional use of pedagogical techniques that promote the achievement of student learning outcomes	Explicit, coherent alignment clearly explained in the course materials	Clear and overt specific techniques explicitly addressed to help all students	Creation of an inclusive environment that is characterized by mutual reciprocity and respect	Modeling of excellent student behaviors

FIGURE 3.1. **Summary of the Role of Instructor construct and how the actions transition to greater use of learning-centered teaching along four levels.**

Construct I: Role of Instructor				
Six Separate Actions: • Learning outcomes foster acquisition of knowledge, skills, or values • Teaching/learning methods promote the achievement of student learning outcomes • Course aligned for objectives, teaching/learning methods, assessment • Supportive environment for learning through specific success techniques • Inclusive environment by acknowledging diversity and background differences • Explicit about teaching/learning methods chosen to promote learning				
	Each action is defined through four levels showing a progression toward learning-centered teaching **Progression toward learning-centered teaching →** **Instructor-Centered → Learning-Centered**			
Instructor-centered				
Minimally learning-centered	X			
Mostly learning-centered	X	X	X	
Extensively learning-centered	X	X	X	X

BOX 3.1.
Example of Easy-to-Implement Learning-Centered Practice

On the first day of class and periodically throughout the course, discuss the learning outcomes, how the students will use them, and how you will grade students on these outcomes. This allows the learning outcomes to become real for the students. Explain how focusing on the learning outcomes can help students to be successful in this course. Post these messages on your learning management system.

Personal Reflection for Your Own Use

How could this example work with your type of teaching?

What modifications would improve its use?

Where might you use this example?

BOX 3.2.
Case Study of a Comprehensive Template for a Learning-Centered Course
That Uses Many Aspects of the Role of Instructor Construct

The student-centered activities for large enrollment undergraduate programs (SCALE-UP) model (Beichner et al., 2007) is a learning-centered approach to teaching STEM courses. This is a National Science Foundation (NSF) and Fund for the Improvement of Postsecondary Education (FIPSE)-funded project that began with physics courses at North Carolina State University and has now been incorporated in more than 24 other institutions with large enrollment introductory STEM courses. This model focuses on pedagogy, teaching materials, and classroom environment, where 2 to 4 instructors (a single faculty member with TAs) can monitor and interact with classes of 100 students.

Pedagogy

Instead of lectures, labs, and recitations, students, working in small groups, are actively engaged with the content in cooperative learning for four to six hours per week.

Teaching Materials

Required readings largely replace the lectures. Students complete online homework problems, motivating them to come to class prepared to discuss the material. Instructors prepare a series of different types of activities that promote student understanding and deep learning. Many of the tasks focus on difficulties of previous students. Students work together to perform these tasks and can ask for assistance from their peers or an instructor.

Classroom Environment

Groups of students collaborate at round tables where they have access to technology and can perform small laboratory experiments. Instructors circulate around the room to interact with the students.

Elements of SCALE-UP

Several elements of SCALE-UP specifically relate to the Role of Instructor construct:

- All elements of the course are aligned.
- Learning outcomes are consistent with American Board of Engineering and Technology accreditation standards.
- Evidence-based teaching/learning methods were chosen because they improve learning in STEM and they promote the achievement of learning outcomes, problem-solving, and the application of content.
- Classes are high challenge but low threat to push the students to master the content in a supportive environment.
- The course structure respects diversity. Groups are created so that there are always two women or two people of color in each five-to-six-person group.
- The course begins with an orientation on how to work collaboratively. The objectives and list of expected activities are posted online prior to every class.

After implementing the SCALE-UP model, faculty report that students have increased conceptual mastery, better problem-solving skills, and a higher pass rate, especially for females and minorities.

Personal Reflection for Your Own Use

What elements of this comprehensive course design could you implement in your teaching?

Where might you use this element?

Action: The Instructor Develops and Uses Challenging, Reasonable, and Measurable Learning Outcomes That Foster the Acquisition of Appropriate Knowledge, Skills, or Values. These Learning Outcomes Are Consistent With the Goals of the Educational Program

Because learning outcomes specify what students should know, be able to do, or value upon completion of the course or program, they are the foundation of good teaching, useful for both instructors and students (Felder & Brent, 2016). Identifying the intention of the learning provides a direction for instruction and should be the first step in designing a course (Gronlund & Brookhart, 2009). The regional accreditation agencies require that educational programs measure whether students meet learning outcomes. Specialty accreditation agencies in business, engineering, the health professions, and primary and secondary education teacher preparation have established criteria for educational programs (Board on Science Education, Division on Behavioral and Social Sciences and Education, National Research Council, 2015). These criteria, by setting clear expectations, direct the student learning outcomes. Professional associations in disciplines within the liberal arts are establishing guidelines for undergraduate and graduate educational programs. For example, the Society for the Teaching of Psychology developed teaching criteria for a model, learning-centered, face-to-face or online undergraduate psychology major (Richmond et al., 2014). The leaves in Illustration 3.1 represent the four levels characterizing each action. Each action is a branch on the tree shown at the beginning of the chapter. Table 3.2 lists the instructor characteristics for the use of learning outcomes on the four-level continuum from instructor-centered to learning-centered approaches.

You may be more familiar with the term *learning objectives* than *learning outcomes*. They are similar. Generally learning outcomes refer to student expectations for a course, an educational program, or an entire curriculum. Learning outcomes vary depending on the discipline and may include knowledge application, critical thinking, and problem-solving or skill acquisition. Suskie (2009) recommends that programs or courses have five to six student learning outcomes. Student learning expectations for classes or units within courses may be referred to as *learning objectives*. Learning outcomes for a course should direct the learning objectives for aspects of the course. Both student learning outcomes and learning objectives are always written in terms of student achievement expectations. Instructor-centered objectives describe what the instructor plans to do or accomplish, such as discuss the content in chapter five.

Using backward course design is a popular way to develop learning outcomes that foster the acquisition of important knowledge, skills, or values (Wiggins & McTighe, 2005). When planning courses, focus on the enduring understanding or the big picture that you want your students to retain years after the course is completed. Enduring understandings provide the students a greater purpose than just learning the content. Instead of selecting a textbook or the content to be covered first, learning-centered instructors first identify the enduring understandings and then determine the learning outcomes that are consistent with them. Using backward course design will help you to do more purposeful course planning and probably lead to more active learning, which does promote better learning.

When you begin to plan a course, ask yourself what the most important concepts, skills, or values are that you want the students to retain and be able to use five years after the course is over. Spend some time constructing a list of about five desired long-term endpoints, as this will determine how the entire course is organized, what content is covered, and what the students will do. Box 3.3 shows how instructors have used backward course design to teach statistics.

ILLUSTRATION 3.1. THE FOUR LEVELS OF CHARACTERISTICS FOR EACH ACTION

TABLE 3.2. Instructor Characteristics for the Use of Learning Outcomes on the Four-Level Continuum From Instructor-Centered to Learning-Centered Approaches

Reading down, each row shows greater use of learning-centered teaching.

Levels	*Action: Learning Outcomes*

Instructor-centered	Instructor:
	
	• Does not develop or use learning outcomes OR
	• Articulates vague or inappropriate learning outcomes that
	  ◦ Are not consistent with the goals of the educational program **OR**
	  ◦ Do not foster the acquisition of appropriate knowledge, skills, or values **OR**
	  ◦ Are not challenging, reasonable, or measurable

Minimally learning-centered	Instructor:
	
	• Develops challenging, reasonable, and measurable learning outcomes but these outcomes
	  ◦ Are not consistent with the goals of the educational program OR
	  ◦ Do not foster the acquisition of appropriate knowledge, skills, or values

Mostly learning-centered	Instructor: • Develops challenging, reasonable, and measurable learning outcomes that are consistent with the goals of the educational program and foster the acquisition of appropriate knowledge, skills, or values **AND** • Places these outcomes in the syllabus, but does not refer to them during the course
Extensively learning-centered	Instructor: • Places in the syllabus challenging, reasonable, and measurable learning outcomes that are consistent with the goals of the educational program and foster the acquisition of appropriate knowledge, skills, or values **AND** • Regularly refers to them throughout the course

Action: The Instructor Uses Teaching/Learning Methods and Educational Technologies That Promote the Achievement of Student Learning Outcomes Such as Knowledge Acquisition, Application, Critical Thinking, or Solving Problems Related to the Content

You can select from numerous teaching/learning methods and educational technologies that should promote the achievement of identified student learning outcomes. For example, Obeid, Schwartz, Shane-Simpson, and Brooks (2017) edited an online anthology that describes how to teach all aspects of psychology, but most of their learning-centered teaching/learning methods generalize to most disciplines. Also, Byrne (2016) edited a book on teaching/learning activities for environmental and sustainability studies that would work in a variety of types of courses. Both books contain examples that may be done in class, online, or as required assignments. However, all of them involve active learning. Active learning requires that the students engage in meaningful activities; it is usually

---

BOX 3.3.
Planning a Statistics Course Using Backward Course Design

Statistics is required for social science and many health professional programs, yet many students dread their statistics course. Renata Strashnaya and Emily Dow (2017) believe that the primary enduring understanding of an undergraduate statistics course is that statistics are used in research. Once Strashnaya and Dow identified this primary purpose of learning statistics, they realized that memorizing equations or applying the steps involved with statistics with nonconcrete data sets would not help students learn how to use statistics in research. Instead, Strashnaya and Dow helped students gain a conceptual understanding of how statistical analyses can compare values and determine if there is a significant probability of the observed phenomena to occur. These instructors focus on how and why statistical tests answer real-life questions. The students work in small groups either in class or online to explain how statistics would shed light on issues or solve problems and then summarize their thought processes of how they arrived at a specific answer, including why they chose specific statistical tests. By using backward course design, Strashnaya and Dow planned a different but more effective undergraduate statistics course.

Personal Reflection for Your Own Use

What five or so enduring understandings do you want your students to retain years from now?

1.

2.

3.

4.

5.

How can you use backward course design in your teaching?

For what course would you like to use this design technique?

---

contrasted with traditional instructional methods where the students are passive recipients of content. Ensuring that the technique or technology fosters the achievement of the learning is the most important selection criteria.

Ellen Goldman (personal communication, August 12, 2017) created an easy-to-use heuristic to help select appropriate teaching/learning methods for different types of learning outcomes and objectives, as shown in Figure 3.2. The bolded words in Figure 3.2 list different types of learning outcomes according to the students' required cognitive processing.

The cognitive processing requirement or demand increases as you read up the stairs toward the right. The words above the stairs list possible teaching/learning methods that can be used with these learning outcomes.

Personal Reflection

Select the stair levels that represent your learning outcomes or objectives.

Are you using the suggested teaching/learning methods for these objectives? ☐ Yes ☐ No

If not, how can you modify your practice to use the suggested teaching/learning methods for your objectives?

How might you expand your teaching/learning methods?

Appropriate methods often include student-student interactions about the content. As I discussed in the previous chapter, the best learning occur-when students discuss the content, as learning is a social activity. Students appreciate and learn more when you select different teaching/learning methods (Schroeder, 2012). Box 3.4 describes how to use blogs with first-generation college students as a success strategy.

Table 3.3 lists the instructor characteristics for the use of teaching/learning methods on the four-level continuum from instructor-centered to learning-centered approaches. Instructors do not intentionally try to impede student learning, but when they use

teaching/learning methods or educational technologies without regard for student learning outcomes or that conflict with the learning outcomes, they may impede learning. If the learning outcome requires analysis, evaluation, or creation and the instructor does all the analysis, evaluation, or creation, without allowing the students to practice these skills, then the teaching/learning methods chosen conflict with the learning outcomes. Because active learning is a well-established best educational practice, it is essential to learning-centered approaches. Freeman and colleagues (2014) did a meta-analysis of 225 studies comparing student performance after experiencing lectures or active learning. The results so overwhelmingly supported the use of active learning that the authors stated,

If the experiments analyzed here had been conducted as randomized controlled trials of medical interventions, they may have been stopped for benefit—meaning that enrolling patients in the control condition might be discontinued because the treatment being tested was clearly more beneficial. (p. 8413)

FIGURE 3.2. **Goldman's heuristic for selection of teaching strategies that fit various learning objectives.**

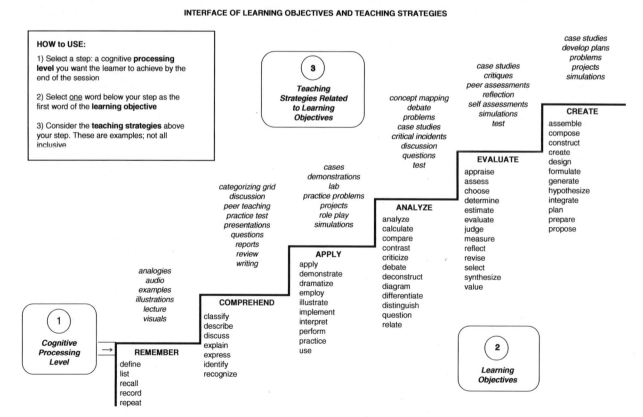

Levels adapted from Anderson et al., 2001.

BOX 3.4.
Using Blogs to Support Beginning College Students

Philip Kreniske and Ralitsa Todorova (2017) use blogs as one type of support system for first-generation college students. They assign a prompt that students respond to weekly. These prompts help students to think through challenging questions. They may ask for reactions to required readings, check on the accuracy of students' understanding of content, or ask how much and how well students are preparing for class. As students are required to respond to their peers' blogs, students can support peers and increase their confidence. Prompts frequently ask about their transition to college. When students respond to prompts about their success or challenges in adjusting to college, their peers share advice and exchange useful ideas. By writing to each other, students begin to develop a social support network of other new college students and acquire cultural capital.

Personal Reflection for Your Own Use

For what course(s) would you like to use blogs?

How can you use blogs in your teaching to ensure students are keeping up to date with their studying and preparation?

How can you use blogs in your teaching to increase student-to-student connections, especially in online courses?

Learning-centered teachers intentionally employ multiple active-learning strategies and use the most appropriate ones for specific situations.

Action: The Instructor Aligns the Three Essential Components of a Course: Learning Outcomes, Teaching/Learning Methods, and Assessment Measures in Terms of Content and Consistent Verbs Representing the Same Cognitive Processing/Intellectual Skill Demands Placed on the Students

Alignment occurs when all three essential aspects of a course (learning outcomes, teaching/learning methods, and student assessment) require the same cognitive demand from the students. For example, if the learning outcome calls for analysis, the students should learn how to analyze, be provided with opportunities to practice such analyses, and be assessed on their ability to perform these analyses. Taxonomies of learning have been used for years to develop learning outcomes or objectives. Anderson and colleagues (2001) introduced a revised version of Bloom's (1956) taxonomy. This revised taxonomy has a hierarchy of six levels of cognitive processing demand or intellectual skill required. The bolded words in Figure 3.2 list these six levels. The words listed below the stair levels are examples of measurable verbs that instructors

can use to develop learning outcomes. Although Goldman's model only suggests teaching and learning activities, which are listed above the line, these same activities can be used for assessments. To align your course, choose appropriate teaching and learning activities and assessment measures in the same column as the learning outcome or objective.

Aligned courses give students direction and provide them with clarity. When courses are aligned, student learning and their demonstration of this learning are maximized. However, misalignment inhibits learning. Misalignment occurs when one or more of the three aspects do not require the same cognitive demand. Two common misalignments occur when the learning outcome requires a higher level of cognitive demand (i.e., apply) than the assessment (i.e., comprehend) or when the teacher only models the intellectual skill but does not give students opportunities to practice the intellectual skills required. If you use backward course design, you are more likely to align the learning outcomes, teaching and learning methods, and assessments.

Table 3.4 lists the instructor characteristics for course alignment on the four-level continuum from instructor-centered to learning-centered approaches. Many instructors have not heard about the concept of course alignment, which may lead them to use the instructor-centered approach on this action. However,

TABLE 3.3. Instructor Characteristics for the Use of Teaching/Learning Methods and Educational Technologies on the Four-Level Continuum From Instructor-Centered to Learning-Centered Approaches

Reading down, each row shows greater use of learning-centered teaching.

Levels	*Action: Teaching/Learning Methods and Educational Technology*
Instructor-centered	Instructor: • Uses teaching/learning methods or educational technologies that impede student learning **OR** • Uses teaching/learning methods or educational technologies that conflict with learning outcomes **OR** • Uses instructor-centered teaching methods which allow students to be passive and memorize material
Minimally learning-centered	Instructor: • Uses teaching/learning methods or educational technologies without regard for student learning outcomes **OR** • Uses active-learning approaches during less than half of the course
Mostly learning-centered	Instructor: • Selects teaching/learning methods or educational technologies that should help students achieve learning outcomes **AND** • Uses active-teaching-learning methods in more than half of the course. Such active learning can occur in class, online, or as out-of-class assignments **OR** • Uses activities where students interact with each other and the instructor about the course content in more than half of the course, with interactions that can occur in class, online, or as out-of-class assignments as in group projects
Extensively learning-centered	Instructor: • Intentionally uses various pedagogical techniques and/or educational technologies that promote the achievement of student learning outcomes **AND** • Uses active-learning approaches in at least 90% of the course **AND** • Explains to students how these methods or technologies promote the achievement of student learning outcomes

once they consider it and try to align the learning outcomes, teaching/learning methods, and assessment measures, students learn more and are more satisfied with the instructor (Pape-Zambito & Mostrom, 2014). Because this concept may be new to you and might require major revisions in how you teach, I suggest you try to incrementally become more learning-centered with this action, as shown in Table 3.4.

Biggs (1999) believes that problem-based learning (PBL) is one of the best examples of an aligned course design, and Weimer (2013) stated that PBL is the learning-centered course design that has the most

evidence to support its use. Learning outcomes and teaching/learning methods are inherently aligned with PBL, which uses an iterative process where dialogue about problems is the focus of student-driven discussions and the primary in-class activity (Blumberg, 2019). Students begin their first discussion of a real problem without advance preparation on the topic. The students identify relevant questions they will address, which motivates them to learn the material. After the students research the answers to the questions that they developed, they begin their second discussion of the same problem. At this second discussion, usually

TABLE 3.4. Instructor Characteristics for the Use of Course Alignment on the Four-Level Continuum From Instructor-Centered to Learning-Centered Approaches

Reading down, each row shows greater use of learning-centered teaching.

Levels	*Action: Course Alignment*
Instructor-centered	Instructor: • Does not align objectives/learning outcomes, teaching/learning methods, and assessment methods **OR** • Does not understand the concept **OR** • Does not think about course alignment
Minimally learning-centered	Instructor: • Aligns two out of the three course actions **OR** • Does not indicate such alignment on the course syllabus
Mostly learning-centered	Instructor: • Aligns objectives/learning outcomes, teaching/learning methods, and assessment methods **AND** • Shows the alignment on a course document but does not explain the alignment to the students or why it is important
Extensively learning-centered	Instructor: • Explicitly, coherently, and consistently aligns objectives/learning outcomes, teaching/learning methods, and assessment methods **AND** • Clearly explains this alignment on the course materials

---

BOX 3.5.
How to Determine If a Problem-Based Learning Course Is Aligned

Stina Jansson, Hanna Soderstrom, Patrik Andersson, and Malin Nording (2015) changed a traditional lecture-based graduate course in environmental chemistry to one that employs PBL. These authors thought that PBL was especially suited to the environmental chemistry content of the course because of its complexity and its interdisciplinary nature. Upon presentation of a short descriptive text and the expected learning outcomes, the students, working in small groups of fewer than 10 people, brainstormed the questions that they wanted to study, prioritized the relevant issues to address, described the problem, identified questions they would address in their own reading, and then independently found the resources to address these questions and came back together to solve the problem. They had to identify and synthesize additional information to solve the problem. They made reports on their solutions to the problems, which were graded. In addition, the students took a final exam which covered all the learning outcomes.

Jansson and colleagues (2015) explained the course alignment with a figure (see Figure 3.3) that they called constructive alignment to show the interrelationships among the objectives, teaching/learning methods, and assessment.

Student performance on the exam was less than expected and the students commented that the exam did not fit with the rest of the course. Therefore, the authors concluded that they had not fully aligned the assessment with the teaching/learning methods. They planned to change their assessment methods to be aligned with the objectives and PBL format.

(Continues)

BOX 3.5. (Continued)

Personal Reflection for Your Own Use

Diagram your course using a similar triangle figure with the three essential aspects of the course. How would you determine if your course is aligned?

Can you use PBL in your teaching? If so, how would you use it?

FIGURE 3.3. Course alignment of the problem-based chemistry course.

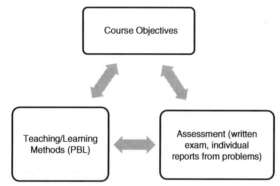

Modified from Jansson et al., 2015.

a few days later, the students synthesize the solution and then move on to a new problem, using the same iterative process. PBL works best in the professions and the sciences, where students encounter real-life problems to discuss. Box 3.5 describes how instructors have determined whether their PBL course was aligned.

Action: The Instructor Creates a Supportive and Success-Oriented Environment for Learning and for Accomplishment for All Students Through Proactive, Clear, and Overt Course-Specific Success Techniques

Because your role as a learning-centered teacher is to facilitate student learning and success, it follows logically that you should create a supportive and success-oriented environment through helping students use specific success techniques. However, this was not always the case and students still believe that courses are intended to weed out several of them. Because students have varied abilities to read, take notes, participate in class discussions, contribute to teams or small group work, study, and organize information, you can help all of them by discussing specific success strategies and techniques. Table 3.5 lists the instructor

characteristics for the creation of a supportive environment on the four-level continuum from instructor-centered to learning-centered approaches.

The following are some evidence-based success techniques that you can teach your students to use (Doyle, 2008; McGuire & McGuire, 2015):

- Create a mnemonic to recall the order of steps or a series.
- Develop a pictorial or graphic representation of what has been stated in words.
- Teach the material to someone else, especially someone who is not in the class.
- Practice good health habits, including well-balanced meals, enough sleep—especially the night before an exam—and exercise.
- Attribute results to one's own actions—not to luck, ability, or the teacher.

There are many others, and you should pick the ones that are most appropriate for your students.

Although outside-of-class reading is required in most college courses, less than one-third of college students regularly read the required materials (Burchfield & Sappington, 2000). Even more troubling is when students attempt to read the material and may not have the ability to extract the relevant information (Kuh, Kinzie, Schuh, & Whitt, 2011; Nilson, 2010). Therefore, an important success strategy is to get the students to read and understand the material. Box 3.6 shows how you can get students to read and understand the main points of the reading.

Because passing exams is an important part of succeeding in many courses, you can help students do well on tests by using the following tips compiled by William Altman and Richard Miller (2017):

- Remind students to review lecture notes, reading assignments, and other materials several

TABLE 3.5. Instructor Characteristics for the Creation of a Supportive and Success-Oriented Environment on the Four-Level Continuum From Instructor-Centered to Learning-Centered Approaches

Reading down, each row shows greater use of learning-centered teaching.

Levels	*Action: Creation of a Supportive and Success-Oriented Environment*
Instructor-centered	Instructor: • Has attitudes or uses instructional methods that do not create a supportive environment for all **OR** • Receives feedback that the environment is not supportive of learning and success for all students because of instructor actions or attitude **AND** • Does not attempt to improve the environment
Minimally learning-centered	Instructor: • Is available to help students to answer questions or provide clarification **OR** • Encourages or invites weaker students to come for one-on-one help or extra sessions or tutoring **OR** • Suggests campus resources where students can get additional help to succeed
Mostly learning-centered	Instructor: • Intentionally strives to create a supportive and success-oriented environment for all students **AND** • Gives clear and overt specific techniques to help students to succeed (not just generic advice) in one-on-one situations or when students ask for help
Extensively learning-centered	Instructor: • Explicitly addresses clear and overt specific techniques to help students to succeed (not just generic advice), with advice given to all students **AND** • Explains to students how these methods promote student success for all

days before the test so they can prepare and discover areas that they might need to clarify with peers or you.

• Help students to see what to focus on by providing a study guide, especially on the reading material.
• Create practice questions so that students can understand the format of the types of questions used.
• Help students to do better if they did poorly, especially on the first test, by critically reviewing test preparation strategies, analyzing the pattern of mistakes made on the exam, and encouraging students to talk to you outside of class.

Although this action points to specific success strategies, the primary purpose of all learning-centered teaching is to facilitate student learning and accomplishment. Thus, all actions promote student learning, but some are more directed to student success. Table 3.6 lists other actions included throughout this book that directly address ways to support students to succeed. Although I describe learning-centered teaching

BOX 3.6.
Motivating Students to Read and Understand the Main Concepts

Kent Divoll and Sandra Browning (2013) effectively used a reading retention strategy to help students read assignments and understand the main points of required reading assignments. In a condensed summer course for undergraduate education majors, students are expected to read the assignments before coming to class and write answers to a few questions about important concepts in the reading. In class students compare their answers to these questions first in pairs and then in trios. Students correct their written answers. According to a student survey, knowing that the answers would be shared with peers motivated the students to read the assignment and try to answer the questions. Even if the students had not read the assignment, they learned from these discussions. The authors used the reading retention exercise on some of the readings and compared student performance on exam questions where the material was discussed though the reading retention strategy and where it was not. Students did significantly better on higher level short answer and essay questions when they discussed the content with peers than on the nondiscussed content. There were no differences on recall-type questions or multiple-choice questions. Therefore, this reading-discussion strategy is a worthwhile time investment for challenging material but may not be worth it for easy-to-comprehend material.

Personal Reflection for Your Own Use

Do you require students to read material that you have found they do not understand? If so, would using the reading retention strategy be appropriate with these assignments?

For what courses and what readings might you use it?

TABLE 3.6. Other Learning-Centered Teaching Actions That Directly Address Supporting Students to Succeed

Actions	*Which Construct Discusses This Action*
The instructor creates an inclusive and welcoming environment for learning and for success for all students by acknowledging and accepting diversity and differences in background	Role of Instructor
The instructor provides scaffolding learning support, then allows for greater student independence as the course proceeds The instructor fosters the development of learning or learning to learn skills for the present and the future The instructor fosters the development of self-directed, lifelong learning skills The instructor fosters students' engagement in reflection and critical review of their learning through well-structured activities The instructor fosters the students' use of meta-cognitive skills and habits of the mind	Development of Student Responsibility for Learning

(Continues)

TABLE 3.6. (Continued)

Actions	*Which Construct Discusses This Action*
The instructor uses organizing schemes that are discipline-specific conceptual frameworks	Function of Content
The instructor helps students acquire discipline-specific methodologies such as how to read primary source material, laboratory skills, or communicate effectively in the discipline	
The instructor provides students with frequent, useful, and timely formative feedback to foster learning gains	Purposes and Processes of Student Assessment
The instructor establishes a safe, moral, and ethical environment that empowers all students	Balance of Power

as a series of separate actions, it really is an integrated approach to teaching.

Many instructors believe that they should teach to be consistent with their students' learning styles. College success courses and tutoring centers often give students inventories of their learning styles. However, Pashler, McDaniel, Rohrer, and Bjork (2008) found from a comprehensive review of the literature very little empirical evidence to support matching instruction to learning style. College students can learn in a variety of ways. However, when instructors use a variety of teaching/learning methods, student learning increases regardless of their preferred method of learning.

Action: The Instructor Creates an Inclusive and Welcoming Environment for Learning and for Success for All Students by Acknowledging and Accepting Diversity and Differences in Background

When students feel they are a welcomed part of a community, they are more open to new perspectives and can question their own assumptions (Haras et al., 2017). Then they can grow and learn. But

we cannot assume that all students feel included or welcome. Black students report that they experience overt and covert racism, prejudice, or intolerance frequently (Sohn, 2016). Many feel alienated and isolated from their peers and the college experience in general. These perceptions of prejudice and alienation are probably also felt by other minority students, but Black students have been studied more. More students of color, first-generation college students, international students, students with physical limitations, and nontraditional-age students are attending all types of higher education. These students may not feel welcome at traditional institutions, but you can help these students by

- treating all your students as people, calling on them by name (and pronouncing it as they do), and encouraging students to do the same;
- using frequent comprehension checks with audience response systems;
- being conscious of names and images you use to explain examples;
- inclusively facilitating whole class discussions;

- establishing fundamental conventions for classroom interactions such as not interrupting, maintaining confidentiality, equitably resolving disagreements, and responding to stereotypes or racist, sexist, disability, or ageist comments; and
- creating connections through personal stories, honesty, and respect among students so that all students can support and validate each other.

Tinto (2010), who has researched college retention for decades, recommends that you try to foster a sense of belonging and connection with all students. Students feel a sense of community when they interact with each other while focusing on a common goal. When students feel connected, they are more motivated to engage with the course requirements, learn more, earn higher grades, and report more satisfaction. Building a sense of community is paramount, but more difficult, in online learning. Without a sense of belonging, online students, especially those who feel different from mainstream students, often feel isolated and frustrated. Box 3.7 offers suggestions on how to build this sense of community and foster engagement in online courses.

You should be particularly mindful of how you teach and create opportunities for students to be open to different perspectives when you are teaching emotionally laden content such as race, political differences, or health disparities or when you are trying to change attitudes. Class discussions in a supportive environment are important venues for students and you to hear their classmates' experiences and perspectives. Students should be encouraged to write their reflections on a variety of real-life topics and on their personal struggles. When students read their peers' reflections, students can begin to develop empathy with others (Kernahan & Chick, 2017).

BOX 3.7.
Building Community in Online Courses

Joann Dolan, Kevin Kain, Janet Reilly, and Gaurav Bansal (2017) reviewed multidisciplinary research and concluded that three complementary concepts are essential to online communities: teaching presence, social presence, and cognitive presence. Student-teacher, student-student, and student-content interactions foster these three types of presence. Discussion boards or forums where students respond to questions about content that help them formulate well thought out and quality responses can build these three presences. To enhance teaching presence, instructors should model appropriate discussion responses; acknowledge individual contributions; draw less active students into the conversation; identify areas of agreement or disagreement to help students reach consensus; provide supportive and respectful comments when students disagree; and, most importantly, provide frequent timely and constructive feedback. Research suggests that when instructors and students create online personas by, for example, posting their pictures and some personal things about themselves, such as favorite movies or hobbies, students can relate to the instructor and their peers more as people, which adds to social presence. They recommend that instructors establish a noncontent or "water cooler" discussion board. Instructors and students can post their personas there. Students can ask and answer technology questions there. Instructors can increase social presence by counting students' engagement in community-building exercises toward the final grade. Instructors can enhance their students' cognitive presence by posing challenging questions, giving real examples for students to respond to, and suggesting alternatives for the students to think about. Collaborative assignments where students must contribute their own work to create an integrated product or where peers critique each other's work increase students' cognitive presence in online courses.

Personal Reflection for Your Own Use

How can you build teaching, social, and cognitive presence in your online courses?

How can you build teaching, social, and cognitive presence in your face-to-face courses?

How would discussion boards enhance the sense of community in both your online and face-to-face courses?

TABLE 3.7. Instructor Characteristics for the Creation of an Inclusive Environment on the Four-Level Continuum From Instructor-Centered to Learning-Centered Approaches

Reading down, each row shows greater use of learning-centered teaching.

Levels	Action: Creation of an Inclusive Environment
Instructor-centered	Instructor: • Receives feedback that the class's or institution's environment is not inclusive of all diverse and different backgrounds **AND** • Does not make changes to be more inclusive
Minimally learning-centered	Instructor: • Does not focus on creating an inclusive or welcoming learning environment **OR** • Teaches without regard to diversity or differences in background
Mostly learning-centered	Instructor: • Intentionally and consistently includes examples that relate to diversity and differences in background **AND** • Intentionally considers diversity while promoting inclusion when requiring students to work in groups or to interact with each other
Extensively learning-centered	Instructor: • Creates an inclusive environment that responds to and benefits from differences to foster the development and learning of all students, an environment characterized by mutual reciprocity and respect **AND** • Promotes discussion of diversity and differences in background and abilities in an inclusive and welcoming environment

Table 3.7 shows the characteristics of instructors who create inclusive and welcoming environments on the four-level continuum from instructor-centered to learning-centered approaches. It is much easier to achieve learning-centered approaches on this action in some disciplines and types of courses than others. If creating an inclusive and welcoming environment means rethinking how and what you teach, I suggest you think of using the two more learning-centered characteristics incrementally. Talk to your disciplinary peers about how they are striving to be learning-centered on this action.

Action: The Instructor Explicitly States Teaching/Learning Methods Chosen to Promote Deep Student Learning and Foster Future Use of Learning

Instructors who use learning-centered teaching have observed that it is essential to explicitly and repeatedly explain why they are using learning-centered teaching and how students should act. Table 3.8 shows the characteristics of instructors who are explicit about their use of learning-centered teaching approaches on the four-level continuum from instructor-centered to learning-centered approaches. The course syllabus and the course site on the institution's learning management system are appropriate venues to explicitly describe your rationale for the learning-centered teaching approaches you use and to define your expectations of what and how the students should perform. As an opening statement on a syllabus, "Knowing is not enough, we must apply. Willing is not enough, we must do" clearly communicates the instructor's intentions and that students will be actively engaged in their learning (Piskadlo, 2016).

Because students in learning-centered teaching courses assume a role other than the traditional one of just being note takers, you should explain your

TABLE 3.8. Instructor Characteristics for Being Explicit About Teaching/Learning Methods Chosen on the Four-Level Continuum From Instructor-Centered to Learning-Centered Approaches

Reading down, each row shows greater use of learning-centered teaching.

Levels	Action: Being Explicit About Teaching/Learning Methods
Instructor-centered	Instructor: • Does not mention anything about teaching/learning methods to students **OR** • Does not explain how chosen teaching/learning methods promote deep student learning and foster future use of learning
Minimally learning-centered	Instructor: • Identifies the teaching/learning methods used on the syllabus without further explanation **OR** • Explains choice of teaching and learning methods without being clear that they promote deep student learning and foster future use of learning
Mostly learning-centered	Instructor: • Describes the teaching/learning methods used in the course on the syllabus, at the course site on the learning management system, and through interactions with students **OR** • Explains how teaching/learning methods have been chosen to promote deep student learning and foster future use of learning
Extensively learning-centered	Instructor: • Explicitly addresses how the students should use the teaching and learning methods employed in the course and explains why they are used to further learning throughout the course **AND** • Models ideal student behaviors to achieve deep learning such as how they should work in groups expectations for participation

expectations. Some students believe that attendance in class or just asking simple clarification questions is enough to yield a good participation grade. However, you can clarify that good participation includes adding significantly to discussions, asking good questions, reflecting on what peers have said, providing personal experiences, and explaining content from readings. As many students have not had good experiences with group work, they might prefer to work alone. Another mistake students make when they are assigned questions to answer is dividing the questions among the group and then copying each other's answers. Both behaviors defeat the purpose of group work. Instead break the larger task into smaller parts and monitor that the students are working together (Felder & Brent, 2016). When students are inexperienced with a learning activity, you should model what you expect

them to do. Box 3.8 explains how to introduce the use of concept maps, a prototypical learning-centered technique. A concept map is a good graphic tool for representing one's understanding and organization of content, even for students with limited English language skills. Concept maps show key concepts, the links between these concepts, and hierarchical structures (Cañas & Novak, 2010). Because concept maps integrate verbal, visual, and spatial information, they enhance encoding and retrieval of information (Schunk, 2016).

Chapter Summary

This chapter discusses how you can begin to change your teaching to be more learning-centered through

---

BOX 3.8.
Introducing Concept Mapping to Chinese Marketing Students

Tania Von der Heidt (2015), through a pre-instruction task, introduced a concept mapping activity to undergraduate marketing students in China, because she knew that they had no experience with the tool and that it contrasted with their traditional Confucian heritage educational system. The students were told the purpose and advantages of concept maps. The instructor presented a simple concept map that had all the necessary characteristics. Then, to test the students' understanding of concept maps, students were asked to individually develop a concept map about what they knew about love. After 10 minutes, the students discussed and shared some of their maps with the whole class. Only then were the students asked to develop marketing-content concept maps.

Personal Reflection for Your Own Use

How can you model behaviors for new learning activities?

How can you use concept mapping in your course?

TABLE 3.9. Summary of the Role of Instructor Construct and Actions Contrasting Instructor-Centered Approaches With Learning-Centered Approaches

For details on each action, see the description in the chapter.

Key to Table

Columns = Action descriptions

Rows = Reading down each column, each successive row shows greater use of learning-centered teaching.

Levels ↓	← *Actions for Role of Instructor* →					
	Learning Outcomes	**Teaching Methods**	**Course Aligned for Objectives, Teaching/ Learning Methods, Assessment**	**Supportive and Success-Oriented Environment**	**Inclusive Enviroment**	**Being Explicit**
Instructor-centered	Vague or inappropriate	Impedes learning	Not aligned	Not supportive	Not inclusive	Not mentioned
Minimally learning-centered	Does not foster learning	Selected without regard for learning outcomes	Aligns two out of the three course actions	Not a focus	Not a focus	Identifies on syllabus
Mostly learning-centered	Fosters learning	Promotes learning	Three are aligned, indicated on course document	Provides techniques for success	Intentional consideration	Describes use of learning-centered methods
Extensively learning-centered	Regularly refers to learning outcomes	Intentionally uses various methods	Alignment is explicit, coherent	Explains how these methods promote success	Mutual respect	Models excellent student behaviors

the construct called Role of Instructor. Table 3.9 summarizes the six core actions of this construct and briefly identifies the characteristics of faculty at four levels going from instructor-centered to learning-centered teaching.

Taking Stock of This Construct and How You Can Implement Learning-Centered Teaching With the Role of Instructor

Table 3.10 gives an example of how a hypothetical instructor reviewed his current learning-centered

---

TABLE 3.10. Example of Completed Status of My Teaching and Plans for Change

Directions

1. Put a ^ in the cell that indicates your status.
2. Put a * in the cell to identify the level to which you aspire to become more learning-centered on this action.
3. Indicate your time line to achieve change for each action on the bottom row.
4. Make comments that will help you make these planned changes.

Levels↓	← *Actions for Role of Instructor →*					
	Learning Outcomes	**Teaching Methods**	**Course Alignment**	**Supportive Environment**	**Inclusive Environment**	**Being Explicit**
Instructor-centered	Vague or inappropriate ^	Impedes learning	Not aligned ^	Not supportive	Not inclusive	Not mentioned ^
Minimally learning-centered	Does not foster learning	Selected without regard for learning outcomes	Aligns two out of the three course actions	Not a focus	Not a focus ^ *	Identifies on syllabus
Mostly learning-centered	Fosters learning *	Promotes learning	Three are aligned, indicated on course document *	Provides techniques for success ^	Intentional consideration	Describes use of learning-centered methods *
Extensively learning-centered	Regularly refers to learning outcomes	Intentionally uses various methods ^ *	Alignment is explicit, coherent	Explains how these methods promote success *	Mutual respect	Models excellent student behaviors
Time line to achieve change	Next year	NA	Next year	Next semester	NA	Next semester

Note: You may not want to plan changes in every action.

Notes/Comments on My Plans

I never thought about the actions where I am instructor-centered but now they make sense to me and I can change to be more learning-centered. The changes that I will make are easy to implement; I just need to be more explicit in what I already do. When I am thinking about alignment, I will also address the learning outcomes and the teaching methods.

teaching status and decided what and when to make changes. This table is provided to illustrate how you will do a similar review and documentation.

Table 3.11 gives you the opportunity to review your current learning-centered teaching status and

decide what and when you want to change. Your proposed changes are only tentative plans. Once you have read through the rest of this book, you will reconsider your plans and prioritize what you will want to change.

TABLE 3.11. Worksheet: Status of Teaching and Plans for Change to Increase Use of Learning-Centered Teaching Approaches

Date_____

Directions

1. Put a ^ in the cell that indicates your status.
2. Put a * in the cell to identify the level to which you aspire to become more learning-centered on this action.
3. Indicate your time line to achieve change for each action on the bottom row.
4. Make comments that will help you make these planned changes.

Note: You may not want to plan changes in every action.

Construct I: Role of Instructor

Levels↓	← Actions →					
	Learning Outcomes	**Teaching Methods**	**Course Alignment for Objectives, Teaching, Assessment**	**Supportive Environment**	**Inclusive Environment**	**Being Explicit**
Instructor-centered	Vague or inappropriate	Impedes learning	Not aligned	Not supportive	Not inclusive	Not mentioned
Minimally learning-centered	Does not foster learning	Selected without regard for learning outcomes	Two thirds aligned	Not a focus	Not a focus	Identifies on syllabus
Mostly learning-centered	Fosters learning	Promotes learning	Aligned, indicated on syllabus	Encourages support	Intentional consideration	Describes use of learning-centered methods
Extensively learning-centered	Regularly refers to learning outcomes	Intentionally uses various methods	Alignment is explicit, coherent	Provides techniques for success	Mutual respect	Models excellent student behaviors
Time line to achieve change						

Notes/Comments on My Plan

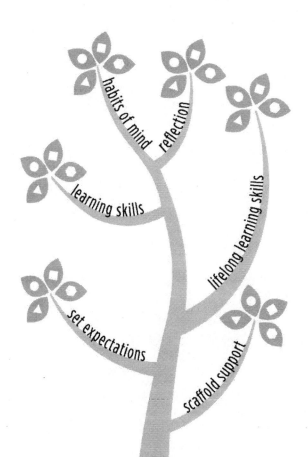

habits of mind

reflection

learning skills

lifelong learning skills

set expectations

scaffold support

Responsibility

Current Evidence-Based Understanding of Learning

CHAPTER 4

Development of Student Responsibility for Learning

Chapter Highlights

When students assume responsibility for their learning, they become empowered learners. As a learning-centered teacher, you perform the following core actions that facilitate student development of responsibility for learning:

- Set student expectations, which enables the responsibility for learning to be shared between you and the students.
- Help students develop responsibility for learning by scaffolding support.
- Foster the development of learning to learn skills.
- Foster self-directed, lifelong learning skills.
- Foster students' engagement in reflection and critical review of their learning.
- Foster students' use of metacognitive skills and habits of the mind.

Instructors notice that many students lack the skills to take responsibility for their learning. These skills vary depending on the maturity or skill level of the student and the type of course. When instructors encounter students who are not assuming enough responsibility for their learning, some instructors take over this role, almost automatically. An unintended consequence of instructors assuming responsibility is that students remain overly dependent on instructors to learn (Weimer, 2013). They may not become self-directed, self-regulated, autonomous, lifelong learners, a necessary skill to succeed in school and beyond.

The development of responsibility for learning is essential for learning-centered teaching to succeed, especially with undergraduate students. When students assume responsibility through active engagement in their learning rather than passively and compliantly receiving training as directed by their instructors, they become empowered learners. When instructors use learning-centered teaching, students become the owners of their learning, leading to autonomy and continued learning long after formal education ends (Boud, 2012; Lee & Hannafin, 2016). Fostering the development of student responsibility for learning provides graduates the ability to succeed in our ever-changing world and workforce.

Some instructors and students rarely think about who should be responsible for learning (Weimer, 2013). However, learning-centered instructors are conscious of this important construct. Teaching students these skills is not a waste of time and may even be as important as content. Students need repeated and varied opportunities to acquire the skills to learn beyond college. Box 4.1 describes an easy-to-implement learning-centered technique.

BOX 4.1.
Example of Easy-to-Implement Learning-Centered Practice

Model learning and study strategies by creating short videos of how to read the required readings and how to study and succeed in this course. Post these videos to your learning management system. Notify the students about them in your syllabus and on the first day of class. By proactively helping students to read the material or study the content, you are encouraging the weaker students to acquire the necessary skills to succeed without having to ask for help.

Personal Reflection for Your Own Use

How could this example work with your type of teaching?

What modifications would improve its use?

Where might you use this example?

This chapter follows the same format as the previous one, with similar tables. Table 4.1 contrasts instructor-centered approaches with learning-centered teaching on each of the six actions that define Development of Student Responsibility for Learning. Each column represents a separate instructor action of this construct. Note the qualitative difference among these six actions. The first one establishes the tone for how to develop students to take responsibility for learning, and the second one describes a way to teach these skills, whereas the remaining actions specify skills or practices that foster the development of responsibility for learning. These skills and practices are related and may overlap. Classification of these skills and practices varies in the literature. The literature on students' responsibility for learning rarely lists a set of skills that students need to master (Ellis, 2013). I explain each action and provide a published example of its use. To assist you in transforming your teaching to be more learning-centered I describe instructor characteristics using four increasingly learning-centered levels (instructor-centered, minimally learning-centered, mostly learning-centered, and extensively learning-centered). I present each action with its characteristics for the four increasingly learning-centered levels in separate tables.

Box 4.2 is a case study of an instructional design framework that draws on the theoretical constructs supporting this model of learning-centered teaching as discussed in chapter 2.

Action: The Instructor Sets Student Expectations, Which Enable the Responsibility for Learning to Be Shared Between the Instructor and the Students, With a Greater Amount Assumed by the Students

Learning-centered teaching is new for many students. This is especially true for beginning, international, and nontraditional students. Many students do not understand that they need to take a more proactive role in their own learning. Students may even question why the instructor "is not teaching" or teaching in the manner they expect. Box 4.3 discusses evidence that students often have different expectations than their instructors and there are differences among different types of students. Therefore, you should carefully explain your expectations to the students.

Greater transparency about responsibility for learning results in improved learning. Although you could feel this transparency about expectations is more like selling the idea than teaching, it may be necessary. You can specify expectations for responsibility in different

TABLE 4.1. Summary of Responsibility for Learning Construct and Actions Contrasting Instructor-Centered Approaches With Learning-Centered Approaches

Each column represents a separate action of the Development of Responsibility for Learning construct. Read down to see use of learning-centered teaching.

Approach	← Core Actions of the Responsibility for Learning →					
	Set Expectations That Responsibility for Learning Is Shared	Provide Scaffolding Support That Helps Students to Develop Responsibility for Learning	Develop Learning or Learning to Learn Skills That Are Directed Toward School Success	Develop Self-Directed, Lifelong Learning Skills	Foster Use of Reflection and Critical Review of Student Learning	Foster Use of Meta-cognitive Skills and Habits of the Mind to Assist Students to Solve Real-Life Problems
Instructor-Centered	Assumes majority of the responsibility for student learning	Does not provide scaffolding support	Considers learning skills irrelevant	Considers self-directed learning skills irrelevant to the course	Provides very occasional opportunities for student reflection, critical review, and self-assessment of their learning	Considers metacognitive skills and habits of the mind irrelevant
Learning-Centered	Provides repeated opportunities for students to assume responsibility for their own learning	Explicitly, intentionally models responsibility, teaching how to take responsibility actively	Explicitly facilitates students to develop various and appropriate skills for further learning	Explicitly facilitates students to develop skills for lifelong learning	Explicitly facilitates students to develop reflection, critical review, and self-assessment skills	Explicitly facilitates students to develop metacognitive skills and habits of the mind

ways. Certainly, your expectations need to be carefully described on your syllabus. To ensure students read the syllabus you can have a syllabus hunt where you ask students to find the answer to questions about information on the syllabus. You might consider developing a learning contract with students at the beginning of the semester to help students comprehend your and their responsibilities. In addition, you remind students of your expectations for their responsibility for learning.

The leaves in Illustration 4.1 represent the four levels characterizing each action. Each action is a branch on the tree shown at the beginning of the chapter. As Table 4.2 shows, the instructor characteristics for this action on the four-level continuum from instructor-centered to learning-centered approaches reflect the instructor's emphasis and explicitness about setting expectations for learning. Common instructor-centered teaching practices, as noted in Table 4.2, do not set the tone for students to take responsibility for learning, and they reinforce instructors assuming far too much responsibility for learning. However, sometimes, especially with immature or unmotivated

BOX 4.2.
Case Study of an Instructional Design Framework That Uses Many Aspects of the
Development of Student Responsibility for Learning Construct

Eunbae Lee and Michael Hannafin (2016) summarized research in constructivism, psychology, and the cognitive sciences and developed three key concepts that are essential for learning-centered teaching: autonomy, scaffolding, and audience.

Autonomy

- Learning autonomy can be achieved only though instructor support.
- When students achieve autonomy, their academic performance increases.

Scaffolding

- Instructors provide the necessary support through scaffolding. Effective instructors provide scaffolding support until student can function without it. Then instructors withdraw the scaffolding support.
- Three types of scaffolding:
  o Procedural for process
  o Conceptual for content organization
  o Metacognitive for goal setting, planning, organizing, self-monitoring, and self-evaluation

Audience

- When students create authentic course materials, they are more motivated to perform at their best.
- Authentic artifacts can be shared with potential users and classmates for feedback.
- Web 2.0 has blurred the distinction between producers and consumers of information.

Using these three concepts, Lee and Hannafin (2016) propose a design framework they call "own it, learn it, and share it." Both the concepts and the design framework can be used in face-to-face and online courses. Each framework element has design guidelines:

Design Framework Element	Example of Design Guidelines That Relate to Responsibility for Learning
Own it	Students should set personal goals that relate to the teacher's goals.
Learn it	Support student efforts through scaffolding.
Share it	Peer review can foster self-evaluation and reflection.

Personal Reflection for Your Own Use

How can you incorporate fostering student autonomy in your teaching?

How can you incorporate scaffolding your teaching?

How can you incorporate authentic audiences in your teaching?

How can you incorporate the design framework of own it, learn it, and share it in your teaching?

BOX 4.3.
Varying Expectations Among Traditional and First-Generation College Students and Their Instructors

Peter Collier and David Morgan (2008) conducted focus groups to study the consistency between instructors' expectations and students' understanding of these expectations. These findings are summarized here:

Expectation	Instructors	Traditional First-Year Student	First-Generation College Student
Role of syllabus	Convey information about the course, venue for describing expectations	Want basic facts like grading and schedule	Want detailed road map that tells exactly what students need to do
Study time	More than two hours out of class for every hour in class every week of the course	Amount of time available, not what was necessary	Fit it in around their other many commitments
Office hours	Help students to solve problems, further understanding of content	Build a relationship with instructor	Build a relationship with instructor
What is appropriate reference to use on assignments	Discipline-specific references, textbook, required readings	Mostly anything on the Internet, including Wikipedia	Wikipedia often primary source
Written assignments	Use accurate English, proper citations, common conventions about papers like margins	Understood proper use of English, although did not always write correctly	Less aware of proper English grammar, syntax and spelling, and common conventions
Time management	Be realistic about time available, prioritize academics	Felt already understood time management	Rejected advice not to take on too much

Instructors expressed frustration that students, especially first-generation college students, did not understand what students were expected to do and how to succeed in college, even after the instructors made their expectations explicit. They found that more traditional students begin college with greater understanding of their roles and responsibilities as college students than many first-generation students. Because first-generation students could not rely on their parents for guidance to understand what is expected in college, they recommend special orientation programs for first-generation college students.

Personal Reflection for Your Own Use

If the data fit with your experience, how can you use these results?

How would you determine your students' expectations about your course?

How would you use such data to align their expectations with yours?

If you teach first-year, first-generation college students, how can you give them the additional help they might need to succeed?

TABLE 4.2. Instructor Characteristics for Setting Expectations for Responsibility for Learning on the Four-Level Continuum From Instructor-Centered to Learning-Centered Approaches

Reading down, each row shows greater use of learning-centered teaching.

Levels	Action: Setting Expectations for Responsibility for Learning, With Instructor Characteristics at Each Level

Instructor-centered	Instructor:
	
	• Assumes responsibility for student learning by any of the following:
	  ○ Does not set student expectations or does not inform students of these expectations
	  ○ Provides detailed notes, complete presentations, extensive reading guides
	  ○ Tells students exactly what will be on examinations or gives students tests in advance of testing time
	  ○ Constantly reminds students of assignments, deadlines, or test dates
	  ○ Provides students with missing papers, syllabi, or another course material **OR**
	• Receives feedback that instructor micromanages students which allows them to not accept responsibility for their learning and does not change behaviors

Minimally learning-centered	Instructor: • States on the syllabus that students and instructors should share responsibility for learning without further explanation **OR** • States expectations for learning, assignments, time commitment **OR** • Encourages students to know where to find information about assignments and deadlines, and so on without telling them the answer
Mostly learning-centered	Instructor's actions illustrate that students should assume the responsibility for learning: • Explains on syllabus and in class what taking responsibility for learning means **AND** • Provides opportunities for students to assume responsibility for their own learning and explains the rationale **OR** • Informally explains how students should take responsibility for their learning, when requested by students. This explanation may be in one-on-one interactions or in an out-of-class experience
Extensively learning-centered	Instructor actively fosters students to take responsibility for their learning: • Explains what taking responsibility for learning means through repeated, concrete examples of how students take responsibility for learning **AND** • Provides opportunities for students to assume responsibility for their own learning throughout the course **AND** • Explicitly, intentionally explains how students assume responsibility and teaching how to take responsibility actively, using explanations and teaching systematically with everyone and not just those who seek extra help

students, instructors have to use some of these instructor-centered practices. Then the instructor could communicate that in the future, students need to take more responsibility for their learning without these prompts.

Action: The Instructor Helps Students to Develop Responsibility for Learning by Scaffolding Support. At the Beginning the Instructor Provides More Support and Feedback and as the Semester Progresses the Instructor Expects Increasing Student Independence

ILLUSTRATION 4.1. THE FOUR LEVELS OF CHARACTERISTICS FOR EACH ACTION

Just as in building construction, scaffolds provide temporary and adjustable support. This concept comes from constructivism, discussed in chapter 2. Scaffolding is effective when interactions between instructors and students are collaborative and the instructor helps students to succeed where they would not have been able to do so on their own or in their zone of proximal development. Because individuals vary in their abilities or zones of proximal development, learning-centered instructors should strive to give more scaffolding support to some students than others. This can be done through providing extra resources, assistance during office hours, or recommending tutoring. Instructors can provide three types of scaffolding: procedural for process, conceptual for content organization, and metacognitive for goal setting, planning, organizing, self-monitoring, and self-evaluation (Lee & Hannafin, 2016). Scaffolding is commonly used in language acquisition. The instructor provides feedback to help the students learn (Felder & Brent, 2016; Schunk, 2016). An essential feature of scaffolding is that the support is gradually removed to help students acquire independent mastery (Ambrose, Bridges, DiPietro, Lovett, & Norman, 2010). Table 4.3 lists the instructor characteristics for scaffolding support on the four-level continuum from instructor-centered to learning-centered approaches.

Instructors can scaffold learning by providing model answers with an explanation as to why the answers are excellent or solving problems while thinking aloud. Instructors may provide the resources students need to find information or create a template for completing an assignment. The instructor might explain the following techniques as a scaffolding exercise. When some students have more skills than others, the more proficient students can demonstrate their knowledge or skills using a fishbowl technique, with the more novice students observing them. Then the novice students discuss what they learned from the observation. (With a fishbowl approach, some students discuss the material while others observe and then afterward the ones who observed offer their own thoughts or critique.) Students can work on a project together in class while the instructor provides guidance and direction. Then in groups students need to create a similar project on another topic. Box 4.4 describes how STEM professors use scaffolding to help beginning chemistry students master the content and solve problems. Box 5.5 (in the next chapter) discusses how instructors intentionally use scaffolding across an educational program to help students acquire scientific literacy.

Action: The Instructor Fosters the Development of Learning or Learning to Learn Skills That Are Directed Toward School Success.

Examples of learning skills include

- study skills;
- time management;
- self-monitoring;
- goal setting; and
- how to read independently.

Learning skills help students to be more efficient and to succeed in school. The necessary learning skills change depending on the course requirements and as students progress through various levels of their student careers. Instructor-centered teachers either assume students already have these skills or feel that they should not take time away from content to teach these skills. However, learning-centered instructors explicitly teach appropriate skills as needed in their courses. You should teach beginning or struggling students evidence-based effective study strategies such as practice testing or distributed practice. You can also discourage the widespread but ineffective use of highlighting and rereading (Dunlosky, Rawson, Marsh, Nathan, & Willingham, 2013). Table 4.4 shows the four-level progression from instructor-centered to learning-centered on the fostering the development of learning

TABLE 4.3. Instructor Characteristics for Scaffolding Support on the Four-Level Continuum From Instructor-Centered to Learning-Centered Approaches

Reading down, each row shows greater use of learning-centered teaching.

Levels	Action: Scaffolding Support, With Instructor Characteristics at Each Level
Instructor-centered	Instructor: • Does not provide scaffolding support **OR** • Does not increase expectations for student independence
Minimally learning-centered	Instructor: • Provides the same amount and type of scaffolding support throughout the semester **OR** • Provides the same scaffolding to all students without recognizing that some students might need more or less support
Mostly learning-centered	Instructor: • Informally models how to do things independently, when requested by students, in one-on-one interactions or in an out-of-class experience **OR** • Provides additional scaffolding support to some students when they request it, providing different types of scaffolding to these students, as needed **OR** • Removes scaffolding support as the semester progresses
Extensively learning-centered	Instructor: • Explicitly, intentionally models responsibility, teaching how to take responsibility actively, systematically done with everyone and not just those who seek extra help **AND** • Provides different types of scaffolding support as needed: procedural for process; conceptual for content organization; and/or metacognitive for goal setting, planning, organizing, self-monitoring, and self-evaluation **AND** • Removes scaffolding support in an intentional manner, thus allowing students to take more responsibility as the course progresses **AND** • Recognizes when students are not yet ready to take such responsibility **AND** • Responds to individual students' needs for scaffolding support throughout the course

---

BOX 4.4.
Scaffolding Support for Students

Madhu Mahalingam and Elizabetta Fasella (2017) use technology and small group activities as scaffolding to help students succeed in their general chemistry course. The scaffolding occurs weekly. During the lectures students answer questions using an audience response system; then the instructor shows the correct answer. Between classes students must complete homework assignments that require them to solve problems and to evaluate their mastery of the content. An online homework monitoring system provides students with immediate feedback on their mastery of the content and accuracy in solving problems and scaffolds success. This system provides students assistance in solving the problem if they are unable to do so. Thus, some students receive more assistance than others. Further scaffolding occurs in small group problem-solving classes where the students solve challenging chemistry problems. The instructor and teaching assistants provide guidance when needed and can individualize how much support is given. Four times during the semester the students need to solve similar problems alone and with no scaffolding support during the in-class exams. The instructors measure the success of their scaffolding supports through student performance on these exams.

(Continues)

BOX 4.4. (Continued)

Personal Reflection for Your Own Use

Can you use an online homework system, perhaps in conjunction with your textbook, to scaffold student mastery of content outside of class?

How can you use small-group problem-solving sessions to prepare students to solve problems individually on tests?

How could scaffolding systems be used to recognize students in need of additional support?

---

skills action. Throughout this book, when benchmark numbers are given on the four-level progression tables, such as the number three on the second bullet of minimally learning centered level of Table 4.4, they should be used as a metric for semester-long courses.

Personal Reflection

What learning skills do you require your students to use to succeed in your courses?

1.
2.
3.

How do you foster the development of these learning skills?

All institutions accredited by the Commission on Colleges of the Southern Association of Colleges and Schools need to create a quality enhancement plan to address the institution's identified shortcomings. The commission needs to approve this plan and then the institution's administrators need to report on their progress. Box 4.5 describes how a university considered these learning skills so essential to their at-risk students that they became a focus for their institutional quality enhancement plan.

Action: The Instructor Fosters the Development of Self-Directed, Lifelong Learning Skills

Examples of lifelong learning skills include the following:

- determining a personal need to know more on a regular basis, or possessing an inquiring mind;
- developing information literacy skills to find, evaluate, and use information ethically (Association of College and Research Libraries, 2016);
- acquiring a range of strategies for learning in diverse contexts;
- determining if personal need to know has been met; and
- fostering a growth mind-set attitude.

Although graduating self-directed lifelong learners has always been a goal of higher education, this goal has taken on greater importance in the last 30 years. Candy, Crebert, and O'Leary (1994) attribute this change to the shift to an information society where technology makes information ubiquitous, coupled with the advent of new careers and occupations. Traditional college education does not prepare graduates for these new careers, perhaps because of the current focus on disciplinary content. Today, more than was the case 50 years ago, instructors must help students learn how to continuously learn (Arceo, 2016). Individuals with inquiring minds constantly need to learn more, know how to get the answers to their questions, and know when they know enough to determine that their need to know has been met. Table 4.5 lists characteristics on the continuum of instructor-centered to learning-centered instructors on the development of self-directed, lifelong learning skills. This table also lists common lifelong learning skills.

TABLE 4.4. Instructor Characteristics for Fostering Development of Learning Skills on the Four-Level Continuum From Instructor-Centered to Learning-Centered Approaches

Examples of these learning skills include

- time management,
- self-monitoring,
- goal setting, and
- how to read independently.

Reading down, each row shows greater use of learning-centered teaching.

Levels	Action: Fosters Development of Learning Skills, With Instructor Characteristics at Each Level
Instructor-centered	Instructor: • Allows students to meet course objectives without developing further learning skills **OR** • Assumes students will develop learning skills without assistance **OR** • Does not consider learning skills **OR** • Considers learning skills irrelevant
Minimally learning-centered	Instructor: • Does not teach the development of any learning or learning to learn skills to foster school success **OR** • Provides three or fewer opportunities for students to practice at least one of these learning skills due to the nature of the course requirements; does not pay much attention to these learning skills
Mostly learning-centered	Instructor: • Intentionally teaches appropriate learning or learning to learn skills to foster school success **AND** • Provides opportunities throughout the course for students to practice at least two learning skills
Extensively learning-centered	Instructor must meet criteria for mostly using learning-centered approaches **AND** • Explicitly facilitates students to develop various and appropriate skills for further learning **AND** • Provides formative feedback to all students on their development **AND** • Assesses these learning skills and not just the product of the use of these skills

The Association of College and Research Libraries (2016) defined *information literacy* as the ability to frame researchable questions, access sources, evaluate the appropriateness of sources to address research questions, evaluate the content in these sources, and use information legally and ethically. The last part refers to paraphrasing, not plagiarizing, and properly citing sources. People need information literacy to continue to learn outside of school.

Carol Dweck (2008) identified two mind-set attitudes: fixed and growth. Which one students have greatly influences how they lead their lives. People with fixed mind-sets believe that they are born with a fixed amount of intelligence or a certain personality. With effort these people think they can reach their own potential but cannot progress beyond that point. These people view difficulties as obstacles that can lower their self-efficacy. They are prone to give up. In contrast, people with growth mind-sets believe that everyone can change and grow through experience, effort, and help from others. These people view difficulties as challenges; they believe they can

BOX 4.5.
How Teaching Learning Skills Promotes College Success

Faculty and administrators at Dalton State University in Georgia chose to focus on helping students in English writing for their five-year quality enhancement plan because only about half of their students successfully complete the developmental (not for college credit) course in English writing the first time they take it and about one-third third never pass the course, even with five or more attempts (Schwenn & Codjoe, 2013). Three of the learning outcomes concerned proper use of English language and writing effective paragraphs, and one learning outcome related to helping students navigate the college system and teaching students skills to succeed both as writers and as students. The faculty and administrators saw both the writing and the learning skills as closely connected, as they both build critical thinking and self-efficacy. Students in these writing courses were part of a learning community which was linked to their first-year experience course. Relevant learning skill objectives included obtain information literacy skills, identify and apply time management strategies, utilize study skills and test preparation strategies, and identify technological resources that aid academic success. Students wrote reflective journal assignments and the instructors graded them using a rubric that included criteria for correct writing and acquisition of learning skills. They further identified required learning strategies: attend class regularly, complete all major assignments, participate in class work and discussions, complete journal entries, and use online writing resources.

Personal Reflection for Your Own Use

How can you link learning skill acquisition to content of a course, especially writing?

How you do help students who may not be prepared for your course because of lack of learning skills?

TABLE 4.5 Instructor Characteristics for the Development of Self-Directed, Lifelong Learning Skills on the Four-Level Continuum From Instructor-Centered to Learning-Centered Approaches

Examples of these lifelong learning skills include

- determining a personal need to know more on a regular basis or possessing an inquiring mind;
- information literacy skills of finding, evaluating, and using information ethically;
- acquiring a range of strategies for learning in diverse contexts;
- determining when need to know about a topic is met; and
- fostering a growth mind-set attitude.

Reading down, each row shows greater use of learning-centered teaching.

Levels	*Action: Fosters Development of Self-Directed, Lifelong Learning Skills, With Instructor Characteristics at Each Level*
Instructor-centered	Instructor: • Allows students to meet course objectives without developing deep, self-directed, lifelong learning skills **OR** • Assumes students will develop self-directed learning skills without assistance **OR** • Does not consider self-directed learning skills **OR** • Considers self-directed learning skills irrelevant to the course **OR** • Does not foster a growth mind-set attitude

(Continues)

TABLE 4.5. (Continued)

Levels	Action: Fosters Development of Self-Directed, Lifelong Learning Skills, With Instructor Characteristics at Each Level
Minimally learning-centered	Instructor: • Does not teach how to develop any of the self-directed or lifelong learning skills **OR** • Does not foster the development of a growth mind-set attitude **OR** • Provides three or fewer opportunities for student to practice at least one of these self-directed, lifelong learning skills due to the nature of the course requirements; does not pay much attention to these learning skills
Mostly learning-centered	Instructor: • Intentionally teaches many of the appropriate self-directed, lifelong learning skills **AND** • Provides opportunities throughout the course for students to practice at least two self-directed, lifelong learning skills **AND** • Provides opportunities for students to acquire a range of strategies for learning in diverse contexts **AND** • Intentionally fosters a growth mind-set attitude
Extensively learning-centered	Instructor must meet criteria for mostly uses learning-centered approaches **AND** • Explicitly facilitates student development of various and appropriate lifelong learning skills and growth mind-set attitude **AND** • Provides formative feedback to all students on their development **AND** • Assesses these learning skills and not just the product of the use of these skills

raise their self-efficacy if they persist and use effective strategies. Instructors can cultivate a growth mind-set in students that leads to a passion for continuous learning.

A distinguishing characteristic of self-directed learning is that the individual takes the initiative for learning. However, self-directed learning, like most learning, usually occurs in a social context and with external assistance (Brookfield, 1985). Acquiring the lifelong learning skills listed here should be fundamental to all undergraduate education (Candy et al., 1994). Graduate, professional, and continuing education should reinforce the need for lifelong learning. Teachers of students at all levels play a critical role in the development of self-directed learning. Box 4.6 discusses how clinical faculty/physicians promote the development of self-directed learning in internal medicine residents. These residents have already earned bachelor's and medical doctor degrees but now they will be functioning more independently as physicians. Although highly educated people were the participants in this study, the insights for how faculty can promote

self-directed learning generalize to all levels of higher education.

Personal Reflection

What lifelong learning skills would you like your students to acquire or master in your courses?

1.
2.
3.

How do you foster the development of these lifelong learning skills?

Action: The Instructor Fosters Students' Engagement in Reflection and Critical Review of Their Learning Through Well-Structured Activities

Reflection and critical review should include self-assessment of learning abilities, mastery of objectives, and strengths and weaknesses. Reflection and critical review help people to make their experiences

---

BOX 4.6.
How Faculty Promote Self-Directed Learning With Advanced Students

Adam Sawatsky, John Ratelle, Sara Bonnes, Jason Egginton, and Thomas Beckman (2017) conducted focus groups with internal medicine residents to determine how their clinical faculty facilitated the residents' further development of self-directed learning. They wanted their faculty members to provide direction to learning, assist in structuring and organizing knowledge, ask challenging questions, help residents to see their knowledge gaps, provide some but not an overwhelming number of resources for further learning, and help the residents assess their new knowledge. However, when the faculty members ask too many questions or else answer all questions with "Look it up," the result is demotivation and less self-directed learning. The residents stressed the importance of the faculty role-modeling their own self-directed learning. They preferred collaborative self-directive learning where they were treated like colleagues.

Personal Reflection for Your Own Use

How can you use the methods identified by these residents with your students?

How do you find a balance between guiding and not overwhelming students?

How can you role-model your own self-directed learning with your students?

How can it be appropriate to treat your undergraduate students like colleagues? When is it inappropriate to do so?

---

meaningful (Kolb, 1984; Schon, 1987). Because it leads to insights about oneself and self-efficacy, reflection plays a powerful role in learning. Reflection could be considered the engine that drives learning (Stevens & Cooper, 2009). For reflections to be effective, James and Brookfield (2014) suggest that instructors ask students to

- consider the assumptions underlining actions or judgments;
- open themselves to different perspectives;
- notice blind spots or omissions in thinking; and
- connect information from one class or discipline to another.

Whereas reflection is introspective, critical review requires learners to integrate perspectives from other people in addition to their own. Critical review is more data-driven than reflection. The combination of inner-focused reflection and other- or outer-focused considerations leads to meaningful learning that might be less biased than otherwise.

Learning-centered instructors require their students to reflect and critically review their learning and experiences because this action helps students to construct knowledge from isolated facts. Once synthesized, this knowledge will be available for use in the future (Fink, 2013). Both reflection and critical review help students to assess their learning abilities, their mastery of objectives, and their strengths and weaknesses. However, before instructors ask their students to engage in reflection and critical review, instructors need to model how it is done. Table 4.6 displays the instructor characteristics for students' engagement in reflection and critical review of their learning on the four-level continuum from instructor-centered to learning-centered approaches.

Instructors use reflection in different ways in a diverse array of courses. Writing instructors often

TABLE 4.6. Instructor Characteristics for Students' Engagement in Reflection and Critical Review of Their Learning on the Four-Level Continuum From Instructor-Centered to Learning-Centered Approaches

Reflection and critical review should include

- self-assessment of learning abilities,
- one's mastery of objectives, and
- one's mastery of strengths and weaknesses.

Reading down, each row shows greater use of learning-centered teaching.

Levels	Action: Students' Engagement in Reflection and Critical Review, With Instructor Characteristics at Each Level
Instructor-centered	Instructor: • Provides no or very occasional opportunities for student reflection, critical review, and self-assessment of their learning **OR** • Receives feedback from students that the reflection, critical review, and self-assessment activities are too unstructured to foster learning and the instructor does not try to improve these activities
Minimally learning-centered	Instructor: • Does not teach how to do reflection, critical review, or self-assessment of student learning **AND** • Provides three or fewer opportunities for student reflection, critical review, and self-assessment of their learning
Mostly learning-centered	Instructor: • Intentionally teaches how to do reflection, critical review, and self-assessment of learning **AND** • Provides opportunities throughout the course for student reflection, critical review, and self-assessment of their learning, using activities that are structured and specific enough to allow students to learn from them
Extensively learning-centered	Instructor must meet criteria for mostly using learning-centered approaches **AND** • Explicitly facilitates student development of reflection, critical review, and self-assessment skills of their learning **AND** • Provides formative feedback to all students on their ability to reflect, conduct critical review, and self-assessment of their learning **AND** • Assesses reflection, critical review, and self-assessment skills of learning and not just the product of the use of these skills **AND** • Explains how and why these periodic opportunities for student reflection, critical review, and self-assessment result in greater student understanding

require reflections. Reflections and critical reviews of student experiences in the community are the critical elements that turn service or volunteering to service-learning. Student journals and portfolios should include reflections (Moon, 2006). Box 4.7 describes a pedagogy that uses reflection in sustained, paired dialogues in different types of courses and for different reasons.

Action: The Instructor Fosters the Students' Use of Metacognitive Skills and Habits of the Mind to Assist Students to Solve Real-Life Problems and Gain a Positive Outcome

Table 4.7 displays the instructor characteristics for students' use of metacognitive skills and habits of the mind to assist students to solve real-life problems and gain a positive outcome on the four-level continuum from

---

BOX 4.7.
Sustained, Paired Dialogues Lead to Effective Reflections on Learning

For many years, high school, college, and rabbinical students at yeshivas (traditional Jewish education) have engaged in *hevruta*-style study. *Hevruta* learning is characterized by sustained pairs who work together for years. During these dialogues the students interpret their close reading of texts, debate their perspectives, and ask each other difficult questions to analyze and synthesize large amounts of detailed reading.

Mary Wright, Jeffrey Bernstein, and Ralph Williams (2013) describe how they used *hevruta* in two different types of classes to heighten reflection and foster students taking responsibility for their learning. In both examples, prior to each class, students read the required readings and were provided prompts for their discussion. In the first example, a large enrollment, upper level literature course at a highly competitive university, graduate students supervised students as they engaged in *hevruta* learning. During these *hevruta* sessions, they discussed controversial topics throughout the semester. Student surveys showed that the students felt this style of learning was effective in promoting reflection because of how deeply they thought about the literature, which led to self-directed learning.

In the second example, students were in an introductory, small enrollment political science course at a university with a diverse student population, whose students often worked up to 20 hours per week. *Hevruta*-style discussions were used to engage and motivate students 6 times during the semester when the topic or the text to be discussed was difficult to understand. Following the paired discussions, students engaged in a full-class discussion of the same material, and they were much better prepared and more willing to speak. Because of these paired dialogues and the full-class discussions, students were significantly better at explaining their political views to others and weighing the pros and cons of political issues than students in other sections of the course.

Personal Reflection for Your Own Use

How could you use *hevruta*-style discussions in your face-to-face courses?

How could you use *hevruta*-style discussions in your online courses?

What modifications would you have to make for this pedagogy to work with your students and your content?

---

instructor-centered to learning-centered approaches. This table also lists 3 metacognitive skills and 10 common habits of the mind. When students use habits of the mind and metacognitive skills, they become adept at applying learning and evaluating their own process of learning.

Metacognition contains three essential skills: planning, monitoring, and evaluating. Planning involves selecting appropriate strategies and allocating resources to get the task achieved, such as learning or completing a project for school. Monitoring is one's awareness of how much one understands one's skills or abilities in relation to the task to be performed. Evaluating occurs after the task is completed to determine if different strategies would have been better and the efficiency of performing the task.

Thinking about one's thinking, or metacognition, leads to being aware of one's own thoughts, feelings,

intentions, and actions. Knowing that what one says and does affects others should cause people to consider the impact of their choices on other people. Metacognitive skills greatly influence how much and how well students learn because they give people awareness of their learning strengths and weaknesses. This awareness leads to active monitoring of learning strategies and resources (Bransford et al., 2000; McGuire & McGuire, 2015).

People employ habits of the mind when there is uncertainty, in challenging situations, or when they do not know the correct answer (Costa & Kallick, 2008). Several or many habits of the mind are usually employed together. Using these good habits of the mind may differentiate between success and fulfillment in one's career or personal life versus not achieving one's goals. Many habits of the mind exist and overlap with the other skills identified as fostering

TABLE 4.7. Instructor Characteristics for Fostering Students' Use of Metacognitive Skills and Habits of the Mind on the Four-Level Continuum From Instructor-Centered to Learning-Centered Approaches

Examples of these metacognitive skills include

- planning,
- monitoring, and
- evaluating.

Frequently cited examples of habits of the mind not previously discussed in this chapter include

- ability to postpone judgment/managing impulsivity;
- creativity/creating, imagining, and innovating;
- curiosity/questioning and posing problems;
- flexibility;
- interdependent learning and working;
- openness/listening with understanding and empathy;
- persistence;
- responsible risk-taking;
- striving for accuracy, clarity, and precision; and
- transfer of learning/applying past knowledge to new situations.

Reading down, each row shows greater use of learning-centered teaching.

Levels	*Action: Fostering Students' Use of Metacognitive Skills and Habits of the Mind, With Instructor Characteristics at Each Level*
Instructor-centered	Instructor: • Allows students to meet course objectives without fostering the use of metacognitive skills or habits of the mind **OR** • Does not consider metacognitive skills or habits of the mind **OR** • Considers metacognitive skills and habits of the mind irrelevant
Minimally learning-centered	Instructor: • Does not teach how to develop any of the metacognitive skills or habits of the mind to solve real-life problems and to gain a positive outcome **AND** • Provides three or fewer opportunities for student to practice at least one of these metacognitive skills and habits of the mind; does not pay much attention to these metacognitive skills and habits of the mind
Mostly learning-centered	Instructor: • Must model or teach intentionally three or more metacognitive skills or habits of the mind **AND** • Provides students opportunities throughout the course for student to practice three or more metacognitive skills and habits of the mind to solve real-life problems and to gain a positive outcome
Extensively learning-centered	Instructor must meet criteria for mostly uses learning-centered approaches **AND** • Explicitly facilitates student development of various and appropriate metacognitive skills and habits of the mind to solve real-life problems and to gain a positive outcome **AND** • Teaches individuals or groups of students how to use metacognitive skills when deficiencies are detected **AND** • Provides formative feedback to all students on their development **AND** • Explains how and why using metacognitive skills and habits of the mind assist students to solve real-life problems and to gain a positive outcome **AND** • Assesses these metacognitive skills and habits of the mind and not just the product of the use of these skills and habits

responsibility for learning. Scholars in this field have not agreed upon a specific list. Table 4.7 identifies commonly cited (Costa & Kallick, 2008; Fletcher, Najarro, & Yelland, 2015) habits of the mind that have not been previously discussed in this chapter.

Box 4.8 describes a modification of a commonly used teaching and learning activity called a jigsaw. A jigsaw is composed of a few steps. Students come to class prepared to discuss material. In the homogenous discussion step, students are assigned to discuss one aspect of the content in small groups. Each group is assigned a different aspect. In the last step students form mixed groups with a student from each aspect coming together. In these new groups, students either solve problems in which all aspects of the material are

needed or make predictions. In the course described in the box, the students participated in an extended jigsaw activity, and they used many metacognitive skills and habits of the mind. Although the activity was used in the social sciences, it could be used in many different types of disciplines.

For further reading on how to foster reflection, use of metacognition, and habits of the mind, I recommend the following practical books:

- *Fostering Habits of Mind in Today's Students: A New Approach to Developmental Education* (Fletcher et al., 2015)
- *Engaging Imagination* (James & Brookfield, 2014)

BOX 4.8.
Group Project With Individual Accountability and Student Use of Metacognition and Habits of the Mind

Olga Blomgren (2015) used an extended jigsaw for parts of 7 classes covering 4 weeks of the semester. There was out-of-class preparation, individual writing, and other preparation throughout. Prior to the first class, students were asked to skim all the articles assigned on one topic in this course. Students pulled one author's name out of a hat. Students formed 4-person content groups with each group discussing the work of only 1 author. Prior to the next class, each student wrote a persuasive essay about their author's main point. During the next class each group had to reach a consensus on the main points of their article. Their homework was to find and bring a visual that represented the author's ideas. In the next class each group had to select 1 visual or media example that best presented the author's ideas. For homework each student had to find another example in the media of what they thought also represented the author's ideas. Because every student had to bring their artifacts to class, it was easy to see if all students were prepared. Next the group had to develop a presentation and activity for the entire class that explained and developed the author's main ideas and showed why the media selection and visual represented their author's ideas. Each group presented to the class for 30 minutes over the course of several classes. After all the presentations, each student wrote a reflective and evaluative essay explaining their own and their peers' contributions to the group discussions and team project and to discuss what they liked or disliked about the project. All aspects of the project were graded.

Personal Reflection for Your Own Use

How could you use either a jigsaw or this extended jigsaw in your courses?

How could you use a jigsaw or this extended jigsaw in your online courses?

What modifications would you have to make for this teaching and learning activity to work with your students and your content?

What metacognition skills or habits of the mind would you want the students to practice during such an activity?

How would you introduce these metacognition skills or habits of the mind and how would you ensure they are practiced?

- *Using Reflection and Metacognition to Improve Student Learning: Across the Disciplines, Across the Academy* (Kaplan, Silver, LaVaque-Manty, & Meizlish, 2013)
- *Teach Students How to Learn: Strategies You Can Incorporate Into Any Course to Improve Student Metacognition, Study Skills, and Motivation* (McGuire & McGuire, 2015)

Personal Reflection

What metacognitive skills and habits of the mind would help your students to succeed in your courses?

1.
2.

3.
4.

How do you foster the development of these metacognitive skills and habits of the mind?

Chapter Summary

This chapter discusses how you can change your teaching to be more learning-centered through the construct called Development of Student Responsibility for Learning. Table 4.8 summarizes the six core actions of this construct and briefly identifies the characteristics of faculty at four levels going from instructor-centered to learning-centered teaching.

TABLE 4.8. Summary of Responsibility for Learning Construct and Actions Contrasting Instructor-Centered Approaches With Learning-Centered Approaches

For details on each action, see the description in the chapter.

Key to Table

Columns = Action descriptions

Rows = Reading down each column, each successive row shows greater use of learning-centered teaching.

Levels↓	← *Actions of Responsibility for Learning* →					
	Expectations	**Scaffolding Support**	**Learning Skills**	**Lifelong Learning Skills**	**Reflection and Critical Review**	**Metacognitive Skills and Habits of the Mind**
Instructor-centered	Assumes responsibility for student learning	Does not provide scaffolding support	Considers irrelevant	Considers irrelevant	Provides no opportunities	Considers irrelevant
Minimally learning-centered	States responsibility for learning without further explanation	Provides the same scaffolding support throughout the course	Provides limited practice	Provides limited practice	Provides limited practice	Provides limited practice
Mostly learning-centered	Provides some opportunities and explains the rationale	Informally models support	Intentionally teaches, provides practice	Intentionally teaches, provides practice	Intentionally teaches, provides practice	Intentionally teaches, provides practice
Extensively learning-centered	Provides repeated opportunities	Explicitly, intentionally models support, removes support	Explicitly facilitates development	Explicitly facilitates development	Explicitly facilitates development	Explicitly facilitates development

Taking Stock of This Construct and How You Can Implement Learning-Centered Teaching by Developing Responsibility for Learning

Table 4.9 gives you the opportunity to review your current learning-centered teaching status and decide what and when you want to change. See Table 3.10 (in chapter 3) for further directions on how to complete this taking stock activity. Your proposed changes are only tentative plans. Once you have read through the rest of this book, you will reconsider your plans and prioritize what you will want to change.

TABLE 4.9. Worksheet: Status of Teaching and Plans for Change to Increase Use of Learning-Centered Teaching Approaches

Date_____

Directions

For more explanation, see Table 3.10.

1. Put a ^ in the cell that indicates your status.
2. Put a * in the cell to identify the level to which you aspire to become more learning-centered on this action.
3. Indicate your timeline to achieve change for each action on the bottom row.
4. Make comments that will help you make these planned changes.

Note: You may not want to plan changes in every action.

Construct II: Development of Student Responsibility for Learning

Levels↓	← *Actions of the Responsibility for Learning* →					
	Expectations	**Scaffolding Support**	**Learning Skills**	**Lifelong Learning Skills**	**Reflection and Critical Review**	**Metacognitive Skills and Habits of the Mind**
Instructor-centered	Assumes responsibility for student learning	Does not provide scaffolding support	Considers irrelevant	Considers irrelevant	Provides no opportunities	Considers irrelevant
Minimally learning-centered	States responsibility for learning without further explanation	Provides the same scaffolding support throughout the course	Provides limited practice	Provides limited practice	Provides limited practice	Provides limited practice
Mostly learning-centered	Provides some opportunities and explains the rationale	Informally models support	Intentionally teaches, provides practice	Intentionally teaches, provides practice	Intentionally teaches, provides practice	Intentionally teaches, provides practice
Extensively learning-centered	Provides repeated opportunities	Explicitly, intentionally models support, removes support	Explicitly facilitates development	Explicitly facilitates development	Explicitly facilitates development	Explicitly facilitates development
Time line to achieve change						

Notes/Comments on My Plan

content methodologies

discipline thinking

conceptual understanding

organizing scheme

engagement with content

why learn

Content

Current Evidence-Based Understanding of Learning

CHAPTER 5

Function of Content

Chapter Highlights

Whereas instructor-centered teachers cover content, learning-centered instructors help students to meaningfully engage with the content, leading to deep learning and the ability to apply the content in the future. As a learning-centered teacher, you perform the following core actions that facilitate student learning:

- Use organizing schemes to integrate material.
- Promote meaningful student engagement with the content.
- Foster the development and use of discipline-specific methodologies.
- Help students understand why they need to learn the content.
- Provide practice using inquiry or ways of thinking in the discipline.
- Help students acquire in-depth conceptual understanding of the content.

Traditionally, instructors considered content coverage or building a knowledge base as the essence of teaching. As learning-centered teachers, content coverage takes a back seat to students' meaningful engagement with the content so that they have deep learning and can apply the content in the future. Content is not just the end, it is an important means to other desired outcomes as defined by the six core actions.

This chapter follows the same format as chapter 3 and chapter 4. Table 5.1 contrasts instructor-centered approaches with learning-centered teaching on each of the six actions that define the Function of Content. Each column represents a separate action of this construct. I explain each action and provide a published example of its use. To assist you in transforming your teaching to be more learning-centered, I define instructor characteristics, for each action, with four increasingly learning-centered levels (i.e., instructor-centered, minimally learning-centered,

mostly learning-centered, and extensively learning-centered). I present each action with its characteristics for the four increasingly learning-centered levels in separate tables.

Before discussing the actions separately, I suggest an easy-to-implement learning-centered technique in Box 5.1 and describe a case study of a course that uses aspects of the Function of Content for learning-centered courses in Box 5.2.

Action: The Instructor Uses Organizing Schemes That Are Discipline-Specific Conceptual Frameworks to Integrate Material and Provide a Context for Further Learning

The content in most disciplines can be summarized into about a dozen organizing schemes. Organizing schemes are discipline-specific conceptual frameworks that help experts integrate already known content and

TABLE 5.1. Summary of Function of Content Construct and Actions Contrasting Instructor-Centered Approaches With Learning-Centered Approaches

Each column represents a separate action of the Function of Content construct. Read down to see use of learning-centered teaching.

Approach	Use Organizing Schemes	Engage in Personal Meaning-Making	Use Discipline-Specific Methodologies	← *Actions of the Function of Content* → Understand Why They Need to Learn	Solve Problems	Facilitate Future Learning
Instructor-Centered	Does not use organizing schemes in teaching	Allows students to memorize content as it was given to them without requiring understanding or without placing into a context	Does not help students acquire discipline-specific methodologies that they need in the course	Does not use content to help students understand why they need to learn the content for use in their careers or personal growth.	Does not teach inquiry or ways of thinking in the discipline to solve discipline-specific or real-world problems	Does not provide opportunities for students to apply knowledge to new content or new contexts
Learning-Centered	Explicitly uses organizing schemes throughout the course to create student learning outcomes, teaching/learning activities, and assessment activities	Uses assessments consistently that require students to demonstrate that they have created meaning from the content	Assesses these discipline-specific methodologies and not just the product of the use of these methodologies	Requires that students' work on applications to their careers or their lives is graded and counts in the final grade	Provides repeated student practice using inquiry or ways of thinking in the discipline to solve discipline-specific or real-world problems	Requires students to learn or integrate content on their own in a large project or paper, in an assignment that counts enough toward the grade that students take it seriously

---

BOX 5.1.
Example of Easy-to-Implement Learning-Centered Practice: A Template for Reading Required Material

If students read material before class, they are better prepared to engage during the class. Unfortunately, few students do the required reading or, even if they do, they may not actively engage with the content (Divoll & Browning, 2013). However, when you require reading notes prior to class, give questions or a template for notes, and count these notes as a small percentage of the grade, students will come prepared. The following template not only helps the students engage with the content but also helps you structure class time more effectively:

Reading Notes for Reading/Chapter/Article		Date_____	
Key concepts from reading			
You can either give students a list or ask them to develop the key concepts from the objectives.			
State concept in your own words or graphically represent the concept.	How does this concept connect to what you have previously learned?	How does this concept relate to your future career or your personal life?	What questions do you have or which aspects would you like explained or discussed in class?

Personal Reflection for Your Own Use

How could this example work with your type of teaching?

What modifications would improve its use?

Where might you use this example?

---

learn new material. The periodic table of chemical elements is probably the best known organizing scheme. The elements are arranged in columns and each of the elements in a column has similar properties, like being a metal or an inert gas that will not combine with other gases. Chemists know how elements relate to each other by their place on the periodic table. Novices have not organized the content well enough to use it unless they are explicitly taught (Bransford et al., 2000). However, if you routinely use organizing schemes throughout your teaching, students will gain a much bigger sense of the whole picture of your discipline and not just have isolated knowledge. They will also be able to integrate new learning into these organizing schemes (Ambrose et al., 2010).

Examples of organizing schemes in different disciplines include the following:

- Homeostasis is an organizing theme in physiology.

- Moving toward modernity is an organizing theme in history.
- Structure-function relationship is an organizing scheme in biology.
- Individual differences in human behavior is an organizing scheme in psychology.
- The Dewey decimal system or the Library of Congress system are organizing schemes for books used by librarians.

Personal Reflection

What are the organizing schemes in your discipline and in the courses you teach?

1.
2.
3.

BOX 5.2.
Case Study of Understanding the Functions of Psalms

Charles Miller (2010), a religion professor, believes that students think they know the Bible, as they know the content of some parts of it, but this knowledge is largely unexamined and often not seen as relevant to their lives outside of their religious observances. They rarely make meaning out of the Bible; rather, they receive meaning from others. Often students parrot back what they have heard from their preachers or their parents. The purpose of a general education, introductory Bible course is to help students learn to engage with the content and to make it meaningful to them and also to encourage further learning.

    Miller found that students do not like studying psalms. This relates to their dislike of all poetry. Therefore, for all of these reasons, Miller changed how he teaches psalms. He focuses on interpretation and psalms as literary genres and their impact on the reader's expectations. He teaches his students discipline-specific methodologies such as strategies to read and interpret types of psalms. Through class discussions, students come to understand that psalms were written and incorporated into the Bible because they serve functions such as ideological purposes or evoking emotions, including lament, praise, or gratitude. Miller helps students to see the world differently through their study of psalms. He uses video clips, art, and music to show how the Bible influences many aspects of our secular culture. Miller compares psalms to popular music with a chord structure, meter, and rhythm and asks students to connect what they know about popular music to poetry. Students come to realize that psalms, like popular music, have common themes, such as lament or love. Once they have made these connections, then he asks them to see the poetic structure of psalms. As an assignment, students are asked to analyze an infrequently recited psalm that they have not studied. Students who have engaged during class do very well on this assignment. When students analyze psalms, and write their own poetry like the psalms, they become motivated to engage in further study of psalms, poetry, and music.

Personal Reflection for Your Own Use

Do you teach content that students do not relate to? What can you do to help students meaningfully engage with this content?

How can you make your content more meaningful and relevant by comparing it to what students already know, such as popular culture?

How can you help students use content to further their own learning?

4.

5.

6.

7.

8.

9.

10.

Box 5.3 shows how a theater instructor uses organizing schemes to make theater history come alive for students. The leaves in Illustration 5.1 represent the four levels characterizing each action. Each action is a branch on the tree shown at the beginning of the chapter. Table 5.2 lists the instructor characteristics for the use of organizing schemes on the four-level

continuum from instructor-centered to learning-centered approaches. Throughout this book, when numbers are given on the four-level progression tables such as the number 10 on the last bullet of the mostly learning centered level of Table 5.2 they should be used as a metric for semester-long courses.

Action: The Instructor Promotes Meaningful Student Engagement With the Content. This Engagement of Content Occurs Through Personal Meaning-Making to Facilitate Mastery

Engagement is defined by the quality of the effort and involvement in productive learning activities (Kuh, 2009). Creating personal meanings and associations

---

BOX 5.3.
Example of How a Course Was Developed Using Organizing Schemes

Katelyn Wood (2017) teaches history of theater courses without being bound by the common linear temporality starting from ancient Greece and moving onward. Instead she presents the units as what she calls *curative pedagogy*. I would call them organizing schemes that allow her to transcend time and genre and get students to appreciate and integrate similarities and differences of theater across time, location, and cultural contexts. Students learn to synthesize many different performance practices within their cultural or historical contexts. Because traditional textbooks take a linear approach, Wood instead requires students to read from various authors and do different types of in-class exercises. These organizing schemes facilitate the study of theater history as a model of deep learning. Some of the organizing schemes in her courses include the following:

- Theater and the State
- Performance and Spirituality
- Transnational Identities
- Power and Control
- Politics of Style and Form

In Theater and the State students study the ancient Greek play *Lysistrata*, modern Western plays, and Kabuki theater. The 2016 election helped students to see the connection between theater and political protest.

The organizing schemes not only direct the organization of the content but also inform how she conducts classes. Students need to reflect or position themselves as critical historiographers. Students question the material and realize that there is not one correct answer. Students revise and restate their arguments as they progress through the course.

Personal Reflection for Your Own Use

How could you redesign your courses around organizing schemes?

How would the organizing schemes differ for introductory courses compared to advanced courses?

Would you focus on different organizing schemes for a course required for the major compared to elective courses?

What readings would you use, knowing that textbooks rarely use organizing schemes enough to be meaningful?

ILLUSTRATION 5.1. The Four Levels of Characteristics for Each Action

greatly increases the likelihood that the content will be able to be retained and retrieved for later use. Active-learning strategies, creating graphic representations of what was originally in prose, stating concepts in one's own words, and teaching content to others promote meaningful engagement. Likewise, content that is memorized without making meaning out of it is easily and quickly forgotten. Although most instructors would agree with these statements, nonengaging lectures still predominate in teaching, especially to large, introductory, or STEM classes (Bok, 2015; Felder & Brent, 2016). Table 5.3 lists the instructor characteristics for engagement in content through

TABLE 5.2. Instructor Characteristics for Using Organizing Schemes on the Four-Level Continuum From Instructor-Centered to Learning-Centered Approaches

Organizing schemes are discipline-specific conceptual frameworks that help experts integrate much of the material and to learn new material. Novices have not organized the content well enough to use them unless they are explicitly taught. Examples include the following:

- *The periodic table of chemical elements is an organizing scheme in chemistry*
- *Homeostasis is an organizing theme in physiology*
- *Moving toward modernity is an organizing theme in history*
- *Dewey decimal system or the Library of Congress system for organizing books for librarians*

Reading down, each row shows greater use of learning-centered teaching.

Levels	Action: Organizing Schemes, With Instructor Characteristics at Each Level
Instructor-centered	Instructor: • Does not use organizing schemes in teaching
Minimally learning-centered	Instructor: • Uses organizing schemes to plan the overall scope and sequence of the course **BUT** • Does not convey these organizing schemes to the students **OR** • Informally models how to use organizing schemes in one-on-one interactions or in an out-of-class experience
Mostly learning-centered	Instructor: • Uses organizing schemes to formulate student learning outcomes and states them on the syllabus **AND** • Teaches students how to learn using organizing schemes. This teaching is done systematically, with everyone and not just those who seek extra help **AND** • Provides students 10 or more opportunities to use organizing schemes
Extensively learning-centered	Instructor must meet criteria for mostly uses learning-centered approaches **AND** • Explicitly uses organizing schemes throughout the course to create student learning outcomes, teaching/learning activities, and assessment activities **AND** • Frequently discusses these organizing schemes to help students learn content **AND** • Provides formative feedback to all students on their use of organizing schemes **AND** • Uses assessments that require students to demonstrate that they can integrate content into organizing schemes

meaning-making action on the four-level continuum from instructor-centered to learning-centered approaches. Box 5.4 describes how foreign language linguistics instructors engage their students in personal meaning-making with their rather abstract content.

Action: The Instructor Fosters the Development and Use of Discipline-Specific Methodologies

Examples of discipline-specific methodologies include how to

- read articles written by scholars in the discipline;

- read primary source material in the discipline;
- evaluate evidence;
- communicate using the conventions of the discipline (e.g., proper citations, use of equations);
- conduct research appropriate for the level of the course; and
- acquire laboratory skills.

Instead of assuming that students have mastered the discipline-specific methodologies that they need to succeed, learning-centered instructors intentionally assist students to acquire these skills. This assistance should include instruction, modeling, giving students

TABLE 5.3 Instructor Characteristics for Promoting Meaningful Student Engagement on the Four-Level Continuum From Instructor-Centered to Learning-Centered Approaches

Reading down, each row shows greater use of learning-centered teaching.

Levels	*Action: Personal Meaning-Making, With Instructor Characteristics at Each Level*
Instructor-centered	Instructor: • Allows students to memorize content as it was given to them without requiring understanding or without placing into a context **OR** • Uses assessments in which students can succeed without knowing the material (e.g., open-book factual exams)
Minimally learning-centered	Instructor: • Requires minimal transformation or creation of their own meaning of the content **OR** • Assesses students such that they can succeed without really understanding or reflecting on the content
Mostly learning-centered	Instructor: • Requires students to articulate concepts in their own words and to develop associations with the content **OR** • Requires students to transform and reflect on the content to make their own meaning **AND** • Uses some assessments that require students to demonstrate meaning of concepts
Extensively learning-centered	Instructor: • Requires students to transform and reflect on all the content to create their own meaning **OR** • Requires students to do something integrative using material from the course in a large assignment or activity **AND** • Uses assessments consistently that require students to demonstrate that they have created meaning from the content

---

BOX 5.4.
Engaging Students in the Content Through Student Collaboration and Applied Projects

Stephanie Knouse, Timothy Gupton, and Laurel Abreu (2015) teach foundations of linguistic analysis through active-learning techniques. Their students are Spanish language learners with widely varied levels of Spanish language ability. They found that when they made the students engage with the content and not just listen to lectures, the students became more interested and achieved greater mastery of the content; moreover, enrollment in their classes increased. The authors employ a collaborative learning approach where students work in small groups. Students are required to take notes in Spanish and each small group creates master class notes. Each set of master notes produced by one group is evaluated by another group on a rubric. Student reaction to this note-taking and sharing process was that they paid more attention in class, improved their spelling, and mastered the linguistic concepts better. Working in groups provided learning support, increased their engagement, and lowered stress levels. After interviewing native Spanish speakers, the students analyzed the linguistic features used by the native speakers, which forced students to use the content of the course. Course evaluations improved. These findings were even more striking because the students claimed to prefer passive lecture-type classes. The authors suggest other ways for students to create their own meaning from Hispanic linguistics content through Spanish online discussion boards and reflective journals.

Personal Reflection for Your Own Use

How can you use collaborative note-taking in your courses?

What application project would require your students to engage with the content and to form their own meaning of it?

---

opportunities to practice using these methodologies, and providing feedback as students practice. As you can see from the list of examples, these methodologies vary considerably and are, as their name implies, related to specific disciplines. They also vary with the level of the course. For introductory courses, instructors might need to explain how to read the textbook, how tables and figures should be studied, and how to use the citation convention (i.e., APA or MLA) expected in the course. Box 5.5 discusses how instructors assist undergraduate students to critically evaluate research or develop scientific literacy. Graduate and professional students might be taught how to evaluate evidence in research reports or legal decisions. Table 5.4 lists the instructor characteristics for the discipline-specific methodologies action on the four-level continuum from instructor-centered to learning-centered approaches.

Personal Reflection

What discipline-specific methodologies do you

require your students to use to succeed in your courses?

1.
2.
3.

Action: In Addition to Building a Knowledge Base, the Instructor Helps Students Understand Why They Need to Learn the Content for Use in Their Careers or Personal Growth

As experienced adults and instructors we understand why students need to take courses in the liberal arts and prerequisites for majors, but students do not see the connections. Career-minded students may want to take courses that only have the name of their major in the title. Therefore, to help students make the content relevant, learning-centered instructors need to help them see connections to their future careers or to their personal lives. I think it is also

---

BOX 5.5.
Teaching Students Scientific Literacy or How to Evaluate Experimental Research Reports Across an Educational Program

Nicholaus Brosowsky and Olga Parshina (2017) use a model with the acronym QALMRI (question, alternative hypotheses, logic, method, results, and inferences) as a discipline-specific methodology in their behavioral science undergraduate educational program. This methodology is a template to help students identify, summarize, and integrate concepts from an empirical research article. These instructors developed a guide for where students can find the information in articles addressing each letter of the acronym and specific questions the students need to answer to summarize the information. Brosowsky and Parshina scaffold the use of the QALMRI acronym across the undergraduate major. The acronym and how it is used are taught in beginning courses. Students in these courses discuss well-done QALMRI summaries written by their professors. In the next level, students read the original articles and well-developed QALMRI summaries and discuss where the information addressed in the summaries was found in the articles. As an intermediate step, students are given articles in which the instructor illustrates where the relevant information is contained and background information such as definitions that were not in the original article. Students construct their own QALMRI summaries of these articles. As advanced undergraduate students, they select their own articles and develop QALMRI summaries. The QALMRI method can be used in different ways as in-class activities or assignments.

Personal Reflection for Your Own Use

How can you use the QALMRI acronym in your discipline to help students acquire scientific literacy?

How can you and your peers in your department develop program-wide scaffolding to help students acquire important but hard-to-master concepts?

---

important to explain that as college graduates they will be expected to be informed and active citizens. Learning content in a wide variety of domains helps them in this role. Box 5.6 describes two easy-to-implement ways to get students more motivated to learn material because they see the connection to their lives or careers. Table 5.5 lists the instructor characteristics for helping students understand why they need to learn the content action on the four-level continuum from instructor-centered to learning-centered approaches.

Action: The Instructor Provides Practice Using Inquiry or Ways of Thinking in the Discipline to Solve Discipline-Specific, Real-World Problems That Are Appropriate for the Level of the Course

Successful implementation of this action results in students thinking differently because of the content they have learned and how they use the content. Disciplines have different ways of thinking and students benefit from learning a variety of inquiry methods. For example, disciplines analyze, evaluate, and use information differently. STEM uses the scientific method to establish the validity of claims; law uses precedent or previous cases to build an argument. Learning-centered instructors address myths and misconceptions that laypeople or other students have about a particular discipline so that they are better informed students and can accurately solve problems or describe phenomena. Students sometimes believe they understand the content, but cannot solve problems accurately. Therefore, learning-centered instructors give students repeated opportunities to practice using inquiry or ways of thinking in the discipline to solve problems that are appropriate for the level of the course. They provide students with feedback on such abilities. Capstone courses often provide students the opportunity to demonstrate that they can use content-driven inquiry methods or ways of thinking in their major. Table 5.6 lists the instructor characteristics for using inquiry or ways of thinking in the discipline to solve problems on the four-level continuum from instructor-centered to learning-centered approaches.

TABLE 5.4. Instructor Characteristics for Fostering the Development and Use of Discipline-Specific Methodologies on the Four-Level Continuum From Instructor-Centered to Learning-Centered Approaches

Examples of discipline-specific methodologies include

- learning how to read articles written by scholars in the discipline,
- reading primary source material in the discipline,
- evaluating evidence,
- communicating by using the conventions of the discipline (e.g., proper citations, use of equations), conducting research appropriate for the level of the course, and
- acquiring laboratory skills.

Reading down, each row shows greater use of learning-centered teaching.

Levels	Action: Discipline-Specific Methodologies, With Instructor Characteristics at Each Level
Instructor-centered	Instructor: • Does not help students acquire discipline-specific methodologies that they need in the course
Minimally learning-centered	Instructor: • Provides three or fewer opportunities to learn or apply **OR** • Encourages or invites weaker students to come for one-on-one help on these discipline-specific methodologies **OR** • Informally models how to use discipline-specific methodologies, when requested by students, in one-on-one interactions or in an out-of-class experience
Mostly learning-centered	Instructor: • Teaches appropriate discipline-specific methodologies with some intent. This teaching is done systematically with everyone and not just those who seek extra help **OR** • Provides repeated opportunities to learn and practice at least two of these methodologies, using activities that are structured and specific enough to allow students to learn from them • Provides assistance when students are practicing discipline-specific methodologies
Extensively learning-centered	Instructor must meet criteria for mostly uses learning-centered approaches **AND**: • Explicitly facilitates students to develop appropriate discipline-specific methodologies **AND** • Provides formative feedback to all students on their ability to use discipline-specific methodologies **AND** • Assesses these discipline-specific methodologies and not just the product of the use of these methodologies

---

BOX 5.6.
Easy Ways to Get Students More Motivated to Learn Content Through Personal Connections

Lynann Butler (2013) begins a new course by asking students to write their personal goals for the course on separate pieces of paper. Because students may be embarrassed to disclose them publicly, she asks them to crinkle their papers into balls and toss them across the room. Students read aloud other people's goals for the course. This exercise gets everyone thinking about why they should learn the content.

Another example is offered by Thomas Davis (2013) who, at the beginning of every new topic, gives students 10 minutes to generate questions they want to address on that topic. Students are encouraged to look in their textbook, do a quick online search of the topic, consider rumors or myths they have heard about the topic, or think of how the topic has been discussed in the media. Once the list of questions is generated, Davis incorporates these questions into the content discussions in class or through assignments where students read about the answers to questions.

Personal Reflection for Your Own Use

How can you get students to ask questions they want to address on the content?

How can you incorporate the questions raised into content coverage?

TABLE 5.5. Instructor Characteristics for Helping Students Understand Why They Need to Learn the Content on the Four-Level Continuum From Instructor-Centered to Learning-Centered Approaches

Reading down, each row shows greater use of learning-centered teaching.

Levels	Action: Understand Why They Need to Learn, With Instructor Characteristics at Each Level
Instructor-centered	Instructor: • Only uses content to build a knowledge base **OR** • Does not use content to help students understand why they need to learn the content for use in their careers or personal growth
Minimally learning-centered	Instructor: • Helps students to recognize why they need to learn the content **OR** • Provides very limited (e.g., three or fewer) opportunities to help students understand why they need to learn the content
Mostly learning-centered	Instructor: • Provides students 10 or more opportunities to help them understand why they need to learn the content for use in their careers or personal growth **OR** • Gives students five or more opportunities to discuss the relevance to their careers or their personal growth **OR** • Gives students five or more opportunities to practice using the content for their careers or personal growth **OR** • Requires students in half or more of their assignments to explain why or to show how they can use content in other contexts that relate to their careers or their personal growth

(Continues)

TABLE 5.5. (Continued)

Levels	*Action: Understand Why They Need to Learn, With Instructor Characteristics at Each Level*
Extensively learning-centered	Instructor must meet the criteria for mostly uses learning-centered approaches **AND** • Provides formative feedback to all students on their ability to explain why or show how they use content in other contexts that relate to their careers or their personal growth **AND** • Requires that student work on applications to their careers or their lives is graded and counts in their final grade

Personal Reflection

What inquiry or ways of thinking in your discipline would you like your students to be able to use to accurately solve problems or describe phenomena?

1.
2.
3.

Although learning-centered instructors want our students to gain ways of thinking in our discipline, this does not imply that all of our students should pursue our careers. Very few people become professors, yet courses may be designed to prepare students to do research in the discipline. Better goals for undergraduate research or methods courses are to allow students to be consumers of research and to develop an appreciation of what research and research methods can do. Box 5.7 describes how instructors transformed a research methods course to meet these more appropriate goals.

Action: The Instructor Helps Students Acquire In-Depth Conceptual Understanding of the Content to Facilitate Deep and Future Learning and Develop Transferable Skills

Table 5.7 lists the instructor characteristics for helping students acquire in-depth conceptual understanding of the content to facilitate deep and future learning and develop transferable skills on the four-level continuum from instructor-centered to learning-centered approaches. As with all of the other actions in this construct, learning-centered instructors teach so that students can acquire in-depth learning. Such

instructors also provide students opportunities to practice and give students feedback on their efforts. In addition, learning-centered instructors require students to demonstrate their deep learning and their ability to learn on their own with a large project. This is often accomplished in application exercises or experiential learning opportunities.

Researchers have found that students use three common approaches to learning: surface, deep, and strategic (Ramsden, 2003). With surface learning, students largely memorize content, which often leads to an inability to retrieve the content later or to apply it to new situations. When students take a deep approach to learning, they try to understand the content, make associations between what they previously learned and new content, and relate it to experiences. Students use a strategic approach to learning when they do whatever it takes to pass or get a good grade in a course, whether surface, deep, or a combination. When learning-centered instructors use the actions suggested in this book, students realize that their strategic approach requires deep learning. The responses of 80,000 senior students on the National Survey of Student Engagement (NSSE) indicated that when students frequently used deep learning, they reported gains in personal and intellectual development. The faculty of these students reported using learning-centered teaching, thus establishing the correlation between learning-centered teaching, deep learning, and improved academic achievement (Piskadlo, 2016).

Learning-centered instructors can convince career-minded undergraduate students and professional students to acquire in-depth conceptual

TABLE 5.6. Instructor Characteristics for Providing Practice Using Inquiry or Ways of Thinking in the Discipline to Solve Discipline-Specific, Real-World Problems on the Four-Level Continuum From Instructor-Centered to Learning-Centered Approaches

Reading down, each row shows greater use of learning-centered teaching.

Levels	*Action: Solve Problems*
Instructor-centered	Instructor: • Does not use content to help students practice using inquiry or ways of thinking in the discipline to solve discipline-specific or real-world problems **OR** • Does not teach inquiry or ways of thinking in the discipline to solve discipline-specific or real-world problems **OR** • Assesses students' ability to use inquiry or ways of thinking in the discipline to solve discipline-specific or real-world problems, without previously providing instruction or practice
Minimally learning-centered	Instructor: • Helps students recognize why and how inquiry or ways of thinking in the discipline can solve discipline-specific or real-world problems **OR** • Provides very limited opportunities (e.g., three or fewer) to help students practice using inquiry or ways of thinking in the discipline to solve discipline-specific or real-world problems **OR** • Informally models how to use inquiry or ways of thinking in the discipline to solve discipline-specific or real-world problems, when requested by students, in one-on-one interactions or in an out-of-class experience
Mostly learning-centered	Instructor: • Teaches inquiry or ways of thinking in the discipline to solve discipline-specific or real-world problems with some intent. This teaching is done systematically with everyone and not just those who seek extra help, **AND** • Provides students 10 or more opportunities to practice using inquiry or ways of thinking in the discipline to solve discipline-specific or real-world problems **OR** • With 50% or more of the assignments, students are required to use inquiry or ways of thinking in the discipline to solve discipline-specific or real-world problems
Extensively learning-centered	Instructor must meet the criteria for mostly uses learning-centered approaches **AND** • Explicitly facilitates students' ability to develop ways of thinking in the discipline to solve discipline-specific or real-world problems independently **AND** • Provides repeated (at least weekly) student practice using inquiry or ways of thinking in the discipline to solve discipline-specific or real-world problems **AND** • Provides formative feedback to all students on their ability to use inquiry or ways of thinking in the discipline to solve discipline-specific or real-world problems **AND** • Requires that using inquiry or ways of thinking in the discipline to solve discipline-specific or real-world problems. This work is graded and counts enough in their final grade for it to matter to the students

---

BOX 5.7.
Aligning Research Methods Courses to Foster Ways of Thinking as a Researcher

Gary Lewandowski, Natalie Ciarocco, and David Strohmetz (2017) found that although their students in traditional research design courses showed they understood the content of the research methods, the students had less respect for research and the discipline after taking the course. Instead of creating future scientists, research methods courses tend to erode students' interest in scientific activities and inquiry in the field. Therefore, these authors revised the course to focus on thinking and problem-solving like a scientist. Students read interesting articles that exemplified specific research methods and then wrote short essays on the purposes, methods, and results of these articles. Working in small groups, the students designed and conducted easy research projects that attempted to answer real and interesting questions. This learning by doing allowed the students to develop a decision-making process that used research methods and statistics. The projects were about the process of doing research with different research methods and not striving for publishable-quality research. Students who took the revised course were compared to students in the more traditional content coverage courses. Grades were similar in both groups. However, students in the revised course had more favorable attitudes toward the research process and had more confidence in their abilities to conduct research.

Personal Reflection for Your Own Use

How can you use learning by doing approaches to encourage your students to think in your discipline?

How can you focus on the inquiry process and not the quality of the end product? How would your assessment of students' work change?

How can nonresearch design courses, such as laboratory courses for nonmajors, be aligned to foster inquiry in the discipline?

---

understanding when they remind them they will be using this content in the future. Authentic learning projects (i.e., that simulate real-world practice) facilitate students' use of deep learning while increasing motivation, engagement, and confidence; all of them together promote more learning and help students learn in the future (Kuit & Fildes, 2014). These authentic learning projects or authentic assessments promote the development of transferable skills. Box 5.8 discusses an authentic learning project and assignment involving a career-focused electronic portfolio project.

Chapter Summary

This chapter discusses how you can change your teaching to be more learning-centered through the construct called Function of Content. Table 5.8

summarizes the six core actions of this construct and briefly identifies the characteristics of faculty at four levels going from instructor-centered to learning-centered teaching.

Taking Stock of This Construct and How You Can Implement Learning-Centered Teaching With Function of Content

Table 5.9 gives you the opportunity to review your current learning-centered teaching status and decide what and when you want to change. See Table 3.10 for further directions on how to complete this taking stock activity. Your proposed changes are only tentative plans. Once you have read through the rest of this book, you will reconsider your plans and prioritize what you will want to change.

TABLE 5.7. Instructor Characteristics for Helping Students Acquire In-Depth Conceptual Understanding of the Content to Facilitate Deep and Future Learning and Develop Transferable Skills on the Four-Level Continuum From Instructor-Centered to Learning-Centered Approaches

Reading down, each row shows greater use of learning-centered teaching.

Levels	*Action: Deep Understanding to Facilitate Further Learning, With Instructor Characteristics at Each Level*
Instructor-centered	Instructor: • Allows students to learn superficially **OR** • Does not provide opportunities for students to apply knowledge to new content or new contexts **OR** • Does not encourage the development of transferable skills
Minimally learning-centered	Instructor: • Provides content so the best students can acquire conceptual understanding of the content to facilitate deep learning, but does not actively teach how to do this **OR** • Provides students with limited (five or fewer) opportunities to apply knowledge to new content **OR** • Provides students with limited (five or fewer) opportunities to gain and practice transferable skills **OR** • Informally models how to acquire in-depth conceptual understanding of the content to facilitate deep and future learning and develop transferable skills, when requested by students, in one-on-one interactions or in an out-of-class experience
Mostly learning-centered	Instructor: • Frames content so all students can see how it can be applied in the future **OR** • Teaches how to acquire in-depth conceptual understanding of the content to facilitate deep and future learning and develop transferable skills, with some intent. This teaching is done, systematically done with everyone and not just those who seek extra help **AND** • Requires all students to use content in other contexts
Extensively learning-centered	Instructor must meet the criteria for mostly uses learning-centered approaches **AND** Instructor: • Frames and organizes content so students can and do learn additional content that is not taught **AND** • Provides repeated (at least weekly) student practice acquiring in-depth conceptual understanding of the content to facilitate deep and future learning and develop transferable skills **AND** • Provides formative feedback to all students on their ability to acquire in-depth conceptual understanding of the content to facilitate deep and future learning and develop transferable skills **AND** • Requires students to demonstrate deep learning and further learning on their own in a large paper or project, in an assignment that counts enough toward the grade that students take it seriously

BOX 5.8.
Using an Electronic Portfolio to Promote In-Depth Understanding and Look to Future Employment

Bob Barrett (2013) requires the students in his human resources management course to develop an electronic portfolio that shows what they have learned about human resources development, training, and consulting. One of the stated purposes of the portfolio is to help students connect content learned in previous courses and help them to use all content as they prepare for their careers. Each week students complete practical projects on these three areas and place the products of these projects in their portfolio. For example, the students develop a training course that they might turn over to a CEO of a corporation. The students need to integrate the content of the course to create acceptable projects. While creating this portfolio, students are asked to reflect on their work and the potential application of their projects to their future careers. Barrett hopes the students see these portfolios as living documents that students can add to or revise. Ultimately, the goal is to be able to share the electronic portfolio on a future job interview.

Personal Reflection for Your Own Use

How can you use electronic learning portfolios to help students gain in-depth understanding of content in your courses?

How can you promote with your peers the idea that students create ongoing learning portfolios that they develop throughout their student careers?

TABLE 5.8. Summary of Function of Content Construct and Actions Contrasting Instructor-Centered Approaches with Learning-Centered Approaches

For details on each action, see the description in the chapter.

Key to Table

Columns = Action descriptions
Rows = Reading down each column, each successive row shows greater use of learning-centered teaching.

Levels↓	← *Actions for Function of Content* →					
	Use Organizing Schemes	**Engage in Personal Meaning-Making**	**Use Discipline-Specific Methodologies**	**Understand Why They Need To Learn**	**Solve Problems**	**Facilitate Future Learning**
Instructor-centered	Does not use	Student can succeed without knowing the material	Does not help students acquire them, although needed in the course	Does not help students understand why they need to learn	Assesses students, without providing instruction or practice	Allows students to learn superficially
Minimally learning-centered	Does not convey them to students	Requires minimal creation of their own meaning	Provides three or fewer opportunities to learn or apply them	Helps students recognize why they need to learn the content	Provides three or fewer opportunities to help students practice them	Provides five or fewer opportunities to apply knowledge to new content
Mostly learning-centered	Teaches students how to learn using them	Requires students to articulate concepts in their own words	Teaches and lets students practice with some intent	Provides 10 or more opportunities to help students	Provides 10 or more opportunities to practice	Requires students to use content in other contexts
Extensively learning-centered	Uses them throughout the course	Requires students to demonstrate that they have created meaning	Explicitly facilitates student development	Requires that student application work is graded and counts in their final grade	Requires that student problem-solving work is graded and counts in their final grade	Requires students to demonstrate deep learning on their own in a large project

TABLE 5.9. Worksheet: My Plans to Increase Use of Learning-Centered Teaching Approaches

Date_____

Directions

1. Put a ^ in the cell that indicates your status.
2. Put a * in the cell to identify the level to which you aspire to become more learning centered on this action.
3. Indicate your time line to achieve change for each action on the bottom row.
4. Make comments that will help you make these planned changes.

Note: You may not want to plan changes in every action.

Construct III: Function of Content

Levels↓	*← Actions for Function of Content →*					
	Use Organizing Schemes	**Engage in Personal Meaning-Making**	**Use Discipline-Specific Methodologies**	**Understand Why They Need to Learn**	**Solve Problems**	**Facilitate Future Learning**
Instructor-centered	Does not use	Student can succeed without knowing the material	Does not help students acquire them, although needed in the course	Does not help students understand why they need to learn	Assesses students, without instruction or practice	Allows students to learn superficially
Minimally learning-centered	Does not convey them to students	Requires minimal creation of their own meaning	Provides three or fewer opportunities to learn or apply them	Helps students recognize why they need content	Provides three or fewer opportunities to help students practice them	Provides five or fewer opportunities to apply knowledge
Mostly learning-centered	Teaches students how to learn using them	Requires students to articulate concepts using own words	Teaches and lets students practice with some intent	Provides 10 or more opportunities to help students	Provides 10 or more opportunities to practice	Requires students to use content in other contexts
Extensively learning-centered	Uses them throughout the course	Requires students to demonstrate that they have created meaning	Explicitly facilitates students' development	Requires that student application work is graded and counts in their final grade	Requires that student-problem solving work is graded and counts in their final grade	Requires students to demonstrate deep learning on their own in large project
Time line to achieve change						

Notes/Comments on My Plan

formative feedback

policies, standards

integrated with learning

peer, self-assessment

learn from mistakes

authentic assessment

Assessment

Current Evidence-Based Understanding of Learning

CHAPTER 6

Purposes and Processes of Student Assessment

Chapter Highlights

Learning-centered instructors consider both the purposes and the processes of assessment and not just the assessment result. As a learning-centered teacher, you perform the following core actions that facilitate student learning:

- Integrate assessment and learning.
- Use fair, objective, and consistent assessment policies and standards.
- Provide opportunities for students to receive formative feedback.
- Promote the use of student peer and self-assessment.
- Allow students the ability to learn from mistakes.
- Use authentic assessment as a vehicle for real-world preparation.

Especially for undergraduate students, assessment drives learning (Brown, 2007). You should align assessment with the learning outcomes and teaching/ learning activities to achieve deep and lasting learning (Angelo & Cross, 1993). For a learning-centered instructor, assigning grades through summative evaluation becomes just one of the functions of assessing students.

This chapter follows the same format as the previous ones with similar tables. Inspecting Table 6.1 shows that the six purposes and processes of student assessment are different for learning-centered compared to instructor-centered teachers. Each column represents a separate action of the construct. I explain each action and provide a published example of its use. To assist you in transforming your teaching to be more learning-centered, I define instructor characteristics, for each action, with four increasingly learning-centered levels (i.e., instructor-centered, minimally

learning-centered, mostly learning-centered, and extensively learning-centered). I present each action with its characteristics for the four increasingly learning-centered levels in separate tables.

Before discussing the actions separately, I suggest an easy-to-implement learning-centered technique in Box 6.1 and describe a case study of perceptions of learning-centered assessments that uses many aspects of the Purposes and Processes of Student Assessment construct in Box 6.2.

Action: The Instructor Integrates Assessment and Learning

The more assessment and learning are integrated, the more learning-centered these assessments are, resulting in greater learning (Suskie, 2009). The three higher levels (minimally, mostly, and extensively learning-centered) in Table 6.2 suggest ways to integrate assessment with learning.

TABLE 6.1. Summary of Purposes and Processes of the Student Assessment Construct and Actions Contrasting Instructor-Centered Approaches With Learning-Centered Approaches

Each column represents a separate action of the construct. Read down to see use of learning-centered teaching.

Approach							
		← *Core Actions of the Purposes and Processes of Student Assessment* →					
	Integrates Assessment and Learning	**Assessment Policies and Standards**	**Formative Feedback**	**Students' Use of Peer and Self-Assessment**	**Students Demonstrate Mastery**	**Authentic Assessment**	
Instructor-Centered	Does not integrate assessment and learning	Does not consistently enforce policies and standards	Provides students with no constructive feedback	Provides no opportunities for peer and self-assessment	Students have one attempt to demonstrate mastery	Rarely or never uses authentic assessment	
Learning-Centered	Continuously integrates assessment within the learning process through regular formal and informal assessments	Standards and policies are explained to the students throughout the course	Discloses the gap between current and desired level of performance and provides opportunities for students to work to reduce the gap	Counts peer and self-assessment enough that they are taken seriously	Students can retake exams or redo all assignments throughout the semester	Authentic assessment counts 80% or more of final grade	

BOX 6.1.
Example of an Easy-to-Implement Learning-Centered Practice

At the end of each class, ask the students to summarize the key points. This summarization can be done as a think-pair-share or as an individual writing exercise. Then give students feedback on the accuracy of their understanding and correct any misunderstandings, either immediately afterward or, if written, at the next class. This is a quick way to determine if the students learned what you wanted them to learn, gives them some formative feedback, and increases their responsibility for their learning.

Personal Reflection for Your Own Use

How can you use this practice?

For which courses or topics is this practice particularly well suited?

BOX 6.2.
Case Study of Students' and Faculty Members' Perceptions of Learning-Centered Assessments

Diana Pereira's (2016) dissertation compared 57 Portuguese faculty members' perceptions and practices with 634 Portuguese students at 5 universities and 72 Swedish undergraduate students' perceptions on assessment. According to these student and faculty definitions, learning-centered assessment methods put the student at the center of the process and emphasize knowledge construction and skill development. Varied methods emphasize connections to real-world contexts and problems and include portfolios, group projects, and presentations. The faculty members and students agreed that learning-centered assessments methods were fairer, were more effective, and had more positive benefits than traditional assessment methods that were largely summative tests. The positive aspects of learning-centered assessment methods included enhancing the learning process, providing formative feedback, occurring continuously, promoting increased student motivation, and increasing student confidence. Students perceived that they received more feedback and it was more appropriately timed, overall more effective, and more relevant than with traditional methods. Students felt that feedback in traditional assessments was mostly given at the end of the course. In contrast, traditional assessment methods led to more memorization without understanding and fewer long-term gains in student learning. When students are assessed using learning-centered methods, they spend more time preparing and focus on deep learning more than with traditional assessments.

Pereira was interested in the effects of implementation of the Bologna Process across the European Union. The Bologna Process mandated that higher education become more learning-centered (Sursock & Smidt, 2010). Consequently, standards and guidelines for quality assurance were developed. These standards required instructors to communicate the assessment methods to be used in advance, state explicit grading criteria, provide formative feedback, and show relevance to future careers (European Association for Quality Assurance in Higher Education, 2009). Although the instructors perceived that they were using more learning-centered assessment methods, exams were still the most common assessment methods used. The instructors felt that their heavy workload and large number of students prevented greater use of learning-centered assessment methods. However, instructors and students noted that exams were increasingly being used in combination with other more learning-centered methods. Although the instructors recognized the positive aspects of peer and self-assessment, these methods were rarely used. In addition, the instructors noted that they changed their teaching practices to become more learning-centered because of changes they made to assessment methods.

(Continues)

BOX 6.2. (Continued)

Personal Reflection for Your Own Use

Has your national or regional government or professional or discipline-based association developed guidelines or standards for assessing students?

How much do you implement these standards or guidelines?

If you agree that learning-centered assessment is more effective and fairer, how can you implement more learning-centered assessment methods?

Even though students spend more time on learning-centered assessments, how would you get your students to see them as fairer and more effective?

TABLE 6.2. Instructor Characteristics for Integrating Assessment and Learning on the Four-Level Continuum From Instructor-Centered to Learning-Centered Approaches

Reading down, each row shows greater use of learning-centered teaching.

Levels	*Action: Instructor Integrates Assessment and Learning, With Instructor Characteristics at Each Level*
Instructor-centered	Instructor: • Does not integrate assessment and learning **OR** • Does not provide students an indication of how well they are doing in time to make changes or improve
Minimally learning-centered	Instructor: • Returns student work in a timely manner with comments that could help students learn from their previous mistakes **OR** • Briefly answers student questions once graded work is returned
Mostly learning-centered	Instructor: • Integrates learning with assessment and assessment with learning **AND** • Spends time going over answers to exams, explaining what constitutes an excellent answer **OR** • Helps students to see assessment as part of the learning process **OR** • Allows students to justify their answers
Extensively learning-centered	Instructor meets the criteria for mostly learning-centered **AND** • Continuously integrates assessment within the learning process through regular formal and informal assessments **AND** • Provides students with standards of what constitutes outstanding, good, and average work

Using learning-centered assessment practices, learning becomes the centerpiece of the evaluation exercise and not the grade assigned. All assessments do not need to be graded. The leaves in Illustration 6.1 represent the four levels characterizing each action. Each action is a branch on the tree shown at the beginning of the chapter. Box 6.3 describes the results of experiments on the retention effects of the testing process.

When you ask students to justify their answers as they take the exam on multiple-choice items by explaining their reasoning or thought process, you are making the assessment more of a learning activity. You can offer points for the justification as well as the correct answer (Schroeder, 2012). Students can also justify their answers on any type of question after handing in the original exam by explaining in their own words why their answer is supported by an appropriate and credible reference.

Action: The Instructor Uses Fair, Objective, and Consistent Policies and Standards to Assess All Students

As a learning-centered instructor, you will establish clear, objective policies and standards for assessing students. These policies and standards should be communicated to the students and consistently enforced. Students should know exactly how their grades will be determined and specific policies such as penalties for

ILLUSTRATION 6.1. The Four Levels of Characteristics for Each Action

BOX 6.3.
Repeated, Practice Testing Improves Long-Term Retention

Cognitive psychologists found that asking student to recall or recognize material, such as done on a test, improves future retrieval; they call this phenomenon the testing effect. In an experimental design, Henry Roediger and Jeffrey Karpicke (2006) compared the effects of repeated testing to repeated studying of the same material. The students in the repeated studying group had the most confidence that they knew the material, but in fact, they did the worst on delayed tests. Repeated testing resulted in better long-term retention than studying the material for the same amount of time as the repeated tests. These repeated tests occurred without receiving feedback on the correctness of their answers. The authors hypothesized that the testing increased the retrieval routes or cues for the content, whereas the repeated study did not do so. Retention is further improved when the testing is spaced apart by as much as a week. The authors cite research that when feedback follows testing, even greater retention occurs.

Personal Reflection for Your Own Use

How can you use repeated testing, even without feedback, to help students retain the content of your courses?

How can you incorporate feedback into these tests without adding to your workload? Check the availability of technology-assisted learning from textbook publishers, online quizzes, or homework systems that provide feedback.

How can you explain to your students that repeated testing is a more effective study technique than repeated study, especially when students may have ineffective study strategies?

lateness or ability to make up missed assessments. Giving your students the test blueprint or grading rubrics in advance of the assessment helps students to understand how they will be evaluated. Ideally, all rubrics could be included in the syllabus. However, distributing blueprints and rubrics one week in advance of the test or due date helps students. A test blueprint is a matrix showing the objectives to be covered and the number of questions or weight of questions at each taxonomy level (i.e., recall, apply, or evaluate) per

objective. Blueprints help you construct a balanced multiple-choice, short answer, or matching exam. Grading rubrics specify the criteria that will be assessed and the standards going from unacceptable through excellent. Nontraditional students believe that when instructors grade using rubrics and when they are graded anonymously, these students are graded fairer than without these methods (Suskie, 2009). Table 6.3 lists the instructor characteristics for using fair, objective, and consistent policies and standards to assess all

---

TABLE 6.3. Instructor Characteristics for Using Fair, Objective, and Consistent Policies and Standards to Assess All Students on the Four-Level Continuum From Instructor-Centered to Learning-Centered Approaches

Reading down, each row shows greater use of learning-centered teaching.

Levels	*Action: Use Fair, Objective, and Consistent Policies and Standards to Assess All Students, With Instructor Characteristics at Each Level*
Instructor-centered	Instructor: • Does not establish policies and standards **OR** • Does not consistently enforce fair and objective policies and standards **OR** • Provides final grades without a rationale for the grade
Minimally learning-centered	Instructor: • Develops fair, objective, and consistent policies and standards to assess all students **OR** • Consistently uses specified grading standards such as grading rubrics and specified weights for projects and assignments
Mostly learning-centered	Instructor: • Maintains consistency, fairness, and equity in applying all policies and standards to all students, using policies and standards listed on the syllabus, but not discussed further **AND** • Consistently uses specified grading standards such as grading rubrics and specified weights for projects and assignments, with students informed of these standards in advance of due dates
Extensively learning-centered	Instructor: • Maintains consistency, fairness, and equity in applying all policies and standards to all students, explained to the students throughout the course **AND** • Consistently uses specified grading standards such as grading rubrics and specified weights for projects and assignments, standards about which students are informed in advance of due dates and about which they can ask questions **AND** • Maintains a policy that allows students to know how they can improve upon previous efforts and have assessments graded prior to handing in the next assessment

students on the four-level continuum from instructor-centered to learning-centered approaches.

Students expect that their assignments will be graded immediately. Learning-centered instructors carefully grade assignments, which can take more time. Even multiple-choice items may be graded twice after throwing out the poorly performing items. Projects and written assignments need to be read carefully and provide students with comments so that they can improve. It is appropriate to give students a time frame for when they can expect to get their graded work back.

As higher education institutions address the needs of diverse student populations and move toward learning-centeredness, many programs are adopting flipped courses (where the information dissemination occurs outside the class and students work together in class), hybrid or blended courses (a combination of online and in-class components), and fully online courses. These course approaches lead to greater flexibility in teaching/learning and student engagement. This flexibility should also extend to assessment. Although flexibility is also important in assessment, instructors need to state and consistently apply consistent assessment policies to maintain academic integrity and rigor. Minimizing opportunities for students to utilize outside resources during assessments, like exams, could be aided by setting exam expectations and requirements up front. Potential strategies include taking exams on secure computers without the Internet or using exam technology software. Instructors need to be very explicit about how they define cheating. Even better, online exams should require students to apply factual material and not just recall or recognize it. Box 6.4 discusses some assessment policy considerations for flipped, hybrid, and personalized courses.

Action: The Instructor Provides Opportunities for Students to Receive Frequent, Useful, and Timely Formative Feedback to Foster Learning Gains

Table 6.4 lists the instructor characteristics for formative feedback on the four-level continuum from instructor-centered to learning-centered approaches. The effective feedback qualities listed on the instructor characteristics reflect the literature on assessment (Bean, 2011; Nicol, Thomson, & Breslin, 2014), which describes effective feedback qualities, including the following:

- Make positive comments.
- Deliver high-quality and information-rich feedback to students about their progress toward meeting the learning outcomes in a way such that students can understand and process the information.
- Help clarify what good performance is in terms of goals, criteria, and expected standards.
- Disclose the gap between current and desired level of performance and provide opportunities for students to work to reduce the gap between these two levels.
- Encourage a dialogue around learning. This dialogue occurs between the feedback giver and receiver; it should not be a one-way transmission of feedback.
- Focus the student on the assignment requirements.
- Provide recommendations for improvement without grades or praise.
- Avoid offering too much feedback which overwhelms students. You can ask students as they hand in papers or projects to tell you what feedback would be most helpful (e.g., how to improve the overall paper or specific aspects including logic, organization, development of the argument, reporting data, conclusion, etc.).
- Facilitate the development of self-assessment and reflection in learning.
- Encourage students to have positive motivational beliefs and good self-esteem.
- Provide information to students that can be used to help shape learning.

Mazur (1997) introduced a now popular method to provide feedback while promoting greater learning. Students answer questions about the reading the night before the class. The instructor can adjust the class depending on how well students have understood the material. In class students answer challenging questions by using an audience response system, which can be an app on their phones. When most of the students do not get the answer correctly, they discuss their answers in small groups and then the instructor re-polls the students on the same question. Generally, students do much better after the small group discussion.

BOX 6.4.
Assessment Policy Recommendations for Flexible, Personalized, and Hybrid Courses

Thomas Wanner and Edward Palmer (2015) describe assessment policy considerations coming from the literature, based on their experiences teaching hybrid, or flipped courses. Survey results from students and faculty indicate that students

- value choices and control over assessment deadlines, although some found the process of determining their own deadlines confusing;
- need clear structure and guidelines for assessment; and
- want input into the assessment process.

Wanner and Palmer make the following assessment policy recommendations for personalized, flexible, hybrid, or online courses. Instructors should

- align assessment methods and products with the identified student learning outcomes;
- set and specify clear guidelines and structure;
- focus on assessment for learning and not of learning (Keamy, Nicholas, Mahar, & Herrick, 2007);
- rethink what assessment measures, with the focus on using knowledge in a real context instead of assessing factual content that can be easily found online;
- use individually or course cohort negotiated assessments in flexible courses, because students want choices in the method (e.g., essay, report, or projects), timing, and how much assessments count, while being clear what cannot be negotiated;
- give students only a few choices in what they can do;
- specify equivalencies in assignment methods and products;
- allow students as a group to decide what kind of assessments they prefer (exams, essay, or projects), the deadlines for submissions, and the weights of assessments, decided by majority rule, with the entire class following the decisions, which need to be conveyed in writing to the students through a revised and final syllabus; and
- set grading criteria in advance and inform the students of these criteria.

Note that some students lack the ability to make assessment decisions. Therefore, instructors need to aid in setting the context for development of the skills to do these assessments well.

Personal Reflection for Your Own Use

How can you set clear expectations, structure, and limits as you allow for assessment flexibility?

How can you use individually or course cohort negotiated assessments?

Although formative feedback increases student learning, it can be time-consuming for the instructors if they provide individualized feedback. Recorded verbal feedback saves instructor time and may engage students. Box 6.5 shows how nonindividualized, standardized but detailed feedback on drafts can promote significant improvement on final products. Once the instructor develops the feedback, they do not provide individualized feedback and perhaps may not even have to read most drafts.

Action: The Instructor Promotes Students Use of Peer and Self-Assessment
Instructors should provide useful feedback to students, but peer-to-peer and self-assessments can foster significant learning gains also. Advanced students can

TABLE 6.4. Instructor Characteristics for Formative Feedback on the Four-Level Continuum From Instructor-Centered to Learning-Centered Approaches

Reading down, each row shows greater use of learning-centered teaching.

Levels	*Action: Provide Formative Feedback, With Instructor Characteristics at Each Level*
Instructor-centered	Instructor: • Grades assignments without offering recommendations for improvement **OR** • Overwhelms students with too much feedback, especially on repeated mistakes, spelling, and grammar **OR** • Provides students with no constructive feedback **OR** • Does not return student work in a timely way **OR** • Is aware of complaints that the students have no idea what grade they are getting or how they earned their final grade and does not attempt to remediate the situation
Minimally learning-centered	Instructor: • Provides students with limited or not useful constructive feedback **AND** • Makes positive comments only or never makes positive comments **OR** • Helps clarify what good performance is in terms of goals, criteria, and expected standards **OR** • Provides formative feedback only to students who seek it and not to the entire class
Mostly learning-centered	Instructor: • Delivers high-quality and information-rich feedback to students about their progress toward meeting the learning outcomes **AND** • Makes recommendations for improvement without grading or praising **OR** • Gives all students formative feedback that provides insights into how to improve **OR** • Provides all students with constructive feedback following assignments **AND** • Provides constructive feedback in a timely and beneficial manner
Extensively learning-centered	Instructor must meet the criteria for mostly uses learning-centered approaches **AND** • Discloses the gap between current and desired level of performance and provides opportunities for students to work to reduce the gap between these two levels **AND** • Encourages a dialogue around learning between the feedback giver and receiver **AND** • Integrates formative feedback and constructive feedback to all students consistently **AND** • Grades recent student performance considering if students incorporate previous formative feedback

---

BOX 6.5.
Nonindividualized Feedback on Drafts Promotes Significant Improvement on Final Product

Anastasiya Lipnevich, Leigh McCallen, Katharine Pace Miles, and Jeffrey Smith (2014) studied whether providing nonindividualized, detailed, standardized feedback on a draft of a research proposal would improve students' final proposal. After the students handed in their draft proposals, they were randomly assigned to 1 of 3 standard feedback groups to receive (a) a detailed grading rubric specifying 10 criteria with unacceptable to excellent standards defined; (b) 3 exemplars showing weak, average, and excellent research proposals; or (c) both the rubrics and the exemplars. The students did not receive any feedback on the quality of their drafts. The students were asked to revise their drafts based on the nonindividualized feedback they received. The instructors graded both drafts but did not inform the students how they did on the first draft. All three feedback conditions led to significant improvement of the final product over the drafts. However, the students who received the rubrics alone made the largest improvements. Follow-up focus groups with these students indicated that they did not look at the average or good exemplars; they tried to imitate the excellent example. The students who received the exemplars and the rubrics focused more on the excellent exemplar than the rubrics. The students who got the rubrics alone were the most engaged in how they could revise their proposals by checking their work against the requirements. The authors felt that the rubric was more effective after the students completed a draft than just giving the students the rubrics without the draft.

Personal Reflection for Your Own Use

Are you comfortable not providing individualized feedback on drafts? How has this well-designed study helped you to realize that nonindividualized but detailed feedback may be helpful enough to justify saving your time?

What kind of student products would be helpful to have the students complete a draft and receive nonindividualized feedback?

If you currently give students grading rubrics in advance of the assignment deadlines, how can you make these rubrics more effective as learning improvement aids?

How could you provide grading rubrics to all students but still provide individualized feedback on drafts to the students who might benefit from your attention the most?

---

create their own rubrics and then assess themselves on their rubric. Peers may provide more accessible and understandable feedback than instructors, provided they receive training on how they can give feedback and are provided grading rubrics or guidelines (Nicol et al., 2014). Creating and receiving peer assessments can enhance student learning while not increasing instructor time. Box 6.6 describes peer review on drafts of reports.

Table 6.5 lists the instructor characteristics for peer and self-assessment on the four-level continuum from instructor-centered to learning-centered approaches. Throughout this book, when numbers are given on the four-level progression tables such as five times on the second bullet of the mostly learning-centered level of Table 6.5, they should be used as a metric for semester-long courses. Peer and self-assessments or critiques are commonly used in performing and visual arts and in writing courses (Gray, 2013). However, learning-centered instructors in all disciplines should employ more peer and self-assessments. The previous example in Box 6.6 uses a fundamental principle of peer

---

BOX 6.6.
Effective Peer Assessments

David Nicol, Avril Thomson, and Caroline Breslin (2014) studied peer review with undergraduate students in an engineering design class. Each student worked on a unique design task. The authors defined *effective peer review* as both creating and receiving reviews from peers and then having students make revisions based on the reviews they received. Students evaluated a draft report of design projects from two of their peers and wrote a review for each one. The instructor defined the criteria and questions that the students addressed in their review. Students did not grade the overall quality of design documents. After receiving the reviews, students revised their detailed product design specification documents. When students received multiple summaries, they made more improvements to their drafts than if they only received one review. The review process can be completed online, and students should not know who provided the review. Students stated that they learned just as much from the process of creating reviews as from receiving the reports. They came to recognize the different quality of the design projects. While providing peer assessments, the students compared their own reports to those of their peers. This peer review process has also been used effectively in the social and life sciences.

Personal Reflection for Your Own Use

How can you incorporate this peer review and revision process in your teaching?

What type of assignment (i.e., reports, summaries of the literature, persuasive argument, and creative activities) would work well and require that students have a unique task?

How could this peer review and revision process work effectively in online classes?

---

assessment: students should not grade each other or make judgments; they should only provide feedback.

Action: The Instructor Allows the Students to Demonstrate Mastery of the Objectives and Ability to Learn From Mistakes

When tests are returned, students are engaged and motivated to learn, making the return of tests a teachable or learning moment. The characteristics of instructors on this action reflect the extent to which they allow students to learn from their mistakes and to demonstrate mastery as shown in Table 6.6. These characteristics are once again on the four-level continuum from instructor-centered to learning-centered approaches. Exhibit 6.1 shows a posttest analysis that I provide to all students after the first test, allowing those who have done poorly on exams to complete their posttest analysis to get a few extra points. If you keep the exams so you can reuse questions, students

can complete this in office hours or in class. Instructors who allow students to look up wrong answers or discuss items after the test find that the students are very engaged and motivated to learn. Box 6.7 lists different ways instructors let students learn from their mistakes and then go on to demonstrate mastery of the content. You may choose to use these suggestions routinely, only when students do poorly, or on an exam that is heavily weighted. The in-class time might be better spent after the test rather than a review prior to the test.

Action: The Instructor Uses Authentic Assessment (What Practitioners/Professionals Do)

Authentic assessment can occur in campus or online courses and in practice settings. When students are asked to perform real-life tasks, such as keeping laboratory notes of experiments, analyzing real data sets, developing information brochures for a nonprofit agency, or creating a marketing campaign for a new

TABLE 6.5. Instructor Characteristics for Promoting Students to Use Peer and Self-Assessment on the Four-Level Continuum From Instructor-Centered to Learning-Centered Approaches

Reading down, each row shows greater use of learning-centered teaching.

Levels	*Action: Students Use Peer and Self-Assessment, With Instructor Characteristics at Each Level*
Instructor-centered	Instructor: • Does not consider peer and self-assessment relevant **OR** • Does not provide students opportunities for peer and self-assessment **OR** • Allows students to determine their own or peer's grade without the instructor's oversight
Minimally learning-centered	Instructor: • Requires students to use peer and self-assessments once or twice **OR** • Does not factor peer and self-assessments into final grade
Mostly learning-centered	Instructor: • Teaches students how to meaningfully conduct peer and self-assessments **AND** • Requires students to use peer and self-assessments five times or more during a course **AND** • Counts peer and self-assessment in the final grade, guided by the instructor's oversight
Extensively learning-centered	Instructor meets the criterion for mostly learning-centered **AND** • Models how to conduct meaningful peer and self-assessments **AND** • Routinely requires students to use peer and self-assessments **AND** • Provides feedback to students on how well they have conducted peer and self-assessments **AND** • Counts peer and self-assessment enough that they are taken seriously, providing oversight on accuracy of feedback

product, they are engaged in authentic assessment (Suskie, 2009). The more authentic assessments are used and the more they count in the final grade, the more learning-centered the instructor is, as shown on Table 6.7. These real-life tasks can be completed within a regular undergraduate or graduate course. However, students take their assignments more seriously when they are assessed by people in the field and not just their teacher. When the goal of research projects is to share the work beyond the classroom, through conference presentations or publications, then the assessment is authentic. Practitioners in the field evaluate the quality of the research.

Student performances on simulations are also authentic assessments. Clinical placements and field or community practicums or capstone experiences often require students to do real tasks. Senior design projects have been a traditional requirement of engineering programs. With intention, they can be made into even more authentic experiences, as Box 6.8 describes.

Chapter Summary

This chapter discusses how you can begin to change your teaching to be more learning-centered through

TABLE 6.6. Instructor Characteristics for Allowing Students to Demonstrate Mastery of the Objectives and Ability to Learn From Mistakes on the Four-Level Continuum From Instructor-Centered to Learning-Centered Approaches

Reading down, each row shows greater use of learning-centered teaching.

Levels	Action: Demonstrate Mastery of the Objectives and Ability to Learn From Mistakes, With Instructor Characteristics at Each Level
Instructor-centered	Instructor: • Does not provide any opportunities for students to demonstrate that they have learned from mistakes **OR** • Does not provide any opportunities for students to show mastery beyond the first attempt
Minimally learning-centered	Instructor: • Provides one opportunity for students to demonstrate that they have mastered the material after the first attempt **OR** • Gives all students the option of seeking feedback on one major assignment before it is graded
Mostly learning-centered	Instructor: • Allows all students opportunities to demonstrate that they have learned from mistakes **AND** • Provides practice quizzes, with the correct answers given after the quiz **OR** • Allows students to find the correct answers in materials created by the instructor or required course materials, write the answer in their own words, and receive partial credit for this redone assignment **OR** • Encourages all students to seek feedback on one major assignment before it is graded

Extensively learning-centered	Instructor:
	
	• Provides regular opportunities for students to demonstrate that they have mastered the objectives. Such opportunities might include the following:
	  o Provides practice quizzes with feedback on why answers are incorrect and where to seek more information
	  o Allows students to take online quizzes repeatedly, where the best grade counts, using questions that come from a pool of items, so students get different questions on each attempt
	  o Provides students opportunity to retake an exam or redo an assignment at least three times during the semester **AND**
	• Allows students two or more opportunities to demonstrate mastery of content in an alternative way **AND**
	• Allows students to redo graded products or assignments after feedback **AND**
	• Allows students to retake exams or exam sections by discussing the content and handing in a group answer

EXHIBIT 6.1 Making Performance on Tests a Learning Experience

Posttest Self-Assessment

Name_____   **Test Date____**

Please review your wrong answers to help you study more effectively and do better on the next test.

For each question you got wrong, indicate the reasons why you got it wrong by placing a check in the appropriate column. Then indicate your top three reasons why you got items wrong and any comments to explain your reasons.

Careless mistake	Unfamiliar material	Misinterpreted/ misread	Calculation error	Did not understand material	Did not understand question	Keyed answer wrong	Narrowed answer to two alternatives, then guessed	Changed answer from right to wrong	Did not answer item
Comments									

How can you avoid these mistakes in the future?
How can you take tests more effectively?

Indicate the type of question and source of the material covered in the items you got wrong.

Type of Question →	Where This Content Was Covered? (Check as Many as Apply)				
	Lecture, in class	Reading text, prose	Tables, figures, pictures, charts in reading	Lab	Student presentation	Other—indicate
Factual knowledge					
Application					
Problem-solving or evaluation					

How will you study and prepare for tests differently after doing this posttest self-assessment analysis?

BOX 6.7.
Suggestions on How to Let Students Learn From Their Mistakes and
Then Go On to Demonstrate Mastery of the Content

William Altman and Richard Miller (2017) compiled suggestions from peers. After the instructor grades the test, without the instructor going over the answers, students can correct their mistakes in the following different ways:

- Students are informed of their wrong answers and have until the next class to make corrections by citing the page in the textbook or the class date when the concept was explained. Students need to explain the reasons why they made the mistake and how they now have changed their mind. All questions are worth two points. Items that are corrected get a point; items that were not corrected or changed to another wrong answer lose one more point.
- Students get just the grade they received on the test and no further feedback using the following two methods:
  o Students are placed in pairs (one who did well and one who did not do well). Students who got Cs are grouped together, by default. Using notes, the student pairs retake the test during class time as they engage in peer learning. They need to cite page numbers in the text or topic headings from class notes for correct answers. Because this is now an open book, students do better. The grade is the average of the two attempts on the exam.
  o The instructor selects a subset of items for students to discuss. These questions are application or problem-solving items that students did not do well on or items that focus on important concepts. Students do not yet know how they did on these items when they engage in this exercise. Students work in small groups discussing the answers to these selected items and turn in one sheet with their agreed-upon answers. Then the instructor reviews these items during that same class. Students earn credit for correct answers on the group answer sheet.

Personal Reflection for Your Own Use

How can you use the out-of-class look-up-the-answers strategy in your courses?

How can you use either in-class discussion strategy for students to learn after a test?

What would be your practice: (a) use routinely, (b) tell students in advance that is your practice, or (c) only use when students do poorly or a combination, depending on the course? Why?

---

the construct called Purposes and Processes of Student Assessment. Table 6.8 summarizes the six core actions of this construct and briefly identifies the characteristics of faculty at four levels going from instructor-centered to learning-centered teaching.

Taking Stock of This Construct and How You Can Implement Learning-Centered Teaching With Purposes and Processes of Student Assessment

Table 3.10 gives an example of how an instructor reviewed their current learning-centered teaching status

and decided what and when to make changes. Table 6.9 gives you the opportunity to review your current learning-centered teaching status and decide what and when you want to change on this construct. Your proposed changes are only tentative plans. Once you have read through the rest of this book, you will reconsider your plans and prioritize what you will want to change.

TABLE 6.7. Instructor Characteristics for Authentic Assessment (What Practitioners/Professionals Do) on the Four-Level Continuum From Instructor-Centered to Learning-Centered Approaches

Reading down, each row shows greater use of learning-centered teaching.

Levels	*Action: Uses Authentic Assessment (What Practitioners/Professionals Do), With Instructor Characteristics at Each Level*
Instructor-centered	Instructor: • Rarely or never uses authentic assessment
Minimally learning-centered	Instructor: • Uses a single authentic assessment that is weighted less than 20% of the final grade **OR** • Uses assessments that have authentic elements that count less than 20% of the final grade
Mostly learning-centered	Instructor: • Uses authentic assessment that is weighted 50% or more of the final grade **OR** • Uses assessments that have authentic elements that count 50% or more of the final grade **AND** • Explains to students how these assessments simulate real situations if done in non-real-life situations
Extensively learning-centered	Instructor: • Uses authentic assessments throughout the course that count 80% or more of the final grade **AND** • Asks practitioners to review these authentic assessments and provide feedback

BOX 6.8.
Adding More Authentic Aspects to Design Projects

Faculty at Eindhoven University of Technology in the Netherlands have reframed their undergraduate engineering curriculum to be more aligned with what engineers currently do (Bekkers & Bombaerts, 2017). The professors developed an elective three-course sequence on patents and standards. Prior to registering, students learn about these courses and why this content is important for engineers to learn through written descriptions of the content and how the course is conducted. The final course has two authentic learning and assessment aspects. In one, the students participate in a simulation in which they must develop standards for a future product. Students propose and negotiate about proposed standards as if they represent organizations with conflicting goals and interests, such as product manufacturers, regulators, or end users. In the other project, students can work in small groups to develop an innovative concept into a project that might lead to a patent. The project is peer-reviewed using a detailed review form. The students develop nearly finished patent proposals on their inventions and then they receive feedback from patent attorneys on the viability of their inventions.

Personal Reflection for Your Own Use

How can you incorporate simulations in your course? You might be able to find and adapt simulations that other professors or trainers in industry have developed instead of creating a new simulation.

How can you require students to develop a product that is used beyond the course?

How can you integrate practitioners who are not academics to participate in the assessment process?

TABLE 6.8. Summary of Purposes and Processes of the Student Assessment Construct and Actions Contrasting Instructor-Centered Approaches with Learning-Centered Approaches

For details on each action, see the description in the chapter.

Key to Table

Columns = Action descriptions
Rows = Reading down each column, each successive row shows greater use of learning-centered teaching.

← Actions for Purposes and Processes of Student Assessment →

Levels ↓	Integrates Assessment and Learning	Assessment Policies and Standards	Formative Feedback	Students Use of Peer and Self-Assessment	Students Demonstrate Mastery	Authentic Assessment
Instructor-centered	No integration	Not consistently enforced	No constructive feedback	No peer and self-assessment	Does not provide any opportunities to show mastery beyond the first attempt	Rarely or never uses authentic assessment
Minimally learning-centered	Returns work with comments that can help students to learn	Consistently uses specified grading standards	Provides formative feedback only to students who seek it	Students use peer and self-assessments once or twice	Students can get feedback on one major assignment before it is graded	Authentic assessment counts less than 20% of final grade
Mostly learning-centered	Spends time going over answers to exams	Informs students of specified standards in advance	Provides constructive feedback in a timely and beneficial manner	Teaches how to meaningfully conduct peer and self-assessments	Provides practice quizzes, with the correct answers given	Authentic assessment counts 50% or more of final grade
Extensively learning-centered	Continuously integrates assessment within the learning process through regular assessments	Explains standards and policies throughout the course	Grades recent student performance considering if students incorporated previous formative feedback	Counts peer and self-assessment enough that they are taken seriously	Provides regular opportunities for students to demonstrate that they have mastered the objectives	Authentic assessment counts 80% or more of final grade

TABLE 6.9. Worksheet: My Plans to Increase Use of Learning-Centered Teaching Approaches

Directions

1. Put a ^ in the cell that indicates your status.
2. Put a * in the cell to identify the level to which you aspire to become more learning-centered on this action.
3. Indicate your time line to achieve change for each action on the bottom row.
4. Make comments that will help you make these planned changes.

Note: You may not want to plan changes in every action.

Date _____

Construct IV: Purposes and Processes of Student Assessment

← *Actions for Purposes and Processes of Student Assessment* →

Levels↓	Integrates Assessment and Learning	Assessment Policies and Standards	Formative Feedback	Students Use of Peer and Self-Assessment	Students Demonstrate Mastery	Authentic Assessment	
Instructor-centered	No integration	Not consistently enforced	No constructive feedback	No peer and self-assessment	Does not provide any opportunities to show mastery beyond the first attempt	Rarely or never uses authentic assessment	
Minimally learning-centered	Returns work with comments that could help students to learn	Consistently uses specified grading standards	Provides formative feedback only to students who seek it	Students use peer and self-assessments once or twice	Students can get feedback on one major assignment before it is graded	Authentic assessment counts less than 20% of final grade	
Mostly learning-centered	Spends time going over answers to exams	Informs students of specified standards in advance	Provides constructive feedback in a timely and beneficial manner	Teaches how to meaningfully conduct peer and self-assessments	Provides practice quizzes, with the correct answers given	Authentic assessment counts more than 50% of final grade	
Extensively learning-centered	Continuously integrates assessment within the learning process through regular assessments	Explains standards and policies throughout the course	Grades recent student performance considering if students incorporated previous formative feedback	Counts peer and self-assessment enough that they are taken seriously	Provides regular opportunities for students to demonstrate that they have mastered the objectives	Authentic assessment counts more than 80% of final grade	
Time line to achieve change							

Notes/Comments on My Plan

syllabi explanation

freedom of expression

learning opportunities

flexibility

safe environment

student feedback

Power

Current Evidence-Based Understanding of Learning

Balance of Power

We now come to the last construct, the Balance of Power. Some instructors find this construct the most challenging, or the most controversial, with undergraduate students (Eliason & Holmes, 2012). Instructors report that they feel disempowered or more vulnerable when they share power with students (Piskadlo, 2016). However, redistributing power is one of the pillars of true learning-centered teaching. Although challenging, once power is shared, teaching can be more rewarding as students grow into their power. I defined the Balance of Power in ways that should help students become more engaged, leading to motivated learners who are empowered but not entitled students. This Balance of Power should not be threatening to you and will not result in chaos in the course.

Surprisingly, students also resist sharing balance with instructors. They may even question why they have to pay so much tuition to teach themselves. This remark shows a lack of understanding of the liberating and empowering value of sharing power with instructors. As students mature, you can share more power with them.

Table 7.1 contrasts instructor-centered approaches with learning-centered teaching. Each column represents a separate action of the Balance of Power construct. I explain each action and provide a published example of its use. To assist you in transforming your teaching to be more learning-centered, I define instructor characteristics, for each action, with four increasingly learning-centered levels (i.e., instructor-centered,

TABLE 7.1. Summary of the Balance of Power Construct and Actions Contrasting Instructor-Centered Approaches With Learning-Centered Approaches

Each column represents a separate action of the Balance of Power construct. Read down to see use of learning-centered teaching.

Approach				← *Core Actions of the Balance of Power* →			
	Safe, Moral, and Ethical Environment	Syllabus Demonstrates Power Is Shared	Flexibility in Course Requirements	Opportunities to Learn	Appropriate Freedom of Expression	Responds to Student Feedback
Instructor-Centered	Uses inappropriate behaviors or expresses inappropriate attitudes	Tone sets up authoritarian relationship	Allows some students flexibility in deadlines or how they earn grades but does not let other students know about these possibilities	Frames all learning as required for grade	Does not allow freedom of expression in any form	Does not use feedback provided by students
Learning-Centered	Models appropriate moral and ethical behaviors and teaches their importance to students	Uses a welcoming tone that shows that the instructor is approachable and a human being	Is flexible on aspects of at least four of the following: course policies, learning processes, assessment methods, deadlines, and how students earn grades	Fosters learning to occur beyond the course or learning for life, not just learning for school	Encourages and empowers students to express alternative perspectives, when appropriate, even when instructor disagrees	Makes changes because of student feedback

minimally learning-centered, mostly learning-centered, and extensively learning-centered). I present each action with its characteristics for the four increasingly learning-centered levels in separate tables. I suggest an easy-to-implement learning-centered technique in Box 7.1 and describe a case study of a comprehensive template for learning-centered courses that uses many aspects of this construct in Box 7.2.

Within the last decade, the United States Department of Defense refined the use of language for its personnel. The desired outcome of all current language programs in the military is fostering a basic level of communication to improve their relations with local people and decrease the need for interpreters. In addition to learning a language, military personnel learn cultural sensitivity. Box 7.2 describes a new language program designed to meet these new requirements while being learning-centered.

Action: The Instructor Establishes a Safe, Moral, and Ethical Environment That Empowers All Students

Shockingly, this action needs to be included because there are so many examples in society today where moral and ethical violations occur. When all students do not feel safe, they are stripped of their power. Nonmale, non-White, LGBTQ students, and people with disabilities can feel threatened in

higher education settings (Sohn, 2016). Therefore, for this action, instructor-centered behaviors are unacceptable, as listed in Table 7.2. However, the prevention of, or responding to, violations of moral and ethical behaviors gives all students power. Learning-centered instructors devote time and effort to building trust and creating a sense of a safe community among all students and between students and the instructor. The leaves in Illustration 7.1 represent the four levels characterizing each action.

ILLUSTRATION 7.1. The Four Levels of Characteristics for Each Action

BOX 7.1.
Example of an Easy-to-Implement Learning-Centered Practice

Create two possible dates (e.g., before or after a weekend or before or after a break) for major exams or due dates for big assignments that you are comfortable with in terms of the schedule of the course content and your other responsibilities. Tell the students they have one week to vote on their preferences, and majority wins. The students should consider their responsibilities in their other courses. After the voting, post the agreed-upon test dates and due dates. This small measure sends a strong message that you care about your students as people and want them to succeed. It also may relieve pressure when they have several midterms on the same day.

Personal Reflection for Your Own Use

How much flexibility can you offer students in terms of dates for exams or assignments?

Can you move an exam around within a week or postpone to the next week?

Will you use the semester breaks from classes to grade assignments, or can you receive the assignments immediately after the break?

BOX 7.2.
Case Study of Balance of Power in Military Language Acquisition Program

Traditional military language programs use general proficiency curricula where military personnel learn a general body of knowledge such as common vocabulary and grammar. These curricula often focus on listening and reading. In contrast, Marla Federe and Clay Leishman (2014) report on a practical, purpose- and objective-driven, learning-centered curriculum designed to teach Navy SEALs functional Pashto. This program adheres to quality assurance surveillance process teaching criteria, which have the following balance of power attributes:

- Providing a positive and safe learning environment that encourages all students to actively participate
- Ensuring flexibility to be adaptive to student's learning needs
- Making students active agents in their own learning process

The curriculum is based on a detailed needs assessment of which language skills the Navy SEALs need when they are functioning in Pashto-speaking areas. Instead of trying to acquire a body of knowledge, the goal was to foster the acquisition of mission-focused language skills. This change made the course learning-centered. Instructors discuss the daily and hourly objectives and students constantly reflect on how they would use the objectives and the content operationally. Thus, the course allowed multiple opportunities for the students to learn. Class time focused on practical exercises in a simulated village. Students reflected on how well they were doing and what they needed to achieve their objectives. Flexibility is an inherent feature of this teaching method. The instructors have the authority to adapt and update the curriculum to suit the needs of the students enrolled.

The participants in this intensive 12-week course did statistically significantly better on tests of listening, reading, and speaking than military personnel who took the traditional general proficiency curricula. The authors see this model as a work in progress and are using the test results and students' feedback to improve the program and generalize it to other languages and other cultures. This new teaching method has the potential to save the military both time and money in language training.

Personal Reflection for Your Own Use

If training in the military can employ the Balance of Power construct, how can you overcome any personal resistance to sharing some power with students?

How could you envision your teaching as primarily a process of acquiring necessary skills and secondarily as acquiring a body of knowledge? How does this change your learning outcomes?

How can you get students to actively reflect on how they will use the content operationally to foster their realization of opportunities to learn?

Each action is a branch on the tree shown at the beginning of the chapter.

Personal Reflection

What do you do to create a safe environment for all students?

What do you do to create a moral environment for all students?

What do you do to create an ethical environment for all students?

Professional schools, such as the health professions, were the first educators to teach moral and ethical

TABLE 7.2. Instructor Characteristics for Establishing a Safe, Moral, and Ethical Environment on the Four-Level Continuum From Instructor-Centered to Learning-Centered Approaches

Reading down, each row shows greater use of learning-centered teaching.

Levels	*Action: Establishes a Safe, Moral, and Ethical Environment*
Instructor-centered	Instructor: • Uses inappropriate behaviors or expresses inappropriate attitudes **OR** • Has received feedback that the class or institution is not a safe, a moral, and an ethical environment for all students **AND** • Does not make changes to correct these inappropriate behaviors and attitudes
Minimally learning-centered	Instructor: • Abides by ethical and moral standards and laws **AND** • Provides accommodation for students with disabilities
Mostly learning-centered	Instructor meets the criteria for minimally using learning-centered approach **AND** • Maintains consistency, fairness, and equity in applying all policies and standards to all students **AND** • Maintains privacy of student records **AND** • Maintains proper relationships with all students, including on social media
Extensively learning-centered	Instructor meets the criteria for mostly uses learning-centered approach **AND** • Encourages and abides by ethical and moral standards and laws **AND** • Encourages ethical behaviors in academic student conduct **AND** • Prevents or responds appropriately to harassment or violations of ethical standards **AND** • Models appropriate ethical and moral behaviors and teaches their importance to students

behaviors, but now more programs are requiring it (Benninga, 2003). Box 7.3 describes moral training for preservice teachers.

Action: The Instructor Provides a Syllabus and Other Course Artifacts Demonstrating That Students and Instructors Share Power to Promote Learning

A syllabus serves as a framework for the course for both students and faculty (Palmer, Bach, & Streifer, 2014). Most instructors provide students with a syllabus that offers contact information, a schedule of classes, course requirements, policies, and how

students will be graded. Is your syllabus too authoritarian? It might have unintentionally morphed into a long, detailed production that reads like a legal document, defining many strict rules, consequences, and policies. Is this the first impression you want to create for your students about you and your course? Instead, as a learning-centered instructor, you will want to create what Bain (2004) terms a *promising syllabus*. Such a syllabus clearly communicates what students will learn from the course and why. They will be able to know if they are achieving the promise and how they should best spend their time. Learning-centered syllabi are powerful venues to

---

BOX 7.3.
Teaching Morality and Ethics to Preservice Teachers

The National Council for Accreditation of Teacher Education now requires that all preservice teachers receive ethical and moral training. The purpose of the training is to help preservice teachers learn how to model exemplary character traits when they are teachers. Students in introduction to education courses learn about the moral responsibility of teachers to students, parents, colleagues, and community members. Student teacher supervisors are expected to discuss ethical issues they regularly encounter.

Faculty at the University of Minnesota (Benninga, 2003) developed an evidence-based, four-part moral training program aiming to foster moral maturity in preservice teachers, based on the following concepts:

1. Moral sensitivity training focuses on how actions impact other people through role-playing activities.
2. Moral judgment training requires students to make moral and fair judgments about situations.
3. Moral motivation training helps students to prioritize moral values over personal values in school settings.
4. Moral character training fosters students acting on their moral convictions in a series of role-playing professional dilemmas.

Personal Reflection on Applicability for My Use

Does your professional association or disciplinary organization have an ethics or moral code of behavior? If so, are you are adhering to all aspects of this code?

How do you demonstrate exemplary character traits with your students?

---

send the message that students have ownership over their learning.

The tone of the syllabus communicates whether this is a rule-driven course or an opportunity for learning, growth, exploration, and perhaps wonder. The characteristics of the syllabus and other course materials shown in Table 7.3 illustrate different tones. As the characteristics become increasingly more learning-centered, the tone becomes more welcoming and facilitating of student learning and success. Learning-centered syllabi make statements about learning outcomes, receiving feedback, and how the instructor will determine if students are achieving the learning outcomes (Ludwig, Bentz, & Fynewever, 2011). You do not have to completely rewrite your syllabus, but you can revise it to be more learning-centered by changing some language and the tone, as long as it accurately reflects how the course will run.

Personal Reflection

Read your syllabus aloud or ask nonacademic friends to read your syllabus for its tone. What is the impression your document creates?

What can you do to make your syllabus more inviting and empowering for students?

Because each course's syllabus is so important, instructors should consider consulting with faculty developers to develop better syllabi. Box 7.4 describes a course design institute where the participants worked to improve their course syllabi to make them more learning-centered. The faculty developers created a rubric to assess how learning-centered each syllabus was.

Action: The Instructor Allows for Some Flexibility in Course Policies, Assessment Methods, Learning Methods,

TABLE 7.3. Instructor Characteristics for Providing Syllabi and Other Course Artifacts That Demonstrate Students and Instructors Share Power to Promote Learning on the Four-Level Continuum From Instructor-Centered to Learning-Centered Approaches

Reading down, each row shows greater use of learning-centered teaching.

Levels	*Provides Syllabi Demonstrating That Students and Instructors Share Power*
Instructor-centered	Instructor: • Does not mention learning in the syllabus **OR** • States policies, expectations, and assignments as demands, directives, or ironclad rules **OR** • Uses tone that sets up authoritarian relationship
Minimally learning-centered	Instructor: • States reasons why subject/content are worth learning, important, or interesting **OR** • States that students and instructor engage in learning together **OR** • Invites students to learn and grow **OR** • Discusses personal excitement about learning or about this content **OR** • Uses an inviting and less controlling tone
Mostly learning-centered	Instructor meets the criteria for minimally uses learning-centered approach **AND** • States clearly defined and measurable learning outcomes **AND** • States what students must do to meet the learning outcomes and how they can earn their grades **AND** • Explains how and why course will be conducted, what students will do in class or online, and how they will prepare for class **OR** • Explains how students can succeed **OR** • Seeks feedback on the tone of the syllabus

Extensively learning-centered	Instructor meets the criteria for mostly uses learning-centered approach **AND**
	
	• Uses a welcoming tone that shows that the instructor is approachable and a human being **AND**
	• Makes all of the following types of statements:
	  o Clearly defined and measurable learning outcomes and how they fit with the larger educational program's outcomes
	  o How students will get useable feedback on how they are doing throughout the course
	  o How the instructor will know whether teaching is helping students reach learning objectives **OR**
	• Makes an explicit statement about sharing power **OR**
	• Gives motivational messages that set lofty yet achievable goals

---

BOX 7.4.
Learning-Centered Syllabus Rubric

Michael Palmer, Dorothe Bach, and Adriana Streifer (2014) stress the importance of creating a promising syllabus in their week-long course design institute. They created and used an instrument to measure the learning-centered orientation of syllabi. The instrument specified criteria on rubrics and gave a description of what a learning-centered focus would look like on a syllabus. Further, the instrument provided indicators for where to look and examples of what to look for to score syllabi.

The syllabus rubric is organized around the following large-scale criteria, each with associated sub-criteria:

- Learning goals and objectives are the central focus of the course.
- Learning objectives are aligned with major assessments and learning activities.
- Students can use the course schedule as an organizing tool to guide them.
- The course's learning environment supports students and invites them to engage in their learning. The syllabus's tone, promise, and inclusivity indicate the course's learning environment. For example, the tone is positive, respectful, inviting and directly addresses the student as a competent, engaged learner.

The authors measured the pre-/postinstitute syllabi of participants to determine how much impact the institute had. All participants' syllabi became more learning-centered. Gains were larger for the more instructor-centered participants than those who were already more learning-centered prior to the institute. This is logical because the instructor-centered teachers had more room to grow and could employ some easy-to-implement practices to become more learning-centered.

Personal Reflection for Your Own Use

Review your syllabi. How learning-centered are your syllabi?

Are learning goals and objectives the central focus of the course? Explain how.

Do each of your syllabi show that learning objectives are aligned with the major assessments and learning activities? (Alignment is one of the core actions in the Role of Instructor construct, as described in chapter 3.)

Can students use the course schedule as an organizing tool to guide them?

How does the course's learning environment support students and invite them to engage in their learning?

What can you do to improve the learning-centeredness of your syllabi?

Deadlines, or How Students Earn Grades, While Informing Students of Decisions

When instructors allow some flexibility, students perceive that they have greater control over their learning and their grades. This ultimately leads to more learning and higher grades (Weimer, 2013). Flexibility can be demonstrated by giving students options, which increases student motivation (McKeachie, 2007). Easy-to-implement options include choice of due dates for assignments or selecting three out of five exam questions to answer.

Flexibility sends the message that you care about your students and understand that they lead

TABLE 7.4. Instructor Characteristics for Allowing for Some Flexibility on the Four-Level Continuum From Instructor-Centered to Learning-Centered Approaches

Reading down, each row shows greater use of learning-centered teaching.

Levels	*Action: Allows for Some Flexibility*
Instructor-centered	Instructor: • Mandates all policies, learning and assessment methods, and deadlines **OR** • Does not adhere to stated policies **OR** • Allows some students flexibility in deadlines or how they earn grades but does not let other students know about these possibilities
Minimally learning-centered	Instructor: • Informs students of policies, methods, deadlines, and how student earn grades **AND** • Consistently maintains and enforces all the above **AND** • Is flexible on one of the following: course policies, learning processes, assessment methods, deadlines, or how students earn grades **AND** • Allows all students the same flexibility
Mostly learning-centered	Instructor: • Is flexible on at least two of the following: course policies, learning processes, assessment methods, deadlines, and how students earn grades **AND** • Always adheres to what has been agreed upon **OR** • Provides participation options for some activities (e.g., allowing students to participate in class discussions or using online discussion boards after the class) **AND** • Seeks feedback on policies, methods, and deadlines
Extensively learning-centered	Instructor meets the criteria for mostly learning-centered approaches **AND** • Is flexible on at least three aspects of the following: course policies, assessment methods, deadlines, and how students earn grades **AND** • Actively seeks student feedback on policies, processes, methods, attendance options, and deadlines and responds to their feedback with appropriate and considered changes

complex lives. Of course, learning-centered instructors inform their students of where and how they are flexible and where they cannot be flexible. The more process flexibility you allow, the more learning-centered you are, as Table 7.4 shows, listing the instructor characteristics for flexibility on the four-level continuum from instructor-centered to learning-centered approaches.

Numerous variations on policies and practices exist. You need to decide where you can and cannot allow flexibility. Some of this is personal preference or how much you value this policy or practice. Safety and health require some policies, such as wearing protective eyewear when working with chemicals or explosive material or not allowing food in a microbiology laboratory.

Personal Reflection

Rate how you feel about each of the possible policies and practices listed in Table 7.5, as well as any others that are relevant to your courses. Inform students where you do not allow flexibility or policies you are opposed to. Decide if you could allow flexibility on policies you are neutral on; this may depend on the size and level of the class.

Box 7.5 describes a graduate course where the instructors allowed flexibility on reading material, presentation schedule, learning methods, and final assignment to create student ownership.

As a learning-centered instructor, you might consider using one of two flexible grading

methods—mastery or contract grading (Blumberg, 2009). With mastery grading, the instructor selects a high standard to be the minimum acceptable level that students need to reach to pass the assessment. Students can attempt the assessment a few times until they reach this high standard. Instructors do not give any partial credit. Students who do not reach mastery after the allowed number of attempts do not get any credit. Skills where this grading method makes sense, such as those used in the health professions or laboratory safety, are common areas where instructors require mastery. Students may have to reach mastery on all their assignments to pass the course, even if they do well on other aspects. Grades could also reflect the percent of mastered content over a

TABLE 7.5. Self-Assessment of Flexibility Options on Policies and Practices

Policy/Practice	I Am Opposed to Flexibility	I Am Neutral	I Could Allow Flexibility
Ability to make up missed classes			
Ability to make up missed exams			
Allowing extra credit			
Allowing students to get feedback on drafts			
Allowing students to redo less than perfect products			
Collaborating on homework			
Coming late to class			
Drinking coffee or water in class			
Eating in class			
Handing in assignments after the deadline			
Participating in class when student forgot some required equipment			
Participating in class when unprepared			
Providing time frame for providing feedback on assignments			
Recording class lecture or discussion			
Requiring attendance			
Using electronic devices in class			
Wearing professional attire			
Other: Please specify			

BOX 7.5.
Sharing Decision-Making Power with Students

Mariam Abdelmalak and Jesús Trespalacios (2013) teach graduate educational technology courses where the students have shared decision-making power with the instructors to create shared ownership of the class. Prior to the first class, the instructors posted on the learning management system the introduction and table of contents of three possible textbooks. On the first day of class the students read this information, discussed which textbook they preferred, and selected the textbook they would read for the class. Students could read different textbooks. The instructors did not have a complete set of technologies they wanted to cover; instead, students had flexibility in deciding the topics to be discussed. Students chose a topic and a technology tool that they wanted to learn more about. Students were responsible for presenting their topic and technology tool to the class and they agreed on the schedule of presentation dates. During the class where the student presented, that student also facilitated the discussion. Some students planned creative activities for the class discussions. The instructors and the students learned together during the class discussions. The instructors allowed students flexibility in the final assignment by providing assignment options. Each choice had detailed directions and expectations. Halfway through the course, the students submitted a proposal where they identified the major steps they would follow to complete their final assignment. The instructors provided feedback and recommendations on the proposals.

Students liked choosing a textbook and it motivated them to read it more thoroughly. Some students struggled finding a topic and technology they wanted to learn about. However, once they had the topic and prepared to lead the class, they expressed a commitment to doing the best job possible to foster learning for their classmates. They liked having flexibility in their final assignment and chose assignments that were meaningful to them as they related to their interests and goals.

Personal Reflection for Your Own Use

Although this was a graduate course, how can you create ownership through sharing power with undergraduate students?

How could you allow students some choice in the textbook or secondary reading selection? Does it matter to you if all students choose the same textbook or can they read different recommended texts?

How can you allow students choice in the content they learn or that they present to their classmates?

How can you provide choices in assignments yet ensure that they are equivalent?

course. With contract grading, on the other hand, you give students options in the assignments they complete and specify the weights and due dates for each assignment. All assignments might have to be done well to get an A, with fewer requirements for lower grades. Early in the course, student develop a contract that states the assignments they will do and, therefore, the grade they hope to earn. Instructors assign points or grades depending on the quality of the assignment (Nilson & Stanny, 2015). With both systems, instructors need to explain how they work.

Students must adhere to due dates in both grading systems.

Action: The Instructor Provides Students Opportunities to Learn and Helps Students to Recognize When They Have Missed Opportunities to Learn

Although grade reductions are common consequence when students miss opportunities to learn, they send the message that learning is only associated with grades. As a learning-centered instructor, you need to encourage your students to think beyond grades and to realize how learning occurs throughout life. Sadly, missed opportunities to learn may not come again. When students appreciate their opportunities to learn, they rarely miss class (Blumberg, 2009; Weimer, 2013). Early in the semester discuss how the following learning opportunities foster student participation and engagement in the course:

- Attending class
- Participating in class discussions
- Doing optional, ungraded assignments or quizzes
- Going to office hours
- Seeking peer feedback
- Handing in drafts for feedback
- Going for extra tutoring
- Attending out-of-class activities such as lectures, concerts, or going to a museum

Beginning or unmotivated students might benefit from a learning opportunity decision tree to help them become more aware of the numerous learning opportunities available to them. This decision tree would pair every course activity with a metacognition question such as "When I participate how can I learn?" or "What learning opportunity have I missed by not participating?" Table 7.6 lists the characteristics of learning-centered teachers on the opportunities to learn action. When possible, learning-centered instructors create high impact practices. These practices are positively associated with student learning and retention (Kuh, 2008). Service-learning, collaborative assignments or projects, and working with faculty on a research project are examples of high-impact practices that you can incorporate into individual courses.

As instructors practice learning-centered teaching, they often employ more group projects. However, many students do not like group projects and do not see them as opportunities to learn (Felder & Brent, 2016). Therefore, some students may miss learning opportunities throughout the group project experience. Yet, when instructors provide students with guidance and structure about how to work together, students come to appreciate how group projects can be learning opportunities (Millis, 2010). Box 7.6

describes students' insights about their own learning from working in groups.

Action: The Instructor Empowers Student Learning Through Appropriate Freedom of Expression, for Example by Encouraging Alternative Perspectives, Open-Ended Assignments, or the Ability to Determine Some Course Content

Table 7.7 lists the characteristics of learning-centered instructors for the freedom of expression action. Learning occurs when there is open and honest intellectual exchange. Students must feel supported to express themselves without the instructor or students telling them they are wrong or stupid. As a learning-centered instructor, you encourage students to have different perspectives from your own or that of the authors of readings. You can ask students for evidence to support their opinions.

Open-ended assignments are those with more than one correct answer or where there are several paths to a solution. These assignments can be used in all types of courses even in STEM courses. Assignments can be open-ended in terms of content, product format (i.e., essay, presentation, poster, or online product), or when students need to find their own resources to complete the assignment. Open-ended assignments are more likely to be unique and, therefore, less likely to have the potential for students plagiarizing others' work. When students can integrate their interests into open-ended assignments, they become more engaged. Box 7.7 describes how instructors use popular culture to help students express their perspectives about the content of abstract concepts in an introductory international relations course.

Freedom of expression is more encouraged in some disciplines such as the arts, social sciences, and humanities than in other more factual disciplines such as mathematics or physical sciences. Therefore, freedom of expression may be more limited in some contexts, course levels, or disciplines than in others. Introductory courses involving many facts, especially in STEM disciplines, may offer fewer opportunities for freedom of expression. Yet, choice of some content to be learned may be an appropriate freedom of expression in such courses, especially in STEM courses. Students should be able to select an

TABLE 7.6. Instructor Characteristics for Providing Opportunities to Learn on the Four-Level Continuum From Instructor-Centered to Learning-Centered Approaches

Reading down, each row shows greater use of learning-centered teaching.

Levels	Action: Opportunities to Learn
Instructor-centered	Instructor: • Does not allow opportunities to learn beyond what the instructor does or required reading **OR** • Frames all learning as required for grades
Minimally learning-centered	Instructor: • Provides alternative learning opportunities beyond instructor and required reading **AND** • Provides opportunities to learn, such as discussions, peer feedback, or out-of-class experiences that count as 5% to 10% of the final grade
Mostly learning-centered	Instructor meets the criteria for minimally learning-centered approaches **AND** • Explains how varied activities are learning opportunities **AND** • Encourages learning for life in addition to learning for school **OR** • Creates high-impact learning activities that may extend beyond the classroom, activities that count 25% or more of the final grade
Extensively learning-centered	Instructor meets the criteria for mostly learning-centered approaches **AND** • Helps students to take advantage of opportunities to learn even if they are not graded **AND** • Fosters understanding of consequences of not taking advantage of learning opportunities **AND** • Empowers students to recognize why they should learn even if it is not required **AND** • Fosters learning to occur beyond the course or learning for life, not just learning for school

appropriate topic or be given choices of topics for large projects or assignments. Students enjoy learning about controversial topics within the discipline, which can lead to debates, even in introductory courses.

Action: The Instructor Responds to Feedback From Students to Improve Teaching and Learning

Table 7.8 shows the characteristics of instructors regarding responding to student feedback along the four-level continuum from instructor-centered to learning-centered approaches. You can obtain feedback through surveys, focus groups, and casual conversations. However, you should try to gather feedback from as many students as possible and not just the ones who speak out the most. Even more important than collecting feedback, you as a

---

BOX 7.6.
Students Realize That Group Work Can Be Opportunities for All Kinds of Learning

Carol Colbeck, Susan Campbell, and Stefani Bjorklund (2000) investigated what conditions led to positive and negative group learning experiences among undergraduate engineering students at different types of colleges. Students who participated in group design projects were interviewed in focus groups. Out-of-class group experiences such as on jobs or in extracurricular activities and group projects in previous classes helped students realize that group projects increased communication skills, planning, technical skills, self-confidence, time management skills, and resourcefulness. Working together on an open-ended, real-world design project gave the students the opportunity to develop better problem-solving skills. Through discussions they came to believe that multiple solutions might be feasible and that the individual did not always have the right or only answer. Group projects increased engineering students' interpersonal and teamwork skills, including their ability to work with all kinds of people, coping skills in working with difficult people, conflict management, and listening skills. Students learned that people had different goals and motivations for the project and that to be successful they should try to accommodate these different aspirations. These differences allowed leaders to emerge for different aspects of the project. Students learned how to work with the slackers in the group or how to seek assistance when working with them. Because there was too much to do, students learned to trust each other when the tasks got divided and then to come back together to learn from each other.

The authors made the following recommendations for group work:

- Students should have repeated opportunities to engage in group projects because learning effects are cumulative.
- Faculty should receive training on group functioning and then provide students appropriate guidance and support.
- Faculty should assign students to groups and not allow students to pick their teammates.

Although the authors did not state this, I recommend that instructors tell students the benefits of group work to help students realize that they may be missing valuable opportunities to learn when they do not fully participate in group work.

Personal Reflection for Your Own Use

How can you help students to overcome their negative perceptions of group work?

Where can you incorporate group projects into your courses?

What kind of guidance and structure would you give students to make their group projects more meaningful?

---

learning-centered instructor will reflect on student feedback and make appropriate changes. If you ask for feedback early in the semester, you might be able to make changes for the current students. Informing students about the changes you have made because of student feedback assures students that you take their ideas seriously.

Traditional end-of-course evaluations do not correlate with how much or how well students have learned (Nilson, 2012; Weiman, 2015). Instead, the commonly used instruments measure the instructor's popularity and caring. Consider using the Student Assessment of Learning Gains (SALG) instrument instead of or in addition to required end-of-course

TABLE 7.7. Instructor Characteristics for Empowering Students Through Freedom of Expression on the Four-Level Continuum From Instructor-Centered to Learning-Centered Approaches

Reading down, each row shows greater use of learning-centered teaching.

Levels	Action: Freedom of Expression
Instructor-centered	Instructor: • Does not foster freedom of expression in any form **OR** • Demonstrates that the instructor's perspective is the only acceptable one **OR** • Entirely determines course content, including assigning topics to students for large papers, presentations, or projects
Minimally learning-centered	Instructor: • Allows freedom of expression in any form during less than 20% of the course **OR** • Allows students to select their own topics for large papers, presentations, or projects
Mostly learning-centered	Instructor: • Allows students freedom of expression by encouraging alternative perspectives, when appropriate, open-ended assignments, or the ability to determine some course content they want to learn about 50% of the time **AND** • Listens to students' perspectives and does not indicate that they are wrong even if they do not agree with the instructor
Extensively learning-centered	Instructor meets the criteria for mostly learning-centered approaches **AND** • Encourages and empowers students to express alternative perspectives, when appropriate, even when instructor disagrees **AND** • Facilitates students having a voice in determining optional or additional content to be learned **OR** • Evaluates students through assignments that are open-ended or allow alternative paths, using assessments that count 80% of the total grade

evaluation tools. SALG is a free online tool that measures student perceptions of learning activities and the learning environment (SALG, 2013). Instructors pick the relevant course requirements and activities and students rate how much each contributed to their learning. As of 2013, almost 9,000 instructors have used the SALG and over 187,000 students have completed it. Instructors can use it to measure learning gains within a semester or over time. Box 7.8 describes how an instructor responded to student resistance to an innovative assessment and how over time the student SALG scores improved.

Chapter Summary

This chapter discusses how you can change your teaching to be more learning-centered on the Balance

---

BOX 7.7.
Discussions of Popular Culture Empower Student Learning of Content

Professors of international relations see the role of popular culture, especially literature and film, as pedagogical entry points to help students contextualize this content. Jennifer Lobasz and Brandon Valeriano (2015) used popular literature and film throughout their introductory courses in international relations. Assignments usually involved a combination of textbook and popular culture exposure, either reading general literature or viewing a film. Students had freedom of expression in answering the instructor's questions or posing and answering their own questions on the class's blog prior to class. Students were also expected to comment on their peer's posts. Class discussions focused on concepts and how the popular culture illustrated this concept. For the final assignment, students were given a list of the topics covered in most international relations textbooks and the students chose a film, not previously discussed, that illustrated one topic. Students were given a long list of possible films that might have relevancy. The students wrote a detailed paper explaining how their selected film illustrated the topic. The students constructed their argument of how the film connected to the topic. This final assignment helped students to apply and synthesize the essential concepts of international relations. The blog posts, class discussions, and the final assignment were open-ended. Thus, they encouraged freedom of expression and alternative perspectives. Popular culture examples offered more than one correct answer about international relations.

Personal Reflection for Your Own Use

How can you use popular culture as an entry point for your content?

How can you provide open-ended assignments, even in courses with defined theories?

How can you allow freedom of expression or alternative perspective, even in courses where there are correct answers?

---

of Power construct. Table 7.9 summarizes these suggested changes via six actions.

Taking Stock of This Construct and How You Can Implement Learning-Centered Teaching With the Balance of Power

Table 3.10 gives an example of how an instructor reviewed their current learning-centered teaching status and decided what and when to make changes.

Table 7.10 gives you the opportunity to review your current learning-centered teaching status and decide what and when you want to change related to the Balance of Power. Your proposed changes are only tentative plans. In the next chapter you will reconsider all your plans and prioritize what you will want to change.

TABLE 7.8. Instructor Characteristics for Responding to Student Feedback on the Four-Level Continuum From Instructor-Centered to Learning-Centered Approaches

Reading down, each row shows greater use of learning-centered teaching.

Levels	Action: Responds to Student Feedback
Instructor-centered	Instructor: • Does not solicit feedback from students **OR** • Does not use feedback provided by students
Minimally learning-centered	Instructor: • Considers all student feedback offered through standard course evaluation forms **AND** • Reflects on all feedback received, but does not make an action plan to improve **OR** • Makes small changes because of feedback
Mostly learning-centered	Instructor: • Asks for feedback on at least three aspects of the course, including teaching approach; content; assessment methods; and schedule of assignments, readings, policies, or workload. This feedback may be solicited beyond the standard course evaluations **AND** • Uses student feedback to develop an action plan **AND** • Continues to seek student feedback to refine action plan
Extensively learning-centered	Instructor meets the criteria for mostly learning-centered approaches **AND** • Seeks feedback early enough in the course to make changes for the current students, when possible, **OR** • Makes changes to teaching approach, schedule, policies, or assessment methods, because of student feedback **AND** • Tells students about changes made as result of feedback

BOX 7.8.
Using Students' Negative Feedback as a Trigger to Improve

Wendy Keeney-Kennicutt (Keeney-Kennicutt, Gunersel, & Simpson, 2008) introduced several online writing and peer critique assignments in place of a few labs in her general chemistry course. The SALG results for these assignments from the early semesters of use indicated the students strongly disliked all aspects of these assignments. They thought the directions were not clear, they had trouble using the technology, and they stated they were not graded fairly. The students felt that both writing and peer critique had no place in a chemistry course. The instructor used these negative scores and comments as a stimulus for targeted improvements using Schon's (1987) reflection-in-practice process. She continued using the peer critique assignment and collected SALG results for 7 semesters with over 1,500 students.

Keeney-Kennicutt responded to the criticism by incrementally becoming more intentional about communicating to students why she valued the assignment and the potential learning gains. She changed how she explained the assignment, discussed how both writing and peer critique were important to their future careers, gave clearer directions, assured the students that she was available for technology help, increased student trust when she offered to override grades students perceived as unfair, and modeled how to use the technology and how to write a good review. Over time, Keeney-Kennicutt spent more class time discussing the value of the assignment and how to do it successfully because she so much believed that the assignment had value added in addition to demonstrating mastery of chemistry content. By the seventh semester she used this assignment, 71% of the students as indicated by their SALG scores recognized the assignment was a good learning tool. The percentage of students who felt that their writing and critique skills improved because of these assignments nearly doubled from the first semester to the seventh semester of use. The student comments on the assignment went from being mostly negative to majority positive in the fifth, sixth, and seventh semesters she used this peer critique technique.

In their article, the instructor and two faculty developers (Keeney-Kennicutt et al., 2008) stated the following generalizable lessons they learned from the long-term improvement in students' perception of learning gains:

- Expect resistance when course expectations or innovations are introduced. Instead of being discouraged by this resistance, use the feedback to trigger changes.
- Coach students by modeling how to use technology and explain the different aspects of the innovative assignment.
- Be explicit about the rationale for the innovation and how it will benefit students.
- Provide face-to-face and individualized targeted help.
- Count the innovation enough in the course grade so that students realize it is important and valued.

Personal Reflection for Your Own Use

Before you use a very innovative technique, determine the support you have from your chair and other resources. You do not want negative feedback to be held against you for retention or promotion.

What negative feedback have you received that you can use as a stimulus for changing how you teach?

What value-added types of assignments or activities might you introduce that help students meet the larger educational goals beyond mastery of the content of your courses? How can you introduce these types of assignments or activities?

TABLE 7.9. Summary of the Balance of Power Construct and Actions Contrasting Instructor-Centered Approaches With Learning-Centered Approaches

For details on each action, see the description in the chapter.

Key to Table

Columns = Action descriptions
Rows = Reading down each column, each successive row shows greater use of learning-centered teaching.

Levels↓	← *Actions* →					
	Safe, Moral, and Ethical Environment	**Syllabus Demonstrates Shared Power**	**Flexibility in Course Practices**	**Opportunities to Learn**	**Appropriate Freedom of Expression**	**Use of Student Feedback**
Instructor-centered	Uses inappropriate behaviors or expresses inappropriate attitudes	Uses a tone that sets up authoritarian relationship	Does not adhere to stated policies	Frames all learning as required for grades	Does not allow freedom of expression in any form	Does not use student feedback
Minimally learning-centered	Abides by ethical and moral standards and laws	States that students and instructor are engaged in learning together	Is flexible on one course policy or practice	Provides alternative learning opportunities	Allows students to select their own topics for large assignments	Considers course evaluation form feedback
Mostly learning-centered	Maintains fairness and equity in applying all policies to all students	States how students meet learning outcomes and how they earn their grades	Is flexible on at least two policies or practices	Explains how varied activities are learning opportunities	Allows freedom of expression about 50% of the time	Asks for feedback on at least three aspects of the course
Extensively learning-centered	Models appropriate ethical and moral behaviors and teaches their importance to students	Uses a welcoming tone that shows that the instructor is approachable	Is flexible on aspects of at least four course policies or practices, methods, deadlines, and how students earn grades	Fosters learning to occur beyond the course or learning for life, not just learning for school	Empowers students to express alternative perspectives, even when instructor disagrees	Makes changes because of student feedback

TABLE 7.10. Worksheet: Status of Teaching and Plans for Change to Increase Use of Learning-Centered Teaching Approaches

Date_____

Directions

1. Put a ^ in the cell that indicates your status.
2. Put a * in the cell to identify the level to which you aspire to become more learning-centered on this action.
3. Indicate your time line to achieve change for each action on the bottom row.
4. Make comments that will help you make these planned changes.

Note: You may not want to plan changes in every action.

Construct Versus Balance of Power

Levels↓	← *Actions* →					
	Safe, Moral, and Ethical Environment	**Syllabus Demonstrates Shared Power**	**Flexibility in Course Practices**	**Opportunities to Learn**	**Appropriate Freedom of Expression**	**Responds to Student Feedback**
Instructor-centered	Uses inappropriate behaviors or expresses inappropriate attitudes	Uses a tone that sets up authoritarian relationship	Does not adhere to stated policies	Frames all learning as required for grades	Does not allow freedom of expression in any form	Does not use student feedback
Minimally learning-centered	Abides by ethical and moral standards and laws	States that students and instructor are engaged in learning together	Is flexible on one course policy or practice	Provides alternative learning opportunities	Allows students to select their own topics for large assignments	Considers course evaluation form feedback
Mostly learning-centered	Maintains fairness and equity in applying all policies to all students	States how students meet learning outcomes and how they earn their grades	Is flexible on at least two policies or practices	Explains how varied activities are learning opportunities	Allows freedom of expression about 50% of the time	Asks for feedback on at least three aspects of the course
Extensively learning-centered	Models appropriate ethical and moral behaviors and teaches their importance to students	Uses a welcoming tone that shows that the instructor is approachable	Is flexible on aspects of at least four course policies or practices, methods, deadlines, and how students earn grades	Fosters learning to occur beyond the course or learning for life, not just learning for school	Empowers students to express alternative perspectives, even when instructor disagrees	Makes changes because of student feedback
Timeline to achieve change						

Notes/Comments on My Plan

CHAPTER 8

Increasing Your Use of Learning-Centered Teaching

> ### Chapter Highlights
>
> The purpose of this chapter is to help you develop a realistic plan for transitioning to learning-centered teaching or at least for more use of this approach. This chapter discusses different tactics that collectively promote your use of learning-centered teaching. You will find a discussion of how to use learning-centered teaching with the following specific student populations: (a) underprepared, unmotivated, or first-year college students; (b) foreign language learners; and (c) STEM students at all levels. You will have two opportunities to review and revise your plans for increasing your use of learning-centered teaching.

After reading the previous chapters you may have many ideas for how you can use learning-centered teaching. This chapter helps you focus and plan how you will implement your ideas. It also grounds you in your own realities of time, commitments, and departmental and institutional situations.

Suggested Strategies for Transitioning to Learning-Centered Teaching

Depending on your situation you might make incremental, small steps or you might be able to transform your teaching in a course all at once. Regardless of which strategy you use, you should also use critical reflection and documentation about your teaching as you make changes. Social media also can be helpful in connecting with other teachers who are interested in learning-centered teaching.

Incremental, Small Steps
The contrast between the characteristics of the instructor-centered and the learning-centered approaches is so large that they appear to be opposing

paradigms. You may be reticent to make such big changes to how you succeeded in school or how you teach. Instead of seeing these two approaches as different paradigms, you could consider them as a continuum from one approach to the other. To assist you in transitioning to more learning-centered approaches, the model provides two intermediate levels between instructor-centered and learning-centered. Read over the characteristics of instructors at each of the four levels on the actions you wish to change. (Illustration 8.1 represents the four incremental steps within each action.) Decide what level best characterizes your current teaching practices. You will find it easier to make gradual changes to become more learning-centered by transitioning to the next level on each action (Blumberg, 2009). If you change your use of a few actions within these five constructs by transitioning to the next learning-centered level, you will incrementally become a learning-centered teacher. This can be a safe, manageable, and comfortable approach. Yet even small, incremental steps can have an impact on student learning. Often these small steps can motivate you to make further changes (Blumberg, 2015).

ILLUSTRATION 8.1. The Four Levels of Characteristics for Each Action

Take an incremental approach if you

- are alone in transitioning to learning-centered teaching in your department;
- teach a section of a multisection course and need to be similar to the other sections;
- do not have the complete support of your department chair;
- are pretenure and must focus on research or cannot risk having a dip in your student evaluations as you innovate (remember students resist change);
- are an adjunct or part-time professor;
- are teaching a few new-for-you courses;
- may not be teaching the same courses in the future; or
- teach in an accredited or licensed program and you have to work within the constraints of an accrediting body.

Doing a Total Transformation

Whereas incremental changes can be made without much investment of time or resources, total transformations require much more time investment. If you have the opportunity, you might be able to totally transform your teaching or do so within one course. However, to make a transformational change, you must to be willing to give up something (Piskadlo,

2016). When you become a learning-centered teaching instructor, you give up being the chief disseminator of information. Often this sacrifice leads to a loss of control over what is happening and over what the students are doing or what they are thinking. You must be willing to accept that. Yet making a transformational change can be very gratifying. You should see big changes in student learning, as other instructors have experienced. This is a great opportunity to collect some before-change and after-change data that you can use for scholarship of teaching and learning.

You may be able to make a transformational change if any of the following apply:

- You are part of a group of faculty working together to transform their courses
- You are tenured and can afford to take some risks
- You can get release time or a small grant to revise your courses
- You focus on course revision by attending a course design institute where you can work on one course during the institute
- You feel pressure from your administrators to use learning-centered teaching
- You believe that this teaching approach really fits your teaching philosophy or content of your course
- You teach a general education course that is not intended for majors

Critically Reflecting on Your Teaching Supports a Successful Transition

To really grow professionally, you should continuously reflect critically on your teaching (Blumberg, 2014). Personal reflection and critical review are two integrated parts of critical reflection. When you personally reflect, you reconstruct experiences and make them meaningful. As I indicate throughout this book, you should reflect on the examples given to see whether you can incorporate them into your practices. Personal reflection helps you to think about what you are doing day-to-day in your teaching as well as looking at the bigger picture (Blumberg, 2014). Psychologists have found that people who reflect achieve more of their goals (Stevens & Cooper, 2009). As a result of reflection, you will acquire more knowledge about your teaching, which can lead to greater teaching productivity (Blackburn & Lawrence, 1995). Weimer (2010) suggests you ask these questions:

- Who am I as a teacher?
- What do I do well and not so well as a teacher?
- Why do I do what I am doing when teaching?

Although personal reflection is a good first step, it is essential to also consider data or perspectives from other people, especially your students and your peers. When you combine personal reflection with the perspectives of others, you are using critical review. Informal or formal discussions with your colleagues both within your department and across the institution lead to better teaching (Shulman, 2004). Your peers and teaching assistants can offer suggestions about how to handle some of the challenges of transitioning to learning-centered teaching. If you are the pioneer implementing learning-centered teaching in your department, you might want to seek help from faculty in other departments.

Documenting Ideas About Transition
On one level, documentation helps you manage the mundane details of complexity of teaching such as noting a question that led to an engaged class discussion or a note that students need more clarity on an assignment. You can also try to document what you are doing and how that ties to your desire to use more learning-centered teaching. As we tell our students, writing can clarify and organize thinking because it provides a good opportunity to review ideas and experiences (Stevens & Cooper, 2009). I regularly provide space in this book for you to document your ideas about transitioning to more learning-centered teaching as a stimulus for reflecting and as a way to connect it to your own situation and previous experiences (Blumberg, 2014, 2015). Finally, as you review what you have written so far, you have a chance to reexamine your thoughts and plans. The following section provides a structure for you to review your plans for transitioning to more learning-centered teaching.

Using Social Media to Assist in the Transition
As you may already be using social media in your personal and professional life, you can also use it to

support your transition to learning-centered teaching (Blumberg, 2015). Social media enables an exchange of ideas and collaboration with people you know but may not see regularly. Through social media you can also have a social presence and collaborate with people you have never met if you communicate with them often enough (Revkin, 2014; Swan, 2003). You could blog or tweet about your attempts to implement learning-centered teaching and get support, feedback, and suggestions for improvement from an international community of learning-centered teaching instructors. Using social media might be more important if you are trying it alone at your institution or if you are not getting support from your department chair. Be mindful if your chair follows your posts or if they could be forwarded to your chair. Your discussions about learning-centered teaching on social media can help you achieve the teaching ideal of teaching as shared and valued community property (Shulman, 2004).

Planning a New Learning-Centered Teaching Curriculum
Sometimes you are in a good position to start or thoroughly revise an educational program. If you can do this, develop the curriculum using learning-centered teaching. Box 8.1 describes a new undergraduate curriculum where using learning-centered teaching aligned very well with the goals of the program. Therefore, the faculty intentionally designed the program to use many learning-centered teaching aspects. Even if you are not starting from scratch, you can align your educational program or course to be more learning-centered by considering your goals or student learning outcomes and determining what aspects of learning-centered teaching serve your needs.

Taking Stock of Your Plans So Far to Increase Your Use of Learning-Centered Teaching: Part 1

If you have been actively engaged while reading the previous chapters you probably have many ideas of how to increase your use of learning-centered teaching. You might even have too many ideas and may not know where to start. Therefore, before reading the rest of this chapter, review and document your ideas using

---

BOX 8.1.
Case Study of an Undergraduate Curriculum Developed to Be Learning-Centered

Instructors at Ferris State University in Michigan (Njoku, Wakeel, Reger, Jadhav, & Rowan, 2017) developed a new face-to-face and online undergraduate public health curriculum focusing on preparing students to work in underserved rural areas. The faculty intentionally incorporated learning-centered principles throughout the curriculum as they believed that learning-centered teaching would prepare students to have the skills and frameworks to face the somewhat unique challenges and needs of rural areas.

Goal of the Program	Rationale for Value of Learning-Centered Teaching
Be proactive about building collaborative partnerships and teams with other health and service professionals because partnerships are vital in rural areas	Students work in small groups on assignments to learn the benefits of collaboration and practice using successful teamwork strategies.
Prepare students to share power with local stakeholders	Once students learn how to share power and the benefits of doing so, they are more likely to be able to share power in the future.
Be able to solve real rural public health problems Be informed citizens who understand the issues of health and the impact of illness on their region	Students are repeatedly given authentic and complex problems to investigate. Examples include developing a community-based nutrition program for a poor rural area or engagement with service-learning in rural public health agencies.
Take ownership of promoting health in rural areas	Students are empowered to take responsibility for their own learning and their own projects through active-learning activities and choices in project topics.
Be a lifelong learner	By teaching the skills necessary to be lifelong learners, and allowing students to practice these skills repeatedly, students become lifelong learners.
Seek feedback and modify practices as a result of what has been learned	Students participate in Small Group Instructional Diagnoses exercises that give feedback to the faculty midway through the semester so changes can be made. Faculty explain the feedback lead to changes.

   During the curriculum development phase, the public health faculty participated in an intensive one-week workshop to help them develop the program outcomes, a curriculum map, and teaching and learning activities that were consistent with learning-centered teaching. Throughout the implementation of the curriculum, the public health faculty continued to be engaged with faculty developers through attending workshops and participating in a faculty learning community. Some faculty applied for and received a university-funded grant to incorporate service-learning into many courses in the curriculum. Now they are presenting their unique curriculum at conferences and publishing about it (Njoku et al., 2017).

(Continues)

BOX 8.1. (Continued)

Overall the students rated their instructors and their courses very highly on nationally validated end-of-course evaluations. They felt that they had met their learning outcomes and were prepared for their future careers. The students perceived the following benefits of their learning-centered teaching curriculum:

- Acquired ability to access and evaluate resources that were available to them
- Acquired skills that they will be able to use in their careers
- Appreciated flexibility of faculty, policies, and pacing of assignments
- Appreciated that they were treated with respect
- Felt the faculty made the students' learning needs a top priority
- Gained confidence in working with different professionals in rural areas
- Gained real-world experience
- Improved their crucial thinking skills
- Learned from a variety of active-learning experiences
- Valued receiving timely and constructive feedback on their work

Personal Reflection for Your Own Use

How can you intentionally incorporate learning-centered teaching principles and philosophy into your curriculum development or course revision process?

What learning-centered teaching concepts are especially relevant for your revision or development efforts?

How can faculty developers help you to transform your teaching to be more learning-centered focused?

Table 8.1. At the end of this chapter you will prioritize your ideas to develop a specific plan. For now you are cataloguing your possible implementation changes. Follow these directions to document your plans for increasing your use of learning-centered teaching on Table 8.1.

1. Review your notes from the "Taking Stock" end-of-chapter exercises.

   a. Using Table 8.1, circle the name of the actions where you previously thought you wanted to use more learning-centered approaches. You can find these actions listed in the column labeled "Essential Actions Associated With Each Construct." For now, just circle your previous ideas for change. You do not have to choose where to start or what to do in Step 1.

   b. Indicate the level that you thought you might like to become in the next column. For now, just copy what you indicated previously.

2. Review your notes from these end-of-chapter exercises and your answers to the personal reflection questions of your ideas for possible changes from the previous seven chapters. List your implementation ideas in the column

TABLE 8.1. Planning Where You Would Like to Use More Learning-Centered Actions Part 1: Catalogue Your Ideas for Change

See directions in the "Taking Stock" section for noting your plans so far of increasing your use of learning-centered teaching.

Construct	Essential Actions Associated With Each Construct	Learning-Centered Level You Would Like to Achieve: Minimally, Mostly, Extensively	Specific Ideas for Implementation	Indicate Course(s) in Which You Would Like to Use These Ideas	Your Time Line to Achieve Change	Difficulty for You to Make This Change to Achieve Level You Aspire To 1 = Easy 2 = Moderate 3 = Hard
Role of Instructor	Develops learning outcomes					
	Uses appropriate teaching/learning methods					
	Aligns objectives, teaching/learning methods, and outcomes					
	Creates supportive and success-oriented environment					
	Creates inclusive environment					
	Explicitly states teaching/learning methods					

Development of Student Responsibility for Learning	Sets expectations for students' responsibility for learning				
	Provides scaffolding support, then allows for greater student independence as the course proceeds				
	Develops student learning skills				
	Develops student self-directed, lifelong learning skills				
	Fosters student reflection and critical review				
	Fosters students use of metacognitive skills and habits of mind				
Function of Content	Uses organizing schemes				
	Promotes meaningful student engagement with the content				
	Fosters development of discipline-specific methodologies				

(Continues)

TABLE 8.1. (Continued)

Construct	Essential Actions Associated With Each Construct	Learning-Centered Level You Would Like to Achieve: Minimally, Mostly, Extensively	Specific Ideas for Implementation	Indicate Course(s) in Which You Would Like to Use These Ideas	Your Time Line to Achieve Change	Difficulty for You to Make This Change to Achieve Level You Aspire To 1 = Easy 2 = Moderate 3 = Hard
	Fosters thinking in discipline					
	Helps students acquire in-depth conceptual understanding that facilitates future learning					
Purposes and Processes of Student Assessment	Integrates assessment and learning					
	Uses fair, objective, and consistent assessment policies and standards					
	Provides students with formative feedback					
	Uses student peer and self-assessment					
	Allows students to learn from mistakes					
	Uses authentic assessment					

Balance of Power	Creates safe, moral, and ethical environment that empowers all students				
	Provides syllabus that demonstrates that students and instructors share power				
	Allows flexibility in policies and practices				
	Provides varied student opportunities to learn				
	Empowers student learning through appropriate freedom of expression				
	Responds to student feedback				

labeled "Specific Ideas for Implementation" that correspond to the actions within the constructs by noting them on the appropriate row of the table.

3. Review your ideas thus far.

   a. If you put specific ideas into a row where you previously had not indicated you wanted to become more learning-centered, decide if you might become more learning-centered by implementing this idea. Make any appropriate changes to the level you wish to achieve.

   b. Evaluate if the specific ideas you listed fit with your overall plan, revise these specific ideas, or include new ones.

   c. Indicate in which course(s) you would like to use these ideas.

   d. Indicate your time line to achieve each change. Evaluate what you indicated previously.

   e. Indicate how difficult it is for you to make this change to achieve the learning-centered level you desire, using a 3-point scale (1 = easy, 2 = moderate, 3 = hard).

   f. Consider how much time it will take and how much you need to change how you teach.

4. List any overall ideas that do not fit into the taxonomy of constructs.

   a.

   b.

   c.

   d.

   e.

Do you see any clusters of possible changes? If so, describe how you would implement these changes.

Suggestions for Serving Specific Student Populations

My review of the literature of implementation indicates that learning-centered teaching especially appeals to instructors of the following specific student populations: (a) underprepared, unmotivated, or first-year college students; (b) foreign language learners; and (c) STEM students at all levels. Appendix A summarizes the literature.

Underprepared, Unmotivated, or First-Year College Students

Although instructors may feel that learning-centered teaching cannot be used with underprepared, unmotivated, or first-year students, the opposite is true (Weimer, 2013). When you take the time to explain what you are doing, teach and let your students practice learning skills, and use many of the learning-centered teaching actions mentioned here, your underprepared or new students can succeed (Fletcher et al., 2015; McGuire & McGuire, 2015). Learning-centered teaching motivates students because they are more engaged, you provide more frequent formative feedback, and they may be embarrassed to be unprepared for their peers (Weimer, 2013).

First-year experience or college success instructors have used learning-centered teaching in their approach (Schwenn & Codjoe, 2013). When I presented to these instructors and advisers throughout the United States, they tell me they particularly use the actions in the construct of Development of the Responsibility for Learning. These instructors teach first-year students how to use learning skills for school success, embrace self-directed, lifelong learning skills, and engage in metacognitive skills and habits of the mind. They also require students to reflect on their learning. These instructors of first-year students have been pleased with how well students respond to this instruction and how students have profited from learning these skills (Kreniske & Todorova, 2017). Instructors who teach academic success courses to students who are struggling in school as well as their advisers could also teach these skills. Boxes 3.4 and 3.7 describe techniques that are especially helpful for beginning or struggling students.

Foreign Language Learners

Traditionally, the instructor-centered methods used to teach foreign languages to college students or adults have led to disappointing results. Students are expected to learn correct pronunciation and grammar by listening to their teachers as language experts. My review of the literature of foreign language acquisition, both English and other languages, indicates that more progressive language instructors advocate for the use of learning-centered teaching. Instructors of foreign language learners in higher education around the world, in the U.S. military, and for adult English language learners have used many aspects of learning-centered teaching successfully (Federe & Leishman, 2014; Knouse, Gupton, & Abreu, 2015; Mahmoud, 2016). This is even true in cultures where the students are expected to show respect for their teachers and do not have a choice in how or what they learn. For language learners, learning-centered teaching does two things well: it increases students' ability to learn and retain material better, and it fosters a supportive environment for students to become more skillful in their linguistic and communication skills in the language they are acquiring. Because learning-centered teaching is so different from the way education is traditionally conducted in many countries and in the U.S. military, both instructors and students may feel uncomfortable engaging in learning-centered teaching practices. However, when they persist, learning-centered teaching leads to positive outcomes, including scoring higher on traditional tests of language ability compared to traditional teaching methods as well as better communication skills in authentic assessment (Federe & Leishman, 2014; Mahmoud, 2016). Many learning-centered teaching practices have led to greater student involvement in all aspects of courses, less stress, more attention paid to what peers say, greater satisfaction with courses and instructors, and greater cultural sensitivity (Federe & Leishman, 2014; Knouse et al., 2015). Table 8.2 summarizes how foreign language learner instructors have implemented learning-centered teaching actions.

STEM Students
Historically, instructors in the STEM disciplines relied heavily on instructor-centered approaches, especially lectures (Lueddeke, 2003). Perhaps because many STEM instructors have seen the shortcomings of traditional lecture-based courses, they embraced learning-centered teaching. Such shortcomings include poor retention rates of students majoring in STEM and, for those who persisted, a lack of long-term retention of material (Piskadlo, 2016). Extensive research on teaching STEM courses exists (Felder & Brent 2016; Freeman et al., 2014). See Table 1.3 for more details.

Throughout this book, I cite many examples of how STEM instructors use learning-centered teaching. I especially refer you to the case study in Box 3.2 on the SCALE-UP project; hundreds of STEM instructors have used this model to implement learning-centered teaching in large enrollment courses (Beichner

& Isern, 2017). See also Box 1.1 for a modification of this model (Kuit & Fildes, 2014). Scientific literacy, research design, and developing research proposals or design projects are discussed in boxes relating to the actions shown in Table 8.3. Since I only cite published literature here, this probably is a partial list of actions and the authors do not use all the constructs.

Table 8.4 summarizes how STEM instructors at my university employ specific learning-centered teaching actions (Blumberg, 2016a, 2016b; Mahalingam, Schaefer, & Morlino, 2008). Notice that although the STEM and language learner instructors use some of the same actions, they are used differently. These differences reflect the nature of learning the content.

Appendix A offers further suggestions for implementing learning-centered teaching. Table A.1 lists learning-centered techniques or teaching/learning practices that transcend disciplines. Table A.2 lists learning-centered techniques or teaching/learning practices that use online or electronic educational technologies.

Chapter Summary

Figure 8.1 summarizes the main points of this chapter.

Taking Stock: Planning Where You Would Like to Use More Learning-Centered Actions: Part 2—Prioritization

The following directions will help you prioritize your plans for increasing your use of learning-centered teaching.

1. Add any ideas that occurred to you while reading and reflecting on this chapter to Table 8.1.
2. Review your ideas listed in Table 8.1 of changes you want to implement to make them more realistic.
3. Make a realistic change time line for yourself. See if you can cluster these changes to be more efficient. When selecting your intermediate or transformational changes, consider prioritizing according to the implementation progression of constructs given in Figure 8.2. (*Note:* If you are not already at

TABLE 8.2. How Language Acquisition Instructors Implement Learning-Centered Teaching

Learning-Centered Teaching Construct	*Learning-Centered Teaching Action*	*Implementation by Language Learner Instructors*
Role of Instructor	Develops learning outcomes	Develop authentic learning outcomes to reflect how students will use the language.
	Uses appropriate teaching/learning methods	Use active-learning techniques extensively where students need to communicate in the language they are learning. Use small group work where students will collaborate, cooperate, and support each other. Require the students to communicate on social media in the language they are studying.
	Aligns objectives, teaching/learning methods, and outcomes	Give student groups tasks such as explaining in the language they are learning concepts of grammar or communicating in practical scenarios as they would in the different culture.
	Creates supportive and success-oriented environment	Ask students to take class notes in the language they are acquiring and to share their notes with their classmates for correction.
	Is explicit about teaching/learning methods	When giving students tasks, explain that they are learning the appropriate content within these tasks. The tasks organize their learning.
Development of Student Responsibility for Learning	Sets expectations for students to take responsibility for learning Uses scaffolding by providing students decreasing assistance and greater independence as they become more proficient.	Modeled appropriate student behaviors, explained why they help students learn Provide decreasing feedback on how students are doing.
	Fosters student reflection and critical review	Ask students to reflect on how well they are doing in relation to the goals of the course.
Function of Content	Fosters personal meaning-making	Use authentic scenarios such as buying food in the country where this language is spoken or securing safety of citizens for the military.
	Helps students understand why they learn content	
	Facilitates future learning	Because vocabulary, grammar, and syntax are learned in context, they can be recalled better in the future and students can build further vocabulary from these associations.

(Continues)

TABLE 8.2. (Continued)

Learning-Centered Teaching Construct	*Learning-Centered Teaching Action*	*Implementation by Language Learner Instructors*
Purposes and Processes of Student Assessment	Integrates assessment and learning	Throughout an intensive language learning experience, ask students to create a reflective portfolio of their best oral and written work and to assess the progress they have made.
	Provides students with formative feedback	Instructors need to provide frequent feedback on pronunciation, sentence construction, and so on, so that students do not practice and learn faulty language use.
	Uses peer and self-assessment	Peers can provide feedback on grammar and proper use of vocabulary. Students can assess their strengths and weaknesses and then ask for assistance.
	Allows students ability to learn from mistakes	When students work collaboratively, they can make mistakes, receive feedback, and learn from each other.
	Uses authentic assessment	Assessments should reflect what the students will be doing when they use the language in real settings. Multiple-choice questions are not a good way to assess mastery of a language.
Balance of Power	Uses flexibility for course policies, deadlines	Consider the students' background and future use of the language. Do not expect all students to reach the same level.
	Allows freedom of expression	Give students choices in the topics they want to write or speak about.
	Responds to student feedback	Former students can offer insightful feedback on how to improve the course.

Personal Reflection for Your Use

Even if you do not teach language acquisition, how can you apply any of these suggestions to your teaching?

List the suggestions you might use and how you can use them.

Adapted from Al-Zu'be 2013; Federe & Leishman, 2014; Mahmoud, 2016; Knouse et al., 2015.

TABLE 8.3.   Boxes That Discuss Scientific Literacy, Research Methods, or Design Projects Listed by Construct and Action

Construct	*Box Within These Actions*
Role of Instructor	Learning Outcomes
Function of Content	Discipline-Specific Methodologies
	Inquiry Into Ways of Thinking in the Discipline
Purposes and Processes of Student Assessment	Formative Assessment
	Peer and Self-Assessment
	Authentic Assessment
Balance of Power	Opportunities to Learn

Note: Only four constructs are listed because this is a review of the literature discussed in this book.

TABLE 8.4.   How STEM Instructors Implement Learning-Centered Teaching

Learning-Centered Teaching Construct	*Learning-Centered Teaching Action*	*Implementation by STEM Instructors at the University of the Sciences*
Role of Instructor	Uses appropriate teaching/learning methods	Use active-learning techniques extensively in lab courses. Use small group work where students solve content-related problems.
	Aligns objectives, teaching/learning methods, and outcomes	Undergraduate research is an example of alignment.
	Creates supportive and success-oriented environment	An online homework system can provide immediate feedback and assistance in solving problems.
Development of Student Responsibility for Learning	Sets expectations for students to take responsibility for learning	Explained how previous students succeeded in the course by taking responsibility for learning and how to do it
	Uses scaffolding by providing students decreasing assistance and greater independence as they become more capable	Small group in class sessions provided assistance in solving problems. Students expected to solve similar problems on their own on exams
	Fosters student reflection and critical review	Small group discussions foster reflection and critical review

(Continues)

TABLE 8.4. (Continued)

Learning-Centered Teaching Construct	Learning-Centered Teaching Action	Implementation by STEM Instructors at the University of the Sciences
Function of Content	Uses organizing scheme	About 10 organizing schemes, such as evolution or the structure-function relationship, can explain a majority of the topics covered in introductory biology courses.
	Fosters personal meaning-making	Through small group problem-solving sessions, students come to understand the content.
	Fosters discipline-specific methodologies	Lab courses give students opportunities to learn the skills of the discipline.
	Fosters thinking in discipline	Undergraduate research projects allow students to think in the discipline and solve disciplinary problems.
	Helps students understand why they learn content	Providing career and personal life examples can show the importance of learning the content.
Purposes and Processes of Student Assessment	Integrates assessment and learning Provides students with formative feedback	An online homework system can provide immediate feedback and assistance in solving problems.
	Uses authentic assessment	Audience response system integrates assessment and learning and provides immediate feedback Students who have conducted research present posters on campus and at regional meetings

Note: The STEM faculty members do not discuss the Balance of Power construct.

Personal Reflection for Your Use

Even if you do not teach in STEM, how can you apply any of these suggestions for implementing to your teaching?

List the suggestions you might use and how you can use them.

Adapted from Blumberg, 2016a, 2016b; Mahalingam et al., 2008.

least at minimally learning-centered on the first action of Balance of Power—establish a safe, moral, and ethical environment—this needs to be your highest priority. This action is fundamental and essential to all human interactions.)

4. Complete Box 8.2. Come back to these plans iteratively.

FIGURE 8.1. **Summary of the chapter.**

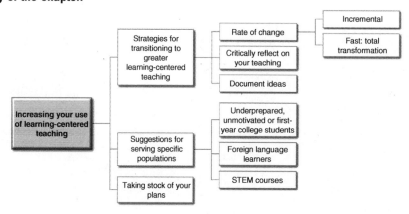

FIGURE 8.2. **Implementation progression of learning-centered teaching constructs.**

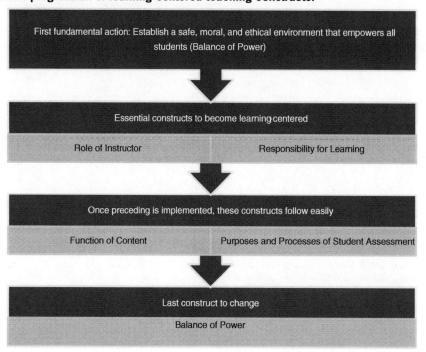

BOX 8.2.
Your Plan for Increasing Your Use of Learning-Centered Teaching Approaches

Date_____

Immediate Changes

Pick no more than five easy-to-change actions just to gain a sense of increasing your use of learning-centered teaching. List these choices and your plan for making these changes.

Pick one or two moderate-to-change actions. List these choices and your plan for making these changes.

Intermediate Changes

Pick one or two intermediate-to-change actions. List these choices and your plan for making these changes.

Transformational Changes

If you were to redesign your teaching to be more learning-centered, what would you do? Try to incorporate as many learning-centered teaching actions from the Role of Instructor or the Responsibility for Learning constructs in this total course design. Outline what you would do, the course(s) where this will be implemented, and the timeline for achieving a transformational change.

Steps You Plan to Take	Course	Time Line
1.		
2.		
3.		

CHAPTER 9

Overcoming Barriers to Using Learning-Centered Teaching

Chapter Highlights

This chapter will help you overcome the following types of barriers to using learning-centered teaching:

- Personal
- Institutional
- Student resistance

It contains practical advice and reviews two models of behavior change.

To employ learning-centered teaching successfully, you should strive to overcome the common barriers listed in Figure 9.1. This chapter will examine varied ways to overcome these barriers.

Overcoming Personal Barriers

Teaching using learning-centered teaching approaches may seem counterintuitive because you may feel that you are not teaching. Some instructors feel they are not teaching if they are not covering the content and if they lose control over what happens in the class. Learning to teach using learning-centered teaching is like learning a foreign language (Harris & Cullen, 2010); it is hard work requiring support and scaffolding. You are most likely to succeed as a learning-centered teaching instructor if you have a real passion for teaching (Verst, 2010). Throughout this book, I have discussed examples of instructors who have overcome their barriers; I hope that you can learn from these instructors.

Beliefs About Teaching

More than a decade ago (Blumberg, 2009), I cited research about the importance of instructors believing that learning-centered teaching was the preferred approach, because philosophies about teaching predict actual teaching behaviors (Polich, 2007). At that time, we were trying to convince instructors that they should change their beliefs about teaching. Now we have research coming from varied disciplines and from North America and Europe that many faculty value learning-centered teaching as a worthwhile teaching approach (D.M. Ellis, 2015; Rice, 2015; Verst, 2010). That is real progress. Self-identification as a learning-centered teaching instructor correlates with implementing this approach (D.M. Ellis, 2015). However, this same literature shows that although faculty value learning-centered teaching, they do not consistently implement it in their teaching. Although beliefs and values may be a necessary condition for action, the literature on the consistency between beliefs and teaching behaviors, summarized in Table 9.1, shows that

153

FIGURE 9.1. **Common barriers to implementing learning-centered teaching.**

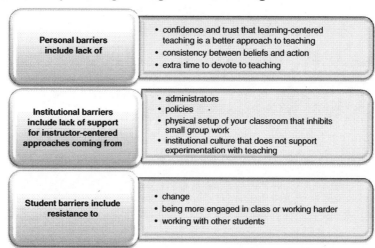

accepting learning-centered teaching is not a sufficient condition for implementation of learning-centered teaching.

Common factors that may prevent you from implementing learning-centered teaching tend to be either personal or institutional. Personal factors include publication pressure and family responsibilities (Rice, 2015; Verst, 2010), belief that inexperienced students cannot learn with learning-centered teaching approaches (D.M. Ellis, 2015), lack of additional time to transform teaching to be more learning-centered (D.M. Ellis, 2015), and belief that instructors must teach content to prepare professional students to pass their board exams (D.M. Ellis, 2015). Institutional barriers include greater teaching time demands (Michael, 2007); class size and classroom configuration (Rice, 2015; Verst, 2010); and budgetary constraints that limit availability of teaching assistants or graders (Rice, 2015). Given these obstacles, your beliefs may not propel you into action. Therefore, I am discussing two frameworks on how to change behaviors.

How to Change Behavior

Much research supports the trans-theoretical model (Prochaska, Redding, & Evers, 2002) and the theory of diffusion of innovations (Rogers, 2003) as effective ways to change behaviors in many different settings.

The trans-theoretical model is a biopsychosocial model of intentional change of behavior that integrates ideas from other theories (Prochaska et al., 2002). It is often used by health professionals and therapists to get people to adopt a healthy lifestyle (i.e., to quit smoking), but I think it applies as you try to adopt learning-centered teaching. Because people often evolve toward a change, the trans-theoretical model describes change as a series of five time-oriented stages: precontemplation (not ready for change), contemplation (getting ready), preparation (ready to make the change), action (the change occurring), and maintenance (change already occurred but needs to be preserved). Although Prochaska and colleagues (2002) describe the stages as linear, researchers have found people can progress in nonlinear ways and may regress to earlier stages. I doubt that you are in the precontemplation stage as you are reading this book. As you progress through the stages, the pros about learning-centered teaching begin to outweigh the cons of adopting it. I believe once you become a learning-centered teacher you will see many more pros than cons and not relapse back to instructor-centered teaching. This model describes 10 processes that need to be implemented to progress successfully through the stages of change and attain the desired behavior change as shown in Table 9.2. According to this model, you should tailor your transition process to meet your needs.

The theory of diffusion of innovations (Rogers, 2003) explains how new ideas or products spread through a population from innovators to laggards along a bell curve. This theory is more successful when individuals are trying to adopt new behaviors

TABLE 9.1. Consistency Between Learning-Centered Teaching Acceptance and Implementation by Discipline

Populations Studied	Knowledge of Learning-Centered Teaching	Valuing Learning-Centered Teaching as Preferred Approach	Teaching Using Learning-Centered Teaching
Agriculture faculty who won outstanding teaching awards at a large public university in the United States and faculty in Sweden (Rice, 2015)	Not clear whether knowledgeable because they received little instruction in how to teach, but they were confident in their teaching ability	Valued the overall concept of learning-centered teaching	Primarily used lecture or lecture integrated with active learning
Arts and sciences faculty who won outstanding teaching awards at a small private university in the United States (Verst, 2010)	Knowledgeable	Valued most actions defined in this book	Implemented the actions within the Function of Content construct For the other four constructs individuals selected which actions they used as perceived to fit the course (i.e., used lecture primarily along with student discussion of content)
Business faculty who won outstanding teaching awards at a small private university in the United States (Verst, 2010)	Knowledgeable	Valued most actions defined in this book	Implemented the actions within the Function of Content construct For the other four constructs, individuals selected which actions they used as perceived to fit the course (i.e., used lecture primarily)
Education faculty who won outstanding teaching awards at a small private university in the United States (Verst, 2010)	Knowledgeable	Valued most actions defined in this book	Implemented majority of the actions within all five constructs
Nursing faculty who taught in the pre-clinical part of the curriculum at a private university (D.M. Ellis, 2015)	Not evaluated	Valued the overall concept of learning-centered teaching	Did not implement learning-centered teaching, especially for beginning students
Nursing faculty who won outstanding teaching awards at a small private university in the United States (Verst, 2010)	Knowledgeable	Valued most actions defined in this book	Implemented the actions within the Function of Content construct For the other four constructs individuals selected which actions they used as perceived to fit the course (i.e., used lecture primarily along with student discussion of content)

TABLE 9.2. Trans-Theoretical Model Processes and How You Can Apply Them to Adoption of Learning-Centered Teaching

Trans-Theoretical Model Process	*Application to Implementation of Learning-Centered Teaching*
Get the facts	Consider the long-lasting learning of students taught by instructor-centered versus learning-centered teaching.
Attend to your feelings	Be sensitive to your feelings, including being anxious about changing how you teach or feeling inspired to teach better.
Notice your effect on others	Observe how the ways that you teach influence how students learn. Notice how your peers and your chair perceive you as a teacher.
Self-evaluate	Consider what kind of teacher you want to be. Create a new image for yourself as a teacher: as a facilitator of learning, not a disseminator of information.
Notice public support	Find policies, resources, and people that support learning-centered teaching within your department, college, or institution. See Box 9.1 discussing such institutional factors.
Make a commitment, become empowered	Believe and feel confident that you can transform your teaching for the better.
Change behaviors	Change how you teach by adapting some of the implementation examples given in this book.
Get support	Seek support from the teaching-learning center or innovative faculty as you transition to learning-centered teaching. Work with another instructor who is also transitioning to learning-centered teaching.
Use rewards	Apply for grants or release time to change your teaching. Apply for teaching awards to get public recognition.
Manage your environment	Create a course syllabus or classroom that reinforces your use of learning-centered teaching.

Note how you can use these processes as you transition to more learning-centered teaching.

rather than stop behaviors. Marketing researchers have used it to track the acceptance of new products. If you are in the contemplation stage of the trans-theoretical model, the theory of diffusion of innovations may help you to get ready to transition to learning-centered teaching. Rogers described five factors that influence adoption of innovations. Table 9.3 shows how you can use each of these factors to help you transition to using more learning-centered teaching.

Practical Advice

Find a like-minded faculty member to work with. You can form a mutual mentoring relationship as you both transition to learning-centered teaching. Your peer can troubleshoot as you plan and review course documents as you prepare them. You can observe each other's class when you are trying a new learning-centered teaching activity or brainstorm why something did not go as well as you anticipated.

TABLE 9.3. How You Can Use Rogers's Factors to Transition to Learning-Centered Teaching

Rogers's Factor	*Explanation*	*Adaptation for Learning-Centered Teaching*
Relative advantage	When you see the innovation as better than what you are doing, you should want to adopt it.	Due to so much research supporting it, educators consider learning-centered teaching as a best practice that all instructors in higher education should adopt.
Compatibility	When you see the innovation as compatible with the teaching to which you aspire, the innovation becomes more acceptable.	Decide what actions within each construct of learning-centered teaching fit with your teaching philosophy, types of course, or discipline. Initially try to change your roles as an instructor and consider how students can assume responsibility for learning in ways that are most consistent with your philosophy of teaching.
Degree of complexity	When you divide complex changes into separate aspects, they become more manageable.	Consider the hierarchy of learning-centered teaching constructs and decide how many changes you can make within your role as an instructor and how students assume responsibility for learning to remain manageable for you.
Trial-ability	When you try innovations in a small and safe way, you are risking less.	Pilot test changes before transforming a whole course. You can pilot changes in one part of an existing course. Explain to students how this is an experiment in how you teach, and you are seeking feedback to improve your teaching.
Observability	When you observe someone else implementing the innovation, you see how the innovation is easier to adopt.	Observe learning-centered teaching instructors at your institution or one nearby. Ask them questions and examine their course artifacts. If you do not know anyone who uses learning-centered teaching, see if you can find someone in your discipline by attending a conference geared to teaching in your discipline.

Adapted from Rogers, 2003.

Note how you can use these factors as you transition to more learning-centered teaching.

Do not be discouraged if the first time you try learning-centered teaching, you encounter a few hiccups. Most innovations take a few tries before they work well. Students may also rank your course, or you, lower than the scores you previously received (Michael, 2007). Some of this is justified as the course may still be rough around the edges and will improve the next time you teach using learning-centered teaching. Some of the lower scores may come from the perception that you are not teaching or their resentment at a change from what they expected. Getting feedback from students during the course and then discussing their complaints and implementing practical suggestions for improvement can lead to better student evaluations. Finally, you and fellow like-minded instructors might pressure committees to change the forms used in end-of-course evaluations so that they are less lecture- and instructor-centered and favor learning-centered teaching behaviors more.

Talk to your chair before you make big changes to how you teach and try to secure support. Perhaps your chair can suggest helpful resources (peers, materials, activities, or monetary support) (D.M. Ellis, 2015). You do not want to blindside your chair if students complain about your teaching. Document how you are making changes and what is happening in the course in your annual performance review. If your students earn higher grades once you implement learning-centered teaching than those prior to implementing learning-centered teaching, your chair may infer that you are engaged in grade inflation. However, to counter this you should be able to show that your students earned these higher grades by greater engagement and learning more. This is actually grade improvement and not grade inflation (Mostrom & Blumberg, 2012).

Role of Educational Developers and Instructional Designers

Instructors cite lack of training in how to use learning-centered teaching as a deterrent to their adopting it (Weimer, 2002). Yet, top-level administrators recognize that faculty developers may be critical to changing the culture from instructor-centered to learning-centered teaching (Piskadlo, 2016). It is far easier to change your teaching in a supportive culture. Faculty developers and instructional designers can be very supportive as you transition to greater use of learning-centered teaching. They can work with you in different ways because they offer a variety of services, including workshops, fellowships, course design institutes, and one-on-one consultations. Use them as a sounding board for your ideas, and they can help you problem-solve when things do not go as planned. Faculty developers can assist you to design new teaching and learning methods and improve syllabi and in-class exercises and assignments as well as assessments (Vaughn, 2014). Educational developers can also help you collect data to demonstrate the effectiveness of your teaching. Instructional designers can aid your use of technology, especially if you flip the course so that the students access the content outside of class and spend time in class working with the content.

Multiday or longer workshops, such as course design institutes, are effective ways to help transform your teaching (Eliason & Holmes, 2012; Njoku et al., 2017; Vaughn, 2014). These workshops can increase your confidence that you are making positive changes. They will also allow you to plan some in-class activities and get feedback on your ideas. If you work outside of North America, you may find these more intense training programs especially beneficial due to many factors including culture and fewer overall training opportunities (Bach, Wei, Inkelas, & Riewerts, 2016; Simon, 2014; Yuan, 2014).

If you do not have a faculty developer or an instructional designer where you work, seek out external resources. Contact the instructor who implemented an example in this book you especially want to adopt. Try to attend teaching conferences in your discipline or across higher education, such as any of the six regional Lilly Conferences on Teaching in Higher Education or alternative training institutes. Pick a training institute that suits your intended teaching including case study teaching, problem-based learning, team-based learning, STEM training through Project Kaleidoscope (PKAL) offered by the American Association of Colleges and Universities (AAC&U), or the summer institute on undergraduate education organized by the National Academies; or other training programs are also sponsored by AAC&U. Organize a visit to a campus that has a reputation for implementing learning-centered teaching. While there, observe classes and talk to instructors.

Instructor Time Commitment

Learning-centered teaching comes with a cost of greater time commitment by the faculty (Michael, 2007). However, learning-centered teachers report that most of the additional time comes up front, as they plan and prepare the course. The same course materials can be used again. Box 9.1 reports on research that considers the time variable and its relationship to institutional culture.

Overcoming Institutional Barriers

The traditional system of higher education and organization, including academic credit and workload policies, all support instructor-centered teaching (Harris & Cullen, 2010; Weimer, 2002). Some of the processes and factors described in Tables 9.2 and 9.3 and Box 9.1 show the interplay between personal and institutional barriers. Instructors cite institutional pressures such as increased class size and the physical structure of the

---

BOX 9.1.
Using Learning-Centered Teaching Assessments

Carrie Myers and Scott Myers (2015) reviewed data from the National Study of Postsecondary Faculty to identify patterns of learning-centered teaching and learning-centered assessment. The learning-centered assessments they considered include extensive writing assignments, multiple drafts of products, team projects requiring a product, peer assessments, and service- or community-based learning that culminate in a report or project. Not surprisingly, they found that both learning-centered teaching and learning-centered assessment practices require more instructor time. At institutions that did not value teaching, or where faculty have higher teaching loads or larger class enrollments, faculty are less likely to engage in learning-centered teaching or learning assessments. However, the extra time commitment is not always a deterrent to their use. When an institution establishes a culture that values effective teaching and assesses student learning outcomes rigorously, then instructors are more likely to adopt learning-centered teaching practices and learning-centered assessment practices. At these teaching-friendly institutions, faculty work harder at all aspects of their jobs, including teaching, advising, research, and administration. Thus, the argument about time constraints as a barrier is not straightforward but may be more contextual or institution-related.

Personal Reflection for Your Own Use

Can you implement any of these learning-centered assessments in your teaching? If so, in what course(s) and how would you use them?

How would you rate your institution in terms of valuing teaching?

If you were to spend more time teaching because you use learning-centered teaching or learning-centered assessments, how would it be recognized or valued at your institution?

---

classroom with fixed seating and podium at the front, as well as the pressure to do many other things besides teaching, as reasons why they persist with instructor-centered teaching practices (Rice, 2015; Verst, 2010).

Although you probably will not be able to reduce class size, you can use the power of learning-centered teaching to your advantage, especially if you have a crucial mass of learning-centered teaching instructors. Administrators want students to learn more and learning-centered teaching provides the vehicle for student success (Haras et al., 2017). You might show administrators some of the vast research that points to learning-centered teaching as an evidence-based best practice. You can also work with your governance body such as faculty senate or unions to convince administrators why they should endorse learning-centered teaching. You can ask for concrete measures of this endorsement by creating a policy that instructors should be recognized and rewarded for teaching using learning-centered teaching. For example, learning-centered teaching courses could count as

an extra contact hour on their workload. Learning-centered teaching instructors could get some bonus pay or could be viewed positively for promotion and tenure.

You can work with other faculty who are implementing learning-centered teaching to convince your department chair or dean that you are teaching more effectively when you use learning-centered teaching. Here again providing literature helps. Once you have taught using learning-centered teaching for a while, you should have your own data to show that it achieves your student learning outcomes. If your institution values the assessment of student learning outcomes, you should analyze your data, such as exam performance on critical thinking or application questions, to demonstrate superior deep learning. If you publish on this teaching as scholarship of teaching and learning, you can count this work as research too. Peer review helps increase your credibility as a good teacher in your institution, and perhaps your bargaining power, such that the labor-intensive nature of your work might demonstrate that you deserve a teaching assistant.

Institutions that are teaching-friendly facilitate instructors overcoming personal barriers more than those that are not as teaching-friendly. Box 9.2 describes two learning-centered, teaching-friendly institutions that foster the widespread implementation of learning-centered teaching.

BOX 9.2.
Case Study of Two Universities That Successfully Implemented Learning-Centered Teaching on a Large Scale

In his dissertation, Kevin Piskadlo (2016) studied two large public universities that successfully adopted SCALE-UP, the large enrollment, STEM learning-centered teaching model described in Box 3.2. He surveyed and interviewed faculty and administration, attended department meetings, observed classes, and reviewed institutional and course documents. The purpose of this dissertation study was to determine how organizational structures and policies supported the institution's transition to learning-centered teaching.

Figure 9.2 summarizes a cascade of influences starting with the highest level administrators who led the campus transition. The senior leadership had the vision to make excellence in undergraduate education a top priority and realized that the university needed a new paradigm to achieve this vision. They were instrumental in the implementation of SCALE-UP and chose it because it was an evidence-based pedagogy with increased student learning and success. They promoted the implementation of learning-centered teaching though organizational policies and structures, in addition to providing the necessary resources. One university created an interdisciplinary department of teaching and learning for faculty to collaborate on innovative ways of implementing learning-centered teaching. The administrators communicated their commitment to learning-centered teaching and undergraduate education to the public.

Although neither institution mandated the use of learning-centered teaching, policies gave the faculty freedom and support to do so. Institutional policies supported learning-centered teaching with explicit signals, including

- expectations about quality teaching and rewarding excellent faculty;
- required participation in faculty development training as part of their jobs;
- multiyear contracts to allow faculty to focus on teaching innovation and improvement;
- budget allocations for implementing learning-centered teaching;
- an acceptance of the scholarship of teaching and learning as legitimate scholarship; and
- valuing the assessment of the impact of the changes.

The resources they provided included construction of active learning classrooms. (See Box 9.3 for a description of active-learning classrooms.) At both campuses, the leaders provided the money to construct a few active-learning classrooms and training opportunities for faculty to learn how to use them. Once the faculty and students recognized their worth, leaders began large-scale construction of active-learning classrooms both for large and medium enrollment courses. At one of these universities, up to one-third of the students had taken a course in at least one active-learning classroom, and these students were requesting more experiences with them.

The chairs of the departments brought life to these organizational policies by

- promoting a culture that valued undergraduate quality teaching along with research,
- supporting faculty to feel safe to experiment with their teaching,
- providing discipline and department-specific training,
- recognizing that teaching using learning-centered teaching takes more time,
- adjusting faculty workloads to transform their teaching,
- recruiting faculty that value undergraduate education and can implement learning-centered teaching,
- providing mentoring opportunities for new faculty, and
- conducting program and course assessments to show value of learning-centered teaching.

(Continues)

BOX 9.2. (Continued)

The universities offered varied training opportunities to learn how to use learning-centered teaching and provided small incentives for faculty to participate. Faculty were given grants to attend national training institutes. Along with peer-to-peer, the teaching and learning center provided varied training that was intended both for novices and for those more experienced with learning-centered teaching, including how to teach effectively in active-learning classrooms, develop a learning-centered syllabus, and create appropriate student activities and assessments.

Interviewed faculty noted repeatedly that the most difficult changes occurred at the beginning of the transformational change. The faculty recognized the leadership's advocacy roles and credited the support of their department chairs, deans, provosts, and presidents to facilitate the transition to learning-centered teaching. These faculty also credited the training opportunities as an important catalyst for transforming their teaching. Without the supportive policies and structures, the faculty did not think they, individually and collectively, would have continued adoption of learning-centered teaching. They cited that being a teaching and learning fellow was prestigious. Although many policies supported this successful adoption of learning-centered teaching, faculty felt that the promotion and tenure policies had not changed enough given the new teaching paradigm. Piskadlo (2016) observed that more tenured professors were involved in learning-centered teaching than pre-tenured faculty.

Personal Reflection for Your Own Use

Although you may not be at an institution that is so proactive about adopting a learning-centered teaching paradigm, you can compare your own institution with those profiled by Piskadlo to identify aspects that are supportive of your transition to learning-centered teaching.

Identify how each of the following can support you as you become a more learning-centered teacher:

- Top-level administrators

- Your department chair

- Peers in your department

- The teaching and learning center

What policies can you use to support your transition?

Piskadlo's (2016) work illustrates the importance of administrative leadership, policies, and structures to achieve large-scale institutional adoption of learning-centered teaching. The faculty in his study stated that if they had not perceived a supportive environment, they might not have continued their hard, transformative work. When policies and structures are not in place, individual motivated instructors can become learning-centered teachers, but it is unlikely that it will become widespread or the norm (Von der Heidt & Quazi, 2013). Large-scale organizational change is more likely to occur where instructors are in a safe environment in which they can experiment and take risks.

The two universities profiled in Box 9.2 created active-learning classrooms. Box 9.3 discusses these classrooms, which are becoming very popular at American institutions (Baepler et al., 2016). Although they were originally intended for large enrollment courses, the same setup can be effectively used for smaller classes as well. Even if your institution does not have active-learning classrooms, you can adapt your classrooms, even auditoriums, to encourage student participation and small group

FIGURE 9.2. How institutional leaders have promoted the use of learning-centered teaching.

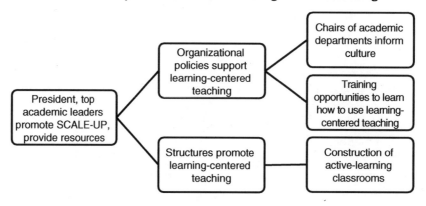

From Piskadlo, 2016.

BOX 9.3.
Active-Learning Classrooms

Many large universities are creating active-learning classrooms because they engage the students and lead to better learning (Baepler et al., 2016; Center for Educational Innovation, University of Minnesota, 2016). Over 100 students may work in a given active-learning classroom but the students work in small groups. Six to 10 students sit in moveable chairs around round tables where they work on problems or answer questions about the content. Each table has a whiteboard and a projection screen to show student work or slides coming from the instructor. Smaller rooms have walls covered with glass and students write on the glass with erasable markers. The active-learning classroom has a teaching station where the instructor can project materials for all students or select student work to be shared with the class. This teaching station may be in the center of the room or can be mobile.

Personal Reflection for Your Own Use

Does your institution have any active-learning classrooms? If so, observe how they are being used.

How can you adapt your present classroom space to be more like an active-learning classroom?

How can you incorporate the principles of active-learning classrooms into online teaching and learning?

---

work by asking students to bring their laptops to class and assigning students to sit in clusters spread out around the large room. If you are in auditorium-type classrooms, assign students to sit every other row so that you can walk around the room and check in with every group. Try to request rooms with moveable tables. Even student cafeterias can be used for small group work.

Lack of administrative support at all levels from your chair to the dean to the chief academic officer inhibits your becoming a learning-centered teaching instructor. Administrative leaders are responsible for policies that may not support change. Try to find like-minded fellow instructors, especially senior faculty, to work with as campus change agents. Your teaching and learning center is a logical place to seek support. Uses the trans-theoretical model processes and Rogers's factors to try to convince administers to be more open to learning-centered teaching. This might be a long process but is worth it in the end.

Overcoming Student Resistance

Students resist change from what has worked for them in the past, as they fear it could result in lower grades (Weimer, 2002). Although individual instructors at your institution may have implemented learning-centered teaching, it is unlikely that most instructors have transitioned. Thus, for students, learning-centered teaching is still a novel experience even if you have been implementing learning-centered teaching for several semesters or in all of your courses. Students may also push back when you require more work or more active participation. Common resistance behaviors, which sabotage your teaching efforts, include not participating in class, complaining to the department chair, and giving low course evaluation scores (D.E. Ellis, 2015).

Therefore, it is essential that you prepare the students for engaging in learning-centered teaching by explaining how the course will function. When you set the proper expectations, you will increase student cooperation. This preparation and setting expectations process needs to be explicit and done repeatedly.

Your syllabus is an important venue for preparing students to become engaged in learning-centered teaching (Piskadlo, 2016). As discussed in chapter 7 on the Balance of Power, be explicit about your use of learning-centered teaching and why you are using it by explaining that learning-centered teaching is superior to traditional methods overall and in your course. Discuss how the students will benefit from it by enhancing their academic success and preparing them for their careers. For example, music instructors might explain that when students experience learning-centered teaching with students sharing power with the instructor and using peer feedback, student performers exhibited increased musical growth, achievement, and greater ability to improve on their own over students in instructor-centered courses (Williams, 2018). Describe how you expect the students to take responsibility for their learning and to pursue deep learning. You can remind students that the syllabus is a contract between you and them and that you expect them to fulfill their end of the contract to succeed.

At the beginning of the course, reinforce what you said in the syllabus. Early on, craft low-stakes learning-centered teaching experiences as students try their new ways to engage and learn. Create a safe and supportive learning environment through providing encouragement and formative feedback. Help students to learn and grow from their mistakes. Be approachable as you guide students to take responsibility for their learning and engage in new behaviors.

Many students have had poor experiences with small group work. This is often due to some nonparticipating or unprepared students. To increase student buy-in and participation, collaboratively define student and instructor roles and responsibilities. If groups are to stay together for a while, students can develop a contract for responsible group work (Oakley, Felder, Brent, & Elhajj, 2004). Students can remind their peers about the contract. Groups should have the ability to fire a member if they have tried to get that individual to cooperate more. Either fired group members have to do all the work alone or you can form a group of similarly fired group members. For further discussion of how learning-centered instructors have successfully used small group work, see Boxes 1.1, 3.5, 7.6, and 8.1.

Chapter Summary

The following suggestions will help you overcome barriers to implementation of learning-centered teaching:

- Believe that this is a superior teaching method
- Seek:
  - Training
  - Small internal grants or release time to transform your teaching
  - Support from
    - leadership or administrators at all levels
    - the teaching and learning center
- Act:
  - Be explicit with your students, explain how and why
  - Start small
  - Work with a partner
  - Try an innovation more than once
  - Get student buy-in and feedback
  - Talk to chair in advance
  - Try to teach in classroom that fosters small group discussions

Overcoming these barriers is worthwhile, because when you use learning-centered teaching, your students will learn more and be more connected to their learning and to their peers, and you will feel more fulfilled as an instructor.

Taking Stock: How You Can Overcome Personal, Institutional, and Student Barriers

A. Identifying personal supports and overcoming personal barriers

1. List your top personal barriers to implementing learning-centered teaching and how you might use the information in this chapter to help overcome them.
   -
   -
   -

2. At what stage of change are you according to the trans-theoretical model?
   - Precontemplation (not ready for change to learning-centered teaching)
   - Contemplation (getting ready to use learning-centered teaching)
   - Preparation (ready to make the change to learning-centered teaching)
   - Action (you have just begun using many learning-centered teaching approaches)
   - Maintenance (you have been using learning-centered teaching and you want to maintain or increase its use)

3. How can you use the trans-theoretical model processes (shown in Table 9.2) to help you transition to further learning-centered teaching?

4. How can you use Rogers's factors (shown in Table 9.3) to help you transition to further learning-centered teaching?

5. What training opportunities can you attend on your campus or elsewhere to help you gain the skills to become an effective learning-centered teacher?

B. Identifying institutional supports and overcoming institutional barriers

1. How do the top administrators support or inhibit your adoption of learning-centered teaching?

2. If they inhibit, what mechanisms do you and other instructors have to promote more support?

3. How does your department chair or head support or inhibit your adoption of learning-centered teaching?

4. If your chair inhibits learning-centered teaching, what mechanisms do you and your colleagues have to promote more support?

5. What policies support your implementation of learning-centered teaching?

6. On a scale from 1 to 5 (5 being most supportive of learning-centered teaching) how supportive is your institution of your use of learning-centered teaching?
   - If your institution is less supportive, perhaps you might scale down your ambitious ideas for total teaching transformation and, even more important, temper your possible frustrations with your lack of major changes.
   - If your institution is more supportive, you might be encouraged to try larger transformations, seeking the assistance from people available to you.

7. What policies inhibit your implementation of learning-centered teaching? How can you work to change these policies?

8. What is the relation of promotion and tenure guidelines to learning-centered teaching—friendly or adversarial?

9. What classroom space that facilitates the use of small group or active learning is available for you to use? How do you go about ensuring that you can teach in these spaces?

C. Overcoming student barriers

1. Describe student resistance, if any, that you encounter or think you might encounter.

2. How can you overcome student resistance?

PART TWO

ASSESSING LEARNING-CENTERED TEACHING USING RUBRICS

CHAPTER 10

How to Use Rubrics as Measurement Tools

Chapter Highlights

This chapter explains how to assess the use of learning-centered teaching with rubrics.

- Each of the five constructs (Role of Instructor, Developing Student Responsibility for Learning, Function of Content, Purposes and Processes of Student Assessment, and Balance of Power) that define learning-centered teaching has a rubric with six parts corresponding to the six actions associated with that construct.
- All rubrics have four levels: instructor-centered, minimally learning-centered, mostly learning-centered, and extensively learning-centered.
- These rubrics can be converted to a Likert ordinal scale.
- Ratings on rubrics can be described using descriptive statistics.
- Graphic displays of data are easy and quick to comprehend.

The earlier chapters of this book discussed how to change teaching to be more learning-centered. An important aspect of the change process is to understand the influence these modifications can have on teaching and student learning. The rest of this book discusses how to assess these changes and their impact. Rubrics are a well-accepted method to communicate expectations and measure the quality of performance. Instructors often use rubrics to grade student work or to assess student learning. Thus, I use rubrics to measure the extent of learning-centered teaching implementation.

Learning-Centered Teaching Rubrics

Rubrics are easy to understand and use as assessment tools. Student work or work products can be evaluated by rubric in whole or in part. Rubrics can be used to mark student performance or to assess student learning without the influence of grading. Rubrics allow the evaluator to judge products or behaviors using specific criteria according to different levels of performance. Because of the explicit criteria and performance levels, rubrics result in objective assessments of what is usually subjectively judged (Walvoord, 1998).

Each of the five constructs (Role of Instructor, Developing Student Responsibility for Learning, Function of Content, Purposes and Processes of Student Assessment, and Balance of Power) that define learning-centered teaching has a rubric with six parts corresponding to the six actions associated with that construct. As you recall and as shown in Illustration 10.1, for each action, I listed characteristics of instructors at the following levels: (a) instructor-centered, (b) minimally learning-centered, (c) mostly

ILLUSTRATION 10.1. THE FOUR LEVELS OF CHARACTERISTICS FOR EACH ACTION

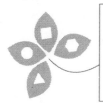

Instructor-centered
Minimally learning-centered
Mostly learning-centered
Extensively learning-centered

learning-centered, and (d) extensively learning-centered. For each construct, these four levels of characteristics become standards for the rubric assessment measures.

In Table 3.10 I gave an example of the learning-centered status of a hypothetical instructor for all six actions of the Role of Instructor construct. According to the first column on this table, he was using an instructor-centered practice on the first action

involving learning outcomes. (The full definition of this action is the instructor develops and uses challenging, reasonable, and measurable learning outcomes that foster the acquisition of appropriate knowledge, skills, or values and are consistent with the goals of the educational program.) Now I provide the following hypothetical information to support his rating: The instructor did not mention learning outcomes in the syllabus. Instead, the focus was on what would be covered in the course. Thus, this would indicate that the instructor uses an instructor-centered practice, as shown by the italics in Table 10.1, because the instructor does not use learning outcomes. I use this example to illustrate how to transition from the tables listing the characteristics that you have seen many times to assessment rubrics.

Table 10.2 explains the three essential elements of descriptive rubrics used to measure learning-centered

---

TABLE 10.1. Example of Rating for One Action by an Instructor on Role of the Instructor

Levels	*Action: Learning Outcomes*

Instructor-centered	Instructor:
	
	• Does not develop or use learning outcomes **OR**
	• Articulates vague or inappropriate learning outcomes that
	   ○ Are not consistent with the goals of the educational program **OR**
	   ○ Do not foster the acquisition of appropriate knowledge, skills, or values **OR**
	   ○ Are not challenging, reasonable, or measurable

TABLE 10.2. Elements of Descriptive Rubrics to Measure the Instructor's Extent of Implementation of Learning-Centered Teaching

Element	*Definition*	*Use in the Learning-Centered Teaching Rubrics*
Assessment criteria	Set of indicators that define behavior or product being measured	Each construct has six assessment criteria. These are the six actions as defined in the chapter on the construct.
Consistent levels of performance	Evaluated by Likert scale May use numbers or words such as "exceeds expectations," "meets expectations," "approaches expectations," "does not meet expectations"	Instructor-centered Minimally learning-centered Mostly learning-centered Extensively learning-centered
Quality definitions for each level	Brief description that explicitly states expectations for each set of criteria	Previously described as characteristics, each level often has more than one characteristic or descriptor.

teaching: assessment criteria, consistent levels of performance, and the quality definitions for each level. The common format for rubrics compares the assessment criteria on the horizontal axis with the levels of expected performance on the vertical axis, resulting in what looks like a table with many boxes and many words within each box.

Instead of using this table format, I prefer one that looks like multiple-choice questions or survey questions with different levels because the descriptions of the quality definitions, like teaching itself, are complex (Blumberg, 2014). This linear format is far easier to read and allows room for comments. They are also similar in format to the tables describing the instructor characteristics given in the previous chapters as shown in Table 10.3. Just as each action described unique characteristics at each of the four levels progressing from instructor-centered to learning-centered, each rubric part for each of these actions lists unique quality definitions for each level. This table shows how the list of characteristics, presented many times in chapters 3 through 7, is converted to a rubric. In Table 10.3 I reproduce Table 3.2 in its original form and show the same characteristics again as a rubric. Table 10.3a shows the list of instructor characteristics for the learning outcomes action on the Role of Instructor construct. Table 10.3b shows the same list of instructor characteristics for the learning outcomes action on the Role of Instructor construct displayed as a rubric.

You use these rubrics to rate how you teach on each action on a scale from 0 to 4. Figure 10.1 shows the correspondence between how the actions transition to greater use of learning-centered teaching (along four levels on the left) and the rubric scoring for assessing learning-centered teaching (on the right). Although you have seen the left side of these figures, the right side shows how this information is used in these descriptive rubrics. Likewise, as you read down either the list of characteristics or the rubrics, each level shows greater use of learning-centered teaching and generally the levels above instructor-centered build upon each other. All rubrics use the same template as shown in Table 10.3b. All the rubrics are in Appendix B and available online.

The hypothetical instructor, referred to previously, uses the instructor-centered practice of not using learning outcomes. The indication on the rubric as shown in Table 10.3b would look similar what is discussed in the following section.

Construct I: Role of Instructor

Action

The instructor develops and uses challenging, reasonable, and measurable learning outcomes that are consistent with the goals of the educational program and foster the acquisition of appropriate knowledge, skills, or values.

Rubric Quality Levels

Uses instructor-centered approaches. Instructor:

- *Does not develop or use learning outcomes* **OR**
- Articulates vague or inappropriate learning outcomes that
  - Are not consistent with the goals of the educational program **OR**
  - Do not foster the acquisition of appropriate knowledge, skills, or values **OR**
  - Are not challenging, reasonable, or measurable

Rubric Scoring

Quality Levels	Score
☐ **Uses instructor-centered approaches**	**0**

How These Learning-Centered Teaching Rubrics Differ From Those Used to Grade Students
The learning-centered teaching rubrics

- do not have minimum passing levels;
- do not have levels like "does not meet expectations," "meets or exceeds expectations," or letter grades;
- are not associated with grades (instead of adding up points to arrive at a grade, consider the individual ratings on each action as potential areas for improvement of teaching); and
- may have several definitions or descriptors at each level. Although this is normally bad assessment practice, especially with rubrics used for student summative assessments, I included several alternative definitions because the criteria are so complex and I do not want to have too many separate actions associated with each construct. When the quality descriptors are connected by *or* statements, you do not have to meet each one. As you complete the

TABLE 10.3. Correspondence Between the Instructor Characteristics on the Learning Outcomes Action and the Rubric Part for Assessing Learning-Centered Teaching

TABLE 10.3A. Instructor Characteristics on the Learning Outcomes Action

Levels	Action: Learning Outcomes
Instructor-centered	Instructor: • Does not develop or not use learning outcomes **OR** • Articulates vague or inappropriate learning outcomes that 　○ Are not consistent with the goals of the educational program **OR** 　○ Do not foster the acquisition of appropriate knowledge, skills, or values **OR** 　○ Are not challenging, reasonable, or measurable
Minimally learning-centered	Instructor: • Develops challenging, reasonable, and measurable learning outcomes but these outcomes 　○ Are not consistent with the goals of the educational program **OR** 　○ Do not foster the acquisition of appropriate knowledge, skills, or values
Mostly learning-centered	Instructor: • Develops challenging, reasonable, and measurable learning outcomes that are consistent with the goals of the educational program and foster the acquisition of appropriate knowledge, skills, or values **AND** • Places these outcomes in the syllabus, but does not refer to them during the course
Extensively learning-centered	Instructor: • The syllabus places challenging, reasonable, and measurable learning outcomes that are consistent with the goals of the educational program and foster the acquisition of appropriate knowledge, skills, or values **AND** • Regularly refers to them throughout the course

rubric just indicate which of the alternatives fits how you teach. Sometimes in the lower three levels and frequently in the extensive use sections, *and* connects each descriptor. Whenever each descriptor is connected to another by *and*, each one needs to be met. This makes the extensively used learning-centered teaching level tightly defined and hard to meet.

Where to Find Evidence to Support Learning-Centered Teaching Ratings

Many different types of evidence about teaching can be used to support learning-centered teaching ratings on the rubrics, as shown in Table 10.4. Your syllabi often contain useful information about how learning-centered your policies and practices are relative

to the five constructs. All course artifacts developed by you including your lesson plans or notes for class activities and the students' artifacts indicate how you implement learning-centered teaching approaches. Peer feedback can also illustrate how you implement learning-centered teaching. Document or attach evidence to support the ratings. The rubrics contain space to note the evidence or where the evidence can be found.

Who Can Rate Teaching?

You can self-report your scores on the rubrics and include this information, along with an explanation of the model and your support for the scores, in your annual performance reviews, teaching portfolios, and dossiers for promotion and tenure. If you self-assess, you need to report on what you are doing, not what

TABLE 10.3B. Rubrics for Assessing Learning-Centered Teaching

Construct I: Role of Instructor

Action: The instructor develops and uses challenging, reasonable, and measurable learning outcomes that are consistent with the goals of the educational program and foster the acquisition of appropriate knowledge, skills, or values.

Rubric Quality Levels

Uses instructor-centered approaches. Instructor:

- Does not develop or not use learning outcomes **OR**
- Articulates vague or inappropriate learning outcomes that
  - Are not consistent with the goals of the educational program **OR**
  - Do not foster the acquisition of appropriate knowledge, skills, or values **OR**
  - Are not challenging, reasonable, or measurable

Minimally uses learning-centered approaches. Instructor:

- Develops challenging, reasonable, and measurable learning outcomes but these outcomes
  - Are not consistent with the goals of the educational program **OR**
  - Do not foster the acquisition of appropriate knowledge, skills, or values

Mostly uses learning-centered approaches. Instructor:

- Develops challenging, reasonable, and measurable learning outcomes that are consistent with the goals of the educational program and foster the acquisition of appropriate knowledge, skills, or values **AND**
- Places these outcomes in the syllabus, but does not refer to them during the course

Extensively uses learning-centered approaches. Instructor:

- Places in the syllabus challenging, reasonable, and measurable learning outcomes that are consistent with the goals of the educational program and foster the acquisition of appropriate knowledge, skills, or values **AND**
- Regularly refers to them throughout the course

Rubric Scoring

- Uses instructor-centered approaches = 0
- Minimally uses a learning-centered approach = 1
- Mostly uses learning-centered approaches = 3
- Extensively uses learning-centered approaches = 4
- No evidence to support rating = NA

Evidence to Support This Rating

FIGURE 10.1. **Correspondence between how the actions transition to greater use of learning-centered teaching along four levels to the rubric scoring for assessing learning-centered teaching.**

Summary of How Each Action Transitions to Greater Use of Learning-Centered Teaching Along Four Levels						Quality Levels/Score
Separate actions	Each action is defined through four levels showing a progression toward learning-centered teaching				→	
Instructor-centered						Uses instructor-centered approaches = 0
Minimally learning-centered	X					Minimally uses learning-centered approaches = 1
Mostly learning-centered	X	X	X			Mostly uses learning-centered approaches = 3
Extensively learning-centered	X	X	X	X		Extensively uses learning-centered approaches = 4

you believe you are doing or what you would like to be doing.

In addition, you can also report on your aspirations or how you want to change your teaching as you may have done in the previous chapters.

Other faculty or faculty developers can also obtain data to rate teaching using these rubrics. This can be done by survey but is probably more appropriate using interviews. In interviews, follow-up and clarification questions can yield more accurate data.

How to Rate Teaching on the Learning-Centered Teaching Rubrics

Use the following methods to rate teaching on the rubrics given in Table B.1 in Appendix B:

- Indicate by highlighting/or underlining all the descriptions that best reflect your actual practices.
- Frequency and use of occurrence is more important to consider than how long the activity takes in a whole class. For example, if you use clickers frequently and discuss the correct answers, even though these clicker questions may take five minutes in a class, you would indicate that you are at the *mostly uses learning-centered* level for the action "the instructor integrates assessment and learning in the assessment construct."
- All items may not apply to all courses. If there is no evidence of an action, rate as NA.
- If you do not use this action, rate it as instructor-centered.
- If a level lists more than one description or definition, you can indicate different levels within the same action.
- If the teaching practices fall on two different levels because of different descriptors, indicate all that apply even though they may be on different levels.
- You will record the rubrics score, supporting evidence and ideas for improvement on Table B.2 in Appendix B.
- You can also highlight any improvement suggestions that you might adapt as you read through the rubrics. Use the descriptors at the

TABLE 10.4. Sources of Evidence About Teaching Used to Support Learning-Centered Teaching Ratings on the Rubrics

Self: Instructor's Evidence and Artifacts	Student Artifacts	Peer/Chair Input
Instructor-developed course materials, including • syllabus • assignment directions • examinations • grading rubrics • assessment plans • assessment tools Personal teaching journals or observations Documentation using critical incident observations Analysis of videos of classroom interactions Review of student work products Concept map of teaching and learning ideas Teaching philosophy statement Teaching portfolio Dissemination of products such as presentations or publications about teaching	Student assessment data Summary or analysis of how students did on assessments End-of-course evaluation data In-course evaluation of teaching Review of students' progress on drafts or large assignments Student reflections on learning or the course Review of student portfolios/ePortfolios Follow-up data on how students did after your course Teaching award nominations submitted by students Feedback from teaching assistants Student perceptions of effectiveness of activities or use of SALG survey (SALG, 2013)	Peer/chair observation of teaching Peer/chair review of teaching, instructor-developed assessment materials Chair report on annual evaluations or promotion letter Teaching award nominations submitted by peers/chair Peer coaching Faculty development coaching Peer review of student work products Peer review of teaching portfolio or dossier

Adapted from Blumberg, 2014.

higher learning-centered teaching levels to direct your next areas of improvement.

• Indicate your rationale and support for these choices on Table B.2 in Appendix B. Because you may be using these rubrics over time or sharing them with others, it is essential that you document how you have reached your ratings. Therefore, each rubric part asks you to provide evidence to support a rating.

Aggregate all of the individual rubric scores from Table B.2 onto Table C.1 in Appendix C.

How to Analyze and Report Data From Rubrics

The learning-centered teaching rubrics are descriptive rubrics and you can analyze the data by turning each level into a Likert ordinal scale with the numbers shown in Table 10.3b. The scale starts with 0 for instructor-centered because this number indicates the absence of learning-centered teaching. Intentionally, this is not an interval scale because there is a large jump in the amount of learning-centered teaching used between minimally and mostly. Table 10.5

contains a sample learning-centered teaching rubric score report. For a full description of each action see the previous chapters. Table C.1 in Appendix C is a summary for all rubric scores. You can use this template to look at your changes over time and to share this summary with others.

Determining the Appropriate Score

Use the following methods to arrive at an appropriate score:

- If you indicated behaviors at two or more levels because of multiple descriptors, pick the level with a majority of the answers.
- If there is a tie, use a number between the levels, such as 3.5.
- If you sometimes (more than minimally, but less than mostly) use a learning-centered teaching approach, you can score it a 2. This may occur with the rubrics that indicate percentage of use, such as the action "the instructor uses authentic assessment."
- If your actions do not quite meet the criteria for extensively using learning-centered teaching, but exceed mostly, you can score it 3.5.

As the sample data shown in Table 10.5 indicate, an instructor or a course can be at all levels on the rubrics, reflecting varying amounts of implementation of learning-centered teaching. Each action's rating is independent. Thus, an instructor can be using extensively learning-centered practices on one action and instructor-centered practices on another action even within the same construct. Using Table B.2 or C.1, you can rank your scores on all the actions from the most learning-centered (those that are extensively learning-centered) to the least (instructor-centered). The top five and the bottom five actions might be the most insightful. You can also compare the five constructs on the percent of mostly or extensively learning-centered. Hopefully, by looking at these summaries of all rubric scores, you will see how you can become more learning-centered on the actions where you have lower ratings.

Reporting on Learning-Centered Teaching Rubric Data

Once you have numbers on these learning-centered teaching ordinal scales you can record these ratings on spreadsheets such as Excel or Google Sheets and then use descriptive analysis to summarize the data. Common analysis yields descriptive statistics, including the range of observed scores and frequency of each score. You can also report the percentage of actions at each of the four levels and the mode or the most frequent response, as shown in Table 10.5 and Table C.1. Since this is intentionally an ordinal rather than an interval scale, do not report the means and standard deviations.

Some people prefer looking at graphs instead of tables, as they convey much information in a small amount of space. Excel or Google Sheets create such graphs easily. Using the data in Table 10.5, I represent these descriptive statistics graphically as shown in Figures 10.2a and 10.2b. The figures illustrate the percent of scores at each level on the rubrics, although they look different. Figure 10.2a is a clustered column chart. It is commonly used to compare values across a few categories. Figure 10.2b shows two different ways of conveying data in a pie chart. Although easy to interpret, the disadvantage of pie charts is that, unlike in Figure 10.2a, you cannot compare all constructs on one chart. Five pie charts would be needed to show performance on all five constructs. When you display charts within Word, even those that were made in Excel, you can change their look by clicking design within the chart. The top ribbon will allow you to change the colors and how the chart looks. You can choose which format to use depending on personal preference and what you are trying to show. Such graphs can help you decide how you want to change to be more learning-centered and similar graphs can show changes made over time. You can also use them to compare the extent of use of learning-centered teaching in different populations such as at different institutions. Colorful charts are easier to interpret than grayscale.

Most common inferential statistical tests require a normal or close to normal distribution. Hopefully your scores, or the scores of many instructors, are not normally distributed; in fact, we would want a negative skew because more scores should be at the higher end. Given the nonnormal distribution, only nonparametric statistical tests should be conducted. However, if you are reporting on the scores on the rubrics, descriptive analysis is sufficient. If you want to see if there is a relationship between learning-centered teaching use and other teacher characteristics, then

TABLE 10.5. Sample Scores on All Actions Using the Learning-Centered Teaching Rubrics

Action	Constructs				
	Role of Instructor	*Responsibility for Learning*	*Function of Content*	*Student Assessment*	*Balance of Power*
Action 1	Learning outcomes 0	Set expectations 0	Organizing schemes 0	Integrate assessment and learning 4	Moral and ethical environment 3
Action 2	Teaching/learning activities 4	Scaffolding 1	Engagement with content 3	Assessment policies and standards 3	Welcoming syllabus 1
Action 3	Course alignment 1	Learning skills 3	Discipline-specific methods 4	Timely formative feedback 3	Flexibility 1
Action 4	Environment for success 4	Self-directed learning 1	Understand why learn 3	Peer and self-assessment 0	Opportunities to learn 0
Action 5	Inclusive, welcoming environment 3	Reflection, review 4	Inquiry in discipline 3	Demonstrate mastery 1	Freedom of expression 1
Action 6	Explicit about methods 0	Metacognitive skills 1	Fosters future learning 1	Authentic assessment 1	Responds to student feedback 4

Construct (Column) Summaries					
Percent Scored at Each Level	*Role of Instructor*	*Responsibility for Learning*	*Function of Content*	*Student Assessment*	*Balance of Power*
Percent instructor-centered (scored as 0)	33%	17%	17%	17%	17%
Percent minimally learning-centered (scored as 1)	17%	50%	17%	33%	50%
Percent mostly learning-centered (scored as 3)	17%	17%	50%	33%	17%
Percent extensively learning-centered (scored as 4)	33%	17%	17%	17%	17%
Range	0–4	0–4	0–4	0–4	0–4
Mode (most frequent score)	0	1	3	1, 3	1

FIGURE 10.2. **Common ways to represent the descriptive statistics coming from learning-centered teaching rubric scores as shown in Table 10.5.**

Figure 10.2a. Clustered column chart.

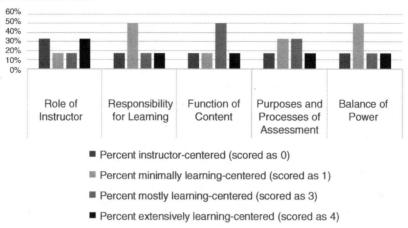

■ Percent instructor-centered (scored as 0)

■ Percent minimally learning-centered (scored as 1)

■ Percent mostly learning-centered (scored as 3)

■ Percent extensively learning-centered (scored as 4)

Figure 10.2b. Pie chart examples.

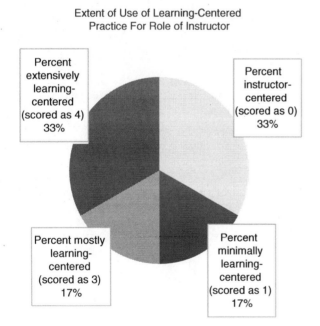

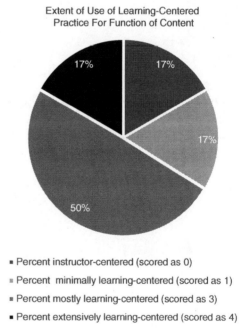

you can use correlational tests. Elder (2014), discussed in Box 10.1, correlated learning-centered teaching rubric scores with teaching demographic data such as years of teaching experience.

The rubrics can be used with a variety of data for scholarship of teaching and learning projects. Some graduate students have used these rubrics in their dissertation research in a variety of ways.

Box 10.1 describes such a dissertation study where faculty members assessed their use of learning-centered teaching. The previous chapter on overcoming barriers gave examples of graduate student and faculty use of these rubrics to study the extent of learning-centered teaching implementation. A team of researchers at the University of Nebraska–Lincoln is investigating whether STEM faculty members use

---

BOX 10.1.
What Demographics Correlate to the Use of Learning-Centered Teaching?

Vivian Elder (2014) wanted to determine whether full-time faculty who taught general education courses at Missouri community colleges used learning-centered teaching. She created a Likert survey in which she turned each action into a separate item that began with "Which best describes your use of _____?" The 4 choices corresponded with the 4 levels on the rubrics. After 106 faculty completed useable surveys in which they self-assessed their use of learning-centered teaching, Elder determined a single level score for each participant by looking at their score distribution. None of these faculty members were rated overall as instructor-centered. The majority of the faculty were using mostly learning-centered practices, with 21% of the faculty classified as extensively learning-centered. Overall, the use of learning-centered teaching did not differ significantly by their years of teaching experience. However, those faculty members who used the most learning-centered teaching had 5 to 10 years of teaching experience, and the faculty who used learning-centered teaching the least had less than 5 years of teaching experience. In addition, faculty who taught oral and written communication courses assessed themselves as using more learning-centered teaching than those teaching STEM, social or behavioral science, or humanities and the arts.

Personal Reflection for Your Own Use

Do you think the instructors at your institution are similar in their use of learning-centered approaches to those in Elder's study? How could you find out?

If you also found that the majority of the instructors at your institution were using learning-centered teaching, how would you or administrators use this data?

How can you use the rubrics to conduct scholarship of teaching and learning?

What faculty demographic characteristics (e.g., rank, years of service, or departmental affiliation) would you choose to determine if it correlates with learning-centered teaching?

---

more learning-centered teaching after a new faculty development orientation where learning-centered teaching is discussed. They are triangulating data from self-report on surveys and are rating classroom observations on these rubrics (Stains, Pilarz, & Chakraverty, 2015). As these examples show, using the rubrics can lead to publications illustrating how learning-centered teaching is used.

You can use the rubrics for one individual, as will be discussed in chapter 11, or aggregate the scores from groups of faculty members such as those that teach in an educational program, discussed in chapter 12.

Chapter Summary

Figure 10.3 explains how you can use rubrics to measure the extent of use of learning-centered teaching.

Taking Stock: Comprehension Check on How to Use the Rubrics and How You Plan to Use the Data You Obtain

1. Consider how you use learning outcomes in your courses, and rate yourself on the rubric shown in Table 10.3b.

FIGURE 10.3. **Chapter summary.**

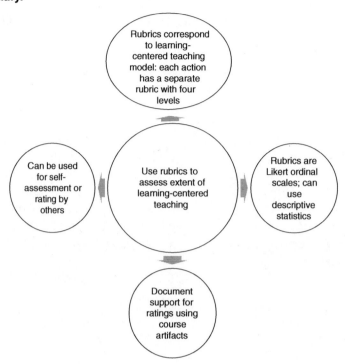

2. What evidence supports your ratings?

3. Suppose you rated your teaching on all of the rubrics. How would you analyze and summarize the data? Consider the templates provided in Table B.2 and Table C.1.

4. How could you use this information in your teaching portfolio or dossier or in the scholarship of teaching and learning?

The next chapter discusses further ways you can assess your teaching to increase your use of learning-centered teaching.

CHAPTER 11

Individual Instructor or Course Assessment of Learning-Centered Teaching

Chapter Highlights

- The assessment cycle is a convenient heuristic you can use to assess your teaching. It has five iterative steps: establish goals, determine a baseline, change teaching, assess changes, and use results for continuous improvement.
- You can use the rubrics described in the previous chapter throughout this assessment cycle to show how you have transitioned to more learning-centered teaching and how to plan further improvements.
- Using this cycle, you can continuously improve your teaching.

Along with many other faculty, you may see assessment as daunting because detailed and highly structured assessment reports are a burden to write (Blumberg, 2017a; Suskie, 2009). To make the assessment process easier, document your thoughts about how and why you are teaching as you go through the semester. Then periodically review your teaching notes and spend about an hour during each semester thinking about the data needed to assess your teaching.

Learning-Centered Teaching Assessment Cycle

I am proposing a manageable assessment of your transition to learning-centered teaching—a literature-based, practical assessment framework that can foster significant changes. This assessment framework is adapted from Suskie's (2009) popular assessment cycle. Figure 11.1 shows the learning-centered teaching assessment cycle. To summarize this process,

establish goals, assess your current practice (baseline), make changes to your teaching and then do a post-intervention assessment. Finally, use these results to make further improvements. You could do a focused post-intervention assessment of just those actions you intentionally changed. However, if you reassess on all actions, you will most likely determine that there were additional improvements because of the specific actions you took.

Establish Your Learning-Centered Teaching Goals

As you read earlier sections of this book, you might have noted how you would like to change your teaching across many actions. Reflect on these many posible actions and try to group them to form your learning-centered teaching goals. At most, you should have one to two comprehensive significant goals that you wish to work on at a time. Depending on what you want to change, you can have different types of goals. Table 11.1 shows examples of different types of goals.

FIGURE 11.1. **Learning-centered teaching assessment cycle**

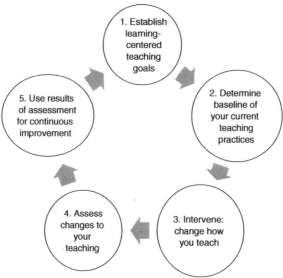

The simplest form of learning-centered teaching goals is to combine several actions within a construct, so your goal might be to become more learning-centered on responsibility for student learning or you might select specific actions within a construct. I will be discussing changes to specific actions within one construct to help you see how to use the assessment cycle. However, as Table 11.1 shows, you can also create a goal that combines several actions across constructs. You can also prioritize or stage your achievement of learning-centered teaching goals.

I illustrate how to employ the learning-centered teaching assessment cycle by using the sample data provided in Table 3.10 for the Role of Instructor construct. Table 11.2 shows the four changes that this hypothetical instructor wants to make and the rubric level the instructor wants to reach; these are the learning-centered teaching goals. To be consistent with how I discussed these actions previously, I state each action in this table and on the following ones by its title that uses learning-centered teaching approach language. This instructor does not want to change behavior on the action of creating an inclusive environment and is already at the extensively learning-centered level for the action on teaching methods; therefore, Table 11.2 lists only four actions for the Role of Instructor.

Establishing goals prior to determining baselines may appear illogical, but it is a recommended assessment practice. These goals should come from your reflections while reading this book, observations, or feedback on your teaching practices. Prior to data collection, you should also have a plan of how you will use the data. Without a plan, data may not be acted upon (Kuh et al., 2015). Establishing goals can lead to better decision-making and more appropriate and streamlined data collection.

Determine Baseline of Your Current Teaching Practices

This baseline can help you determine priorities for change and improvement. You can obtain a rich database by using as many sources as possible, as suggested in Table 10.4. You will have valid comparisons if you use the same assessment methods over time. Use the rubrics introduced in the previous chapter to determine your use of learning-centered teaching approaches. I suggest you complete all the rubrics because, as you make changes relating to one goal, your teaching will also improve in other areas. This is also an interactive process and you will be making more changes in the future. Table 11.3 shows the rubric scores for the baseline of the hypothetical instructor for the Role of Instructor construct.

TABLE 11.1. Examples of Types of Learning-Centered Teaching Goals

Types of Goals	*Actions That Comprise This Goal*
Improve teaching within one construct (e.g., increase the use of learning-centered characteristics on Development of Student Responsibility for Learning)	• Set student expectations to assume responsibility for learning • Provide scaffolding support • Foster the development of learning skills • Foster the development of self-directed, lifelong learning skills • Foster students' engagement in reflection and critical review of their learning • Foster the students' use of metacognitive skills and habits of the mind
Transparency in teaching (these items come from different constructs, as noted in parentheses in the next column)	• Align three components of course (Role of Instructor) • Be explicit about teaching/learning methods in all your courses (Role of Instructor) • Repeatedly explain your expectations for students to take responsibility for learning and how they will take such responsibility (Development of Student Responsibility for Learning) • Discuss with students why they should learn content (Function of Content) • Explain how you use fair, objective, and consistent policies and standards (Purposes and Processes of Student Assessment) • Allow flexibility in course policies, assessment methods, learning methods, and deadlines or how students earn grades (Balance of Power) • Respond to student feedback (Balance of Power)
Supporting students to succeed (these items come from different constructs, as noted in parentheses in the next column)	• Align three components of course (Role of Instructor) • Create an inclusive and welcoming environment for learning and for success for all students (Role of Instructor) • Create a supportive and success-oriented environment for learning and for accomplishment for all students (Role of Instructor) • Implement all of the actions in the student responsibility for learning construct as listed previously (Development of Student Responsibility for Learning) • Use organizing schemes (Function of Content) • Help students acquire discipline-specific methodologies (Function of Content) • Provide students with frequent, useful, and timely formative feedback (Purposes and Processes of Student Assessment) • Establish a safe, moral, and ethical environment (Balance of Power)

Intervene

Your interventions are the changes you will incorporate to be more learning-centered as described in the previous parts of this book. Establish realistic time lines for when you want to try to achieve these changes. Document the changes you make because you will want to reflect on them and put examples into your teaching portfolio or dossier for promotion.

TABLE 11.2. Goals for the Role of Instructor to Use More Learning-Centered Teaching Actions

Action	*Aspirational Rubric Score*[a]
The instructor develops and uses challenging, reasonable, and measurable learning outcomes that foster the acquisition of appropriate knowledge, skills, or values. These learning outcomes should be consistent with the goals of the educational program.	3
The instructor aligns the three essential components of a course—learning outcomes, teaching/learning methods, and assessment measures—in terms of content and consistent verbs representing the same cognitive processing/intellectual skill demands placed on the students.	3
The instructor creates a supportive and success-oriented environment for learning and for accomplishment for all students through proactive, clear, and overt course-specific success techniques.	4
The instructor is explicit about teaching/learning methods chosen to promote deep student learning and foster future use of learning.	3

Legend: 0 = instructor-centered; 1 = minimally learning-centered; 3 = mostly learning-centered; 4 = extensively learning-centered.

[a]Table 3.10 shows these scores.

Assess Changes to Your Teaching Using the Same Rubrics

The same databases and measures should be used both prior to and after the change in order to demonstrate its impact. The rubrics work well here. Table 11.4 shows the before and after intervention rubric scores, as well as the rubric goal aspiration level for this hypothetical instructor.

Use Results of Assessment for Continuous Improvement

Steps 4 and 5 on Figure 11.1 are referred to as closing the assessment loop. It is here that you will obtain and apply the most useful information about your teaching, which should lead to further improvements. Sustained and continuous assessments yield more meaningful information than onetime or sporadic data collection. The data collected such as in Table 11.4 should help you make further changes. You can then try to further improve your teaching on the same

actions within the selected goal or you can choose a different goal to work on.

Inspecting the data in Table 11.4 shows the hypothetical instructor reached or exceeded his goal for all actions except that of alignment of the three essential components of a course. Alignment, then, would be a logical place to try to change. The instructor should review the cognitive demands of the learning outcomes, what the students do during the course, and the assessment methods to see where misalignment occurs. If, for example, he determines that the learning outcome requires a higher level of cognitive demand (i.e., apply) than the assessment (i.e., comprehend), he can change his assessments to require a higher level. Alternatively, he might find that he only models the intellectual skill but does not give students opportunities to practice the intellectual skills required. If that is the case, then he should incorporate more opportunities for students to practice these higher level skills prior to the assessment of them.

TABLE 11.3. Baseline Rubric Scores for the Example of Learning-Centered Teaching for the Role of Instructor

Action[a]	Rubric Score[b]
The instructor develops and uses challenging, reasonable, and measurable learning outcomes that foster the acquisition of appropriate knowledge, skills, or values. These learning outcomes should be consistent with the goals of the educational program.	0
The instructor uses teaching/learning methods and educational technologies that promote the achievement of student learning outcomes such as knowledge acquisition, application, critical thinking, or solving problems related to the content.	4
The instructor aligns the three essential components of a course—learning outcomes, teaching/learning methods, and assessment measures—in terms of content and consistent verbs representing the same cognitive processing/intellectual skill demands placed on the students.	0
The instructor creates a supportive and success-oriented environment for learning and for accomplishment for all students through proactive, clear, and overt course-specific success techniques.	3
The instructor creates an inclusive and welcoming environment for learning and for success for all students by acknowledging and accepting diversity and differences in background.	1
The instructor is explicit about teaching/learning methods chosen to promote deep student learning and foster future use of learning.	0

Legend: 0 = instructor-centered; 1 = minimally learning-centered; 3 = mostly learning-centered; 4 = extensively learning-centered.

[a]All actions stated in the learning-centered format.

[b]Table 3.10 shows these scores.

Also, at this point in the assessment cycle, you can reflect and take a more holistic approach to your transition to more learning-centered teaching. You could perform a personal strengths, weaknesses, opportunities, and threats (SWOT) analysis about your teaching. SWOT analyses are commonly used in project planning. Strengths and weaknesses are internal, so you list what is true about your teaching here or your learning-centered teaching strengths and weaknesses. Under opportunities you list elements either in the larger environment or within your teaching that you can exploit to your advantage. Under threats you would list elements at your institution that could jeopardize further transitioning to learning-centered teaching. I created a hypothetical SWOT analysis for this hypotheical instructor based on my research on learning-centered teaching and the research previously reported as an example. Table 11.5 shows this SWOT analysis. When you can repeat SWOT analyses you show changes over time.

TABLE 11.4. Comparison of Rubric Scores for Learning-Centered Teaching for the Role of Instructor

Action	*Baseline Rubric Score[a]*	*Aspirational Rubric Score[a]*	*Rubric Scoring After Changed Teaching[b]*	*Benchmark Status*
The instructor develops and uses challenging, reasonable, and measurable learning outcomes that foster the acquisition of appropriate knowledge, skills, or values. These learning outcomes should be consistent with the goals of the educational program.	0	3	4	Exceeded goal
The instructor uses teaching/learning methods and educational technologies that promote the achievement of student learning outcomes such as knowledge acquisition, application, critical thinking, or solving problems related to the content.	4	4	4	Maintained status
The instructor aligns the three essential components of a course—learning outcomes, teaching/learning methods, and assessment measures—in terms of content and consistent verbs representing the same cognitive processing/intellectual skill demands placed on the students.	0	3	1	Did not reach goal of mostly learning-centered
The instructor creates a supportive and success-oriented environment for learning and for accomplishment for all students through proactive, clear, and overt course-specific success techniques.	3	4	4	Met goal
The instructor creates an inclusive and welcoming environment for learning and for success for all students by acknowledging and accepting diversity and differences in background.	1	1	1	Maintained status
The instructor is explicit about teaching/learning methods chosen to promote deep student learning and foster future use of learning.	0	3	3	Met goal

Legend: 0 = instructor-centered; 1 = minimally learning-centered; 3 = mostly learning-centered; 4 = extensively learning-centered.

[a]Table 3.10 data.

[b]Hypothetical data.

TABLE 11.5. Personal SWOT Analysis of Learning-Centered Teaching

My Strengths	My Weaknesses
I consciously use and develop the following learning-centered actions within my teaching and class preparation:	I have little awareness of inclusion of the following criteria within my teaching and class preparation:

My Strengths

I consciously use and develop the following learning-centered actions within my teaching and class preparation:

- Using four out of six (66%) either mostly or extensively learning-centered actions for the Role of Instructor construct, including the following:
  - o Develop and use challenging, reasonable, and measurable learning outcomes
  - o Use teaching/learning methods and educational technologies
  - o Create a supportive and success-oriented environment
  - o Be explicit about teaching/learning methods chosen
- Using five out of six (83%) extensively learning-centered teaching actions on the Function of Content construct, including the following:
  - o Promote meaningful student engagement with the content
  - o Help students acquire discipline-specific methodologies
  - o Help students understand why they need to learn the content for use in their careers or personal growth
  - o Use content to practice using inquiry or ways of thinking in the discipline or to solve real-world problems
  - o Help students acquire in-depth conceptual understanding of the content to facilitate deep and future learning and develop transferable skills
- Using some learning-centered teaching actions that support students to succeed, including the following:
  - o Create a supportive and success-oriented environment
  - o Establish a safe, moral, and ethical environment

My Weaknesses

I have little awareness of inclusion of the following criteria within my teaching and class preparation:

- Not using learning-centered teaching with the Responsibility for Learning construct
- Using a mix of instructor-centered and mostly learning-centered actions on the Purposes and Processes of Student Assessment construct
- Using a few learning-centered teaching actions on the Balance of Power construct

(Continues)

TABLE 11.5. (Continued)

Opportunities for Improvement (Both Personal and External)	Institutional Threats
Personal improvement opportunities I can take advantage of: • Reading this book has introduced me to concepts I never thought about. Now that I know about the responsibility for learning, I can incorporate modeling and practice of these skills. • Once I incorporate skills to help students learn better, I will be using more strategies that support students to succeed. • I can change my assessment practices to be more in line with those that are most effective in my discipline. Institutional opportunities I can take advantage of: • A teaching and learning center that supports faculty. • My institution offers a course design institute annually. • My chair encourages faculty to learn about innovative teaching by providing money to attend regional teaching conferences. • The university has active-learning classrooms; perhaps I can teach there.	• College-wide policies make it hard for me to use more learning-centered teaching related to the Balance of Power construct. • My institution values publications in my discipline more than teaching excellence for promotion. • Scholarship of teaching and learning would not count as much as discipline-based research at my university.

More recently, quality experts and organizational developers are recommending the use of more positive-thinking techniques that leverage strengths and opportunities to promote changes. SOAR (identify strengths, opportunities, aspirations, and results) is one such model that can produce greater results than trying to correct the weaknesses as identified in the SWOT analysis. You can summarize a SOAR analysis on a similar 2×2 matrix (American Society for Quality, 2016). Table 11.6 shows a hypothetical SOAR analysis using the same research as the SWOT analysis in Table 11.5. The SOAR analysis makes it easier to implement changes. Again, this can be an iterative process.

Document and Communicate Your Progress With Transitioning to Learning-Centered Teaching

You will want to document your progress along the assessment cycle. Create tables like those in Tables 11.4 through 11.6 and include supportive narrative and examples from your teaching. Your documentation can be placed in your annual performance review, teaching portfolio, or dossier for promotion and tenure. If you are placing these documents in files for others to review, be sure to summarize this learning-centered teaching model; show the rubrics; and, most importantly, describe how you changed your teaching. Provide the evidence you used to arrive at your ratings. Course artifacts such as your syllabi

TABLE 11.6. Personal SOAR Analysis of Learning-Centered Teaching

Strengths—What Do I Do Well? What Are My Abilities and Accomplishments?	**Opportunities—What Are My Best Opportunities That I Can Leverage for Student Success?**
I value learning-centered teaching and have successfully implemented most of the essential actions within the following constructs: • Role of Instructor actions • Function of Content actions **Institutional Resources I Can Take Further Utilize** • Teaching and learning center • Course design institute • Money to attend regional teaching conferences • Observe classes in active-learning classrooms.	• I can model and help students practice the skills necessary for them to assume responsibility for learning in my courses and beyond. • I can change my assessment practices to be more learning-centered by including more in-depth standardized feedback that provides quality formative assessment and also require more peer and self-assessments.
Aspirations—What Do I Want to Be as a Teacher or Achieve in the Future? How my students will remember me or my class: • I want to be an inspiring teacher who motivates all students to engage in the course and to learn more. • I will establish a positive learning environment and give all students the tools to succeed in this course and beyond. • I will be more explicit about what I expect through modeling and discuss why students should engage or learn this way.	**Results—What Tangible Outcomes Will This Bring?** My students will show • increased student engagement; • deep learning; • motivation to continue learning in this discipline; and • an ability to apply knowledge, skills, and attitudes to new situations. **What Measures Will Indicate When My Goals and Aspirations Have Been Achieved?** • Higher scores on application questions, essays, and other more challenging assignments in my course • Increased retention in this discipline from introductory courses • Increased number of students entering graduate school or careers using the knowledge, skills, and attitudes from my courses

are good evidence. Table 10.4 lists many possible sources of evidence. If you want to show how much your teaching has changed you can provide easy-to-understand summary and comparison charts such as those given in Figure 11.2.

Dumbbell charts (Figure 11.3) are another way to show comparisons among baseline, aspirations, and changes after interventions. The data from Table 11.4 are easy to interpret on the dumbbell chart in Figure 11.3. Dumbbell charts are a newer but very

FIGURE 11.2. Summary of extent of use of learning-centered teaching on Role of Instructor construct at different points in the assessment cycle.

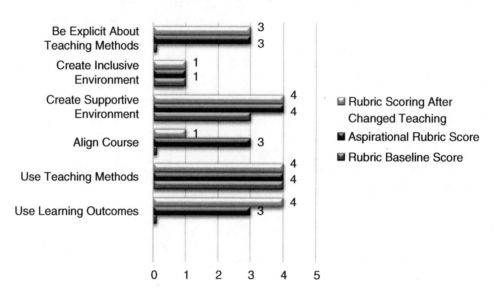

FIGURE 11.3. Comparison of rubric scores on baseline, aspirational goal, and results after changed teaching using a dumbbell chart.

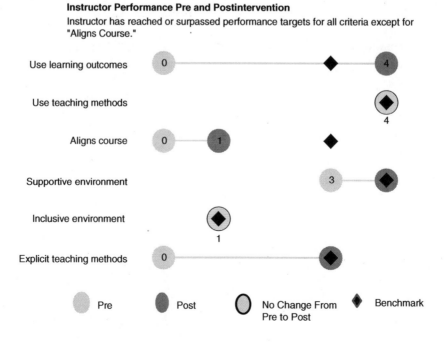

BOX 11.1.
Assessment of Course Redesign Camp

Susan Eliason and Christine Holmes (2012) asked faculty who volunteered for a three-day course redesign camp what they wanted to learn about and used these answers to plan the camp (Step 1 on the assessment cycle). Initially, the participants completed a self-assessment on their use of learning-centered teaching using the rubrics (Step 2). The faculty developers instructing in the camp included many of the topics the participant faculty requested (Step 3). The developers reviewed the syllabi the participants developed during and immediately after the course and rated course assignments on the Function of Content constuct. Six months after the course redesign camp, the participants rated themselves on the learning-centered rubrics. The participants became more learning-centered on Role of Instructor, Function of Content, and Purposes and Processes of Assessment. They did not become more learning-centered on Responsibility for Learning and Balance of Power. Step 4 involved both the course assignment review and the delayed self-assessment on the rubrics. Months after the camp, the developers asked the participants which constucts they wanted to explore further (Step 5). The participants wanted to continue transitioning to more learning-centered teaching practices only on those three constructs where they made progress and had no desire to learn more about student responsibility or balance of power.

Personal Reflection for Your Own Use

Why do you think the participants did not make changes on Responsibility for Learning and Balance of Power? What could have helped them to make changes on these constructs?

Can you develop a project where you can employ the assessment cycle to foster scholarship of teaching and learning?

---

useful way to plot changes over time. They are actually dual-axis combination charts. Excel can make dumbbell charts using a scatterplot, but it is more complicated than the other figures (Evergreen, 2017; Ficek, 2015). They use dot plots with a connecting line that indicates the growth, change, or difference between two points. On Figure 11.3 these points are the baseline or preintervention (shown as a gray circle) and the hypothetical changes made after incorporating learning-centered teaching (shown as black circles). They can also show the benchmark goal (i.e., the dark diamond). This sample chart shows four possible outcomes after an intervention: met goal (i.e., explicit about teaching methods and supportive environment); exceeded goal (i.e., use learning outcomes); did not meet goal (aligns course); and maintained but no change (i.e., inclusive environment and using teaching methods). Fortunately, the other possible outcome, regression to a lower level after intervention, did not occur.

Box 11.1 discusses how faculty developers have used the assessment cycle to determine the effectiveness of a three-day course redesign camp on the participants' use of learning-centered teaching and to plan faculty development activities.

Chapter Summary

Figure 11.4 shows how you can use the assessment cycle to assess your teaching and to document how you have transitioned to more learning-centered teaching.

Taking Stock: Assessing Your Teaching Over Time or Planning for Changes

Start the following exercise now and come back to it when you have collected data or made changes. You

FIGURE 11.4. Chapter summary.

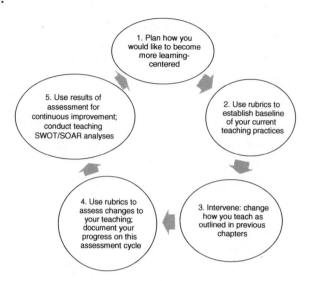

might want to copy this to your working notes in your teaching portfolio.

1. Apply the assessment cycle to your teaching.

   a. What are your improvement goals? State them in terms of the actions within constructs and the aspirational levels you want to reach on the rubrics. Develop one or two goals that incorporate these actions.

   b. Conduct a baseline rubrics assessment for all constructs. Document the results of your baseline rubrics assessment using the summary template in Table C.1 in Appendix C. Date this document and mark it "Baseline."

   c. Document what changes you want to make to your teaching by creating a table similar to Table 11.4.

   d. Document what you did and attach useful course artifacts as supporting evidence.

   e. Conduct a post-intervention rubrics assessment for all constructs or only the actions that you changed. Document the results of your postintervention rubrics assessment using the template in Table C.1. Date these results and mark it "Intervention Round One." Add the new rubric scores to the table you created like Table 11.4.

   f. Use results of assessment for continuous improvement.

      Where would you further like to improve your teaching?

      Conduct personal SWOT or SOAR analyses and mark the date conducted by creating a table or tables similar to Tables 11.5 and 11.6.

   g. Repeat cycle iteratively to fully transform your teaching.

2. Document how you will communicate your steps along the assessment plan and all your data to others. Be sure you explain adequately so that people who are not familiar with this learning-centered teaching model and the assessment cycle understand what you have done.

CHAPTER 12

Program and Institutional Assessment of Learning-Centered Teaching

Chapter Highlights

This chapter explains how to assess educational programs or institutions on their use of learning-centered teaching:

- Program assessments use many of the same concepts, processes, and methods as individual assessment of learning-centered teaching. You can use the same rubrics.
- Align program assessments with the goals of the educational program or current initiatives for improvement.
- Collect data from a large enough sample to represent the educational program; score the data on the rubrics.
- Use a spreadsheet to record and summarize the results of the rubrics.
- Convey results in a manner that is meaningful and easy for others to understand.

After reading the previous two chapters, you should have a good idea of how to assess your practices to determine the extent of implementation of learning-centered teaching. In this chapter, the focus of assessment broadens from individuals to departments and educational programs, college- or institution-wide. Educators often do these larger scale assessments for the purposes of internal or external accountability such as for accreditation. You can also conduct these programs or higher level assessments for the purposes of continuous quality improvement (Ikenberry & Kuh, 2015). In either case, they are also vehicles for scholarship of teaching and learning. The unit of study can be either instructors or courses. You can use the rubrics, the assessment cycle, and concepts previously discussed for review of faculty and courses for program and institutional assessment of learning-centered

teaching. To guide you in conducting program assessments, I discuss how to

- decide what to assess;
- collect programmatic information;
- analyze and summarize programmatic data;
- close the assessment loop by using the data; and
- report programmatic assessment data.

I provide examples of each step.

Instructors who serve on curriculum, assessment, executive, or general education committees within colleges or at the institution level may want to perform a program assessment on the use of aspects of learning-centered teaching. Administrators such as department chairs or deans might find such an assessment useful.

Since faculty members may not be trained to conduct these large-scale assessments or may not have time to conduct them, they can partner with faculty developers, staff in offices of Institutional Effectiveness or Institutional Research. Graduate students in higher education leadership, curriculum development or assessment can be hired to collect and analyze the data. A program evaluation study can be the focus of a master's thesis or doctoral dissertation.

Deciding What to Assess

Align program assessments with the goals of the educational program. Therefore, reviewing the overall goals of educational programs can help to determine what to assess. For example, if an undergraduate program strives to produce graduates who are lifelong learners, then its program assessment should consider the implementation of the following actions:

- The instructor is explicit about teaching/learning methods chosen to promote deep student learning and foster future use of learning. (Role of Instructor)
- The instructor fosters the development of learning or learning to learn skills for the present and the future. (Responsibility for Student Learning)
- The instructor fosters the development of self-directed, lifelong learning skills. (Responsibility for Student Learning)
- The instructor fosters students' engagement in reflection and critical review of their learning through well-structured activities. Reflection and critical review should include self-assessment of learning abilities, one's mastery of objectives, and strengths and weakness of the learning process. (Responsibility for Student Learning)
- The instructor fosters the students' use of metacognitive skills and habits of mind to assist students to solve real-life problems and to gain positive outcomes. (Responsibility for Student Learning)
- In addition to building a knowledge base, the instructor uses content to help students understand why they need to learn the content for use in their careers or personal growth. (Function of Content)
- The instructor helps students acquire in-depth conceptual understanding of the content to facilitate deep and future learning and use transferable skills. (Function of Content)

Strategic planning and institutional initiatives can also indicate what to assess. Many institutions have initiatives related to increased retention and graduation initiatives. Assessment of this initiative should include the actions for supporting students to succeed and persevere, identified on the bottom of Table 11.1.

As the preceding examples illustrate, you can assess the status of selected actions, thus adapting the overall assessment framework for your identified purposes. It would be unwieldy to assess many individual instructors or courses on all rubrics for all actions. Table 12.1 describes examples of different types of programmatic assessments where instructors and faculty developers have or could have used the relevant rubrics to assess specific aspects of learning-centered teaching.

Collecting Programmatic Information

Programmatic assessments tend to use a snapshot of the status at one point in time. When you sustain these assessments over time, you have multiple, data collection times. With such data, you can determine how programs have focused more on learning-centered teaching over time or after development or reform efforts. Educators rarely assess the effectiveness of instructional approaches, such as learning-centered teaching, within routine program assessment based on student learning outcomes. This would be a separate assessment. Since you will be studying how instructors teach, you need to get Institutional Review Board (IRB) approval before you collect data. These reviews will focus on how you treat the data, store it, and keep it confidential. Aggregate data keeps individual responses confidential.

Although individual assessments of use of learning-centered teaching often employ a self-report process, a rigorous programmatic assessment of this approach requires use of consistent standards among all people providing data. In my experience, instructors tend to

TABLE 12.1.   Examples of Different Types of Program Assessment for Aspects of Learning-Centered Teaching

Context and Citation	*Goal of Assessment*	*Which Rubrics Would Provide Appropriate Data?*	*Were Learning-Centered Teaching Rubrics Used?*
Dissertation study of five independent colleges in Kentucky (Johnson, 2013)	Faculty perception and use of learning-centered strategies to assess student performance	Rubrics for all actions within the Purposes and Processes of Student Assessment construct	Yes
Dalton State College's Quality Enhancement Plan for Commission on Colleges, Southern Association of Colleges and Schools (Schwenn & Codjoe, 2013)	Improve students' ability to write accurately	The instructor uses teaching/learning methods and educational technologies that promote the achievement of student learning outcomes (Role of Instructor construct)	No. Rubrics would have provided data to see whether instructors were using these actions that should promote their goals. Such data would have helped to triangulate support for changes in student performance or lack of changes.
	Self-directed learning	The instructor fosters the development of learning or learning to learn skills for the present and the future (Responsibility for Learning construct). The instructor fosters the development of self-directed, lifelong learning skills (Responsibility for Student Learning construct)	
		The instructor fosters the development and use of discipline-specific methodologies (Function of Content construct)	
Review of syllabus after participating in course design institute (Eliason, & Holmes, 2012)	Increased use of learning-centered teaching on the Function of Content construct	Rubrics for all actions within Function of Content construct	Yes

(Continues)

TABLE 12.1. (Continued)

Context and Citation	Goal of Assessment	Which Rubrics Would Provide Appropriate Data?	Were Learning-Centered Teaching Rubrics Used?
Review of recent changes in education program for golf coaches; interviewed coach development administrators involved in the program to determine whether they implemented recommended learning-centered teaching practices (Paquette & Trudel, 2018)	Increased use of learning-centered teaching on the Role of Instructor and Function of Content constructs	Rubrics for all actions within Role of Instructor and Function of Content constructs	Yes
Plan to enhance implementation of learning-centered teaching in undergraduate marketing curriculum (Von der Heidt & Quazi, 2013)	Identify current implementation of learning-centered teaching in a curriculum to make specific curricular change recommendations and identify actions that are not easy to change due to policies	Used all rubrics from all constructs	Yes
Determine whether colleges met their strategic planning initiatives of implementing learning-centered teaching (Blumberg, 2016a, 2016b)	Determine extent of implementation of learning-centered teaching	Selected actions across all constructs that corresponded to those listed in the college strategic plan	Yes

Personal Reflection on Applicability of Table 12.1 for Your Use

Can you identify a similar programmatic assessment that you could do that may be similar to the examples in Table 12.1?

What would you need to be able to do such an assessment?

score themselves more to the learning-centered end than may be justified. Documentation to support the ratings is essential. Then a trained assessor who is familiar with the model and the rubrics can check the ratings. Any discrepancies between the self-assessor and the other assessor can be resolved through discussion. Trained assessors may collect course artifacts or interview the selected population and score the faculty or courses on the rubrics. Establish interrater reliability if more than one person does the scoring.

Especially with large educational programs, it is not necessary to collect data from all instructors or from all classes. Getting a representative sample is enough. Just guard against a convenience sample where you select or invite only the people you interact with regularly or just those who participate in faculty development activities to participate.

I have used two methods to conduct programmatic assessments of learning-centered teaching: review of course material and semi-structured interviews (Blumberg, 2016a, 2016b, 2017b; Blumberg & Pontiggia, 2011). With both methods, establishing interrater reliability of the raters strengthens the validity of the results and conclusions. Syllabic review is a common method for reviewing courses (Eliason & Holmes, 2012; Palmer et al., 2014). When additional course artifacts such as those listed in Table 10.4 are considered, triangulation of support occurs, which yields richer and more valid data. Review of course artifacts, especially syllabi and assignments is especially effective for reviewing online courses.

I begin my one-on-one interviews with the query "Please describe what happens in a typical class." Then I ask questions that direct instructors to talk about the specific actions I want to rate on the rubrics. With semistructured interviews about teaching practices, the interviewer can ask additional clarification questions and review the supporting documentation. An unanticipated but positive outcome of interviews was that they served as faculty development opportunities (Blumberg, 2016b, 2017b). As I asked questions about specific actions, instructors, especially those who did not attend faculty development programs, asked for explanations of these concepts and remarked that they learned from these interviews. I will report on selected rubric ratings from this interview study later in the chapter.

Observation of classes is not only a more ambitious but also a rich data collection method. Use validated observation methods of either recorded segments of class or live occurrences (Lund et al., 2015). Combining these methods leads to even richer, more compelling data. Similarly, you can analyze recorded interactive sessions, online blogs or discussion boards with online instruction.

Analyzing and Summarizing Programmatic Data

Rate each instructor or course according to the method I described in the section called "How to Rate Teaching on the Learning-Centered Teaching Rubrics" in chapter 10. Use a spreadsheet to record your rubric ratings. Create a separate page for every construct you are studying. Each action within that construct gets a separate column. Every instructor or course gets a separate row, with the appropriate rubric scores placed in the corresponding cells, as shown in Table 12.2. Instead of identifying them by name, assign them numbers; this assures anonymity when you share the tables with stakeholders. These numbers may have demographic information associated with them, such as college or departmental affiliation, professional rank, or they just may be number codes. Table 12.2 shows partial data from my research conducted with two colleges at the University of the Sciences. This table lists only four out of six actions in the Role of Instructor construct because these actions were on the strategic plan; the other two were not included in this study. Although I collected data on all five constructs, I list data from only some of the participants for the Role of Instructor construct. My purpose is to show how to set up such a spreadsheet and not to report on the results of this study. Because the possible scores are 0, 1, 3, and 4, do not use means and standard deviation statistics. Box 12.1 explains the program assessment study that I refer to throughout this chapter.

The purpose of discussing this study is to illustrate how you can analyze, report, and use program assessment data, not to describe the results as such. Because only very limited data are given here, you will not be able to follow how the results lead to the conclusions; in fact, some of the figures may appear to contradict the overall conclusion that the colleges had met their learning-centered teaching goals. You can find the full reports published in journals (Blumberg, 2016a, 2016b, 2017b).

TABLE 12.2. Sample Spreadsheet Showing Partial Data From Programmatic Assessment of Two Colleges Using the Rubrics for Role of Instructor

College of Arts and Sciences	*Role of Instructor*			
Faculty Identifier Number	*Teaching and Learning Methods[a]*	*Alignment[b]*	*Supportive Environment[c]*	*Explicit About Teaching Methods[d]*
101	1	1	3	0
102	1	3	3	0
103	4	1	3	3
104	3	3	3	0
105	1	0	4	1
106	4	4	3	1
107	1	3	1	0
108	4	3	3	1
109	1	1	3	0
110	1	0	3	0
…				
140	1	3	3	1
Total percentage instructor-centered (scored as 0)	5%	27%	2%	45%
Total percentage minimally learning-centered (scored as 1)	45%	25%	13%	32%
Total percentage mostly learning-centered (scored as 3)	17%	38%	68%	20%
Total percentage extensively learning-centered (scored as 4)	33%	10%	17%	3%
Total percentage not learning-centered (scored as 0 or 1)	50%	52%	15%	77%
Total percentage learning-centered (scored as 3 or 4)	50%	48%	85%	23%
Range	0–4	0–4	0–4	0–4
Mode	1	1, 3	3	0

(Continues)

TABLE 12.2. (Continued)

| College of Health Professions | Role of Instructor | | | |
Faculty Identifier Number	Teaching and Learning Methods[a]	Alignment[b]	Supportive Environment[c]	Explicit About Teaching Methods[d]
201	1	1	3	1
202	3	1	3	0
203	1	3	3	4
204	4	1	3	3
205	3	1	4	1
206	3	1	3	0
207	4	4	3	3
208	1	1	1	4
209	1	1	3	1
210	4	3	3	1
…				
213	3	1	3	3
Total percentage instructor-centered (scored as 0)	0%	0%	0%	23%
Total percentage minimally learning-centered (scored as 1)	31%	62%	8%	31%
Total percentage mostly learning-centered (scored as 3)	37%	23%	77%	23%
Total percentage extensively learning-centered (scored as 4)	32%	15%	15%	23%
Total percentage not learning-centered (scored as 0 or 1)	31%	62%	8%	54%
Total percentage learning-centered (scored as 3 or 4)	69%	38%	92%	46%
Range	1–4	1–4	1–4	0–4
Mode	3	1	3	1

Legend: These are the four actions on the Role of Instructor construct that were used in the program assessment study described in Box 12.1. Each action is described as using learning-centered practices. Summary statistics are for the entire data set by college.

[a] The instructor uses teaching/learning methods and educational technologies that promote the achievement of student learning outcomes such as knowledge acquisition, application, critical thinking, or solving problems related to the content.

[b] The instructor aligns the three essential components of a course—learning outcomes, teaching/learning methods, and assessment measures—in terms of content and consistent verbs representing the same cognitive processing/intellectual skill demands placed on the students.

[c] The instructor creates a supportive and success-oriented environment for learning and for accomplishment for all students through proactive clear and overt course-specific success techniques.

[d] The instructor explicitly states teaching/learning methods chosen to promote deep student learning and foster future use of learning.

BOX 12.1.
Assessment to Determine Whether Two Colleges Met Their Strategic Plan to
Implement Learning-Centered Teaching

The Colleges of Arts and Sciences and Health Sciences at the University of the Sciences separately developed strategic plans to implement learning-centered teaching. The strategic plan for the College of Arts and Sciences listed specific actions across the 5 constructs that defined how faculty members would implement learning-centered teaching. I created a semistructured interview to collect information so that instructors could be rated on the rubrics that corresponded with these actions (Blumberg, 2016a, 2016b, 2017b). I interviewed 40 out of 69 (58%) full-time faculty members from the College of Arts and Sciences and 13 out of 22 (59%) full-time faculty members from the College of Health Sciences. During the interview, the faculty members showed me course artifacts to support their descriptions of how they taught. Two people rated each interview on the rubrics for the selected actions. Both people were familiar with the model and rated sample sections consistently. The deans and I determined the criteria for success. All scores of 3 (mostly learning-centered teaching) and 4 (extensively learning-centered teaching) were defined as achieving the goal of using learning-centered teaching. We agreed an overall criterion for success to be greater than 50% of the faculty who participated in each college would use mostly or extensively learning-centered teaching practices on most of the selected actions. Of the interviewed faculty in the College of Arts and Sciences, 31 out of 40 (77%) were employing learning-centered teaching practices. Of the interviewed faculty members in the College of Health Professions, 12 out of 13 (92%) were employing learning-centered teaching practices. Both colleges exceeded the benchmark of more than 50% compliance. Faculty in both colleges used the most learning-centered approaches for the Function of Content construct. The faculty in the College of Arts and Sciences also used many learning-centered practices in Responsibility for Learning, probably because they teach many general education courses. No action was scored as instructor-centered for more than 80% of the participants in either college. However, 5 (8%) of the interviewed faculty did not use any learning-centered teaching practices, and they even mentioned overt rejection of learning-centered teaching.

    Both deans were proud that they met their strategic goal of implementing learning-centered teaching and want to maintain this status. They are encouraging further faculty development efforts, especially with new faculty so that they learn to use learning-centered teaching approaches.

Figure 12.1 shows 2 stacked bar charts that total 100%. They compare the faculty from the College of Arts and Sciences to the faculty from College of Health Professions on their use of learning-centered practices related to the Role of Instructor construct. Once again, the actions listed are those that were mentioned in the strategic plan and not all the actions for this construct. The numbers within the bars are the frequency counts for each level—for example, 18 (45%) of the College of Arts and Science faculty were rated as instructor-centered on the action of being explicit about teaching methods. The numbers on the axis on the bottom show the percentages. The bars are stacked together so that they add to 100%, as the name implies. Even though faculty numbers in these 2 colleges are quite different, horizontal 100% stacked bar charts make it easy to compare them.

You can collapse your data into two categories: not learning-centered (scores of 0 and 1) and learning-centered (scores of 3 and 4). Then you can create tables that show the percentage of not learning-centered and learning-centered instructors or courses for each action, for the construct, and overall for all actions combined. Figure 12.2 shows how to graphically display these data. You would construct a figure like this by putting together a series of individual small figures because Excel calculates each one separately. Contrasts between groups, such as in their explicitness about their teaching methods, are easy to observe with vertical stacked bar charts like Figure 12.2.

Figure 12.3 is another example of how you can use a dumbbell chart. You will recall from chapter 11 that dumbbell charts are dot plots with two or more series of data and are an alternative to the stacked bar charts

FIGURE 12.1. **100% stacked bar charts to compare faculty within two colleges on the Role of Instructor construct.**

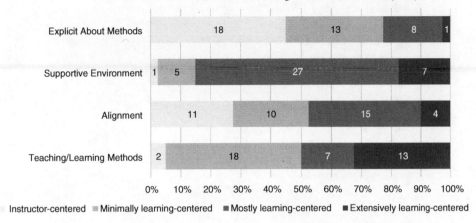

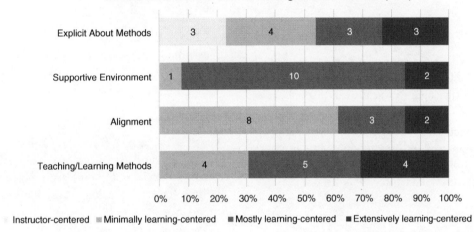

FIGURE 12.2. **Comparing the learning-centeredness of faculty from the two colleges by action.**

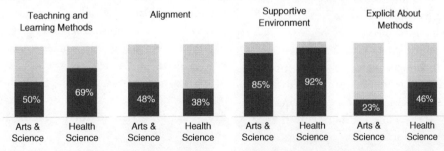

Note: Here the data are collapsed into two dicthomous categories—either instructor-centered (the lighter shade) or learning-centered (the darker shade).

FIGURE 12.3. Comparison of the percentage of learning-centered faculty from the College of Arts and Sciences and the College of Health Sciences on selected actions of Role of Instructor.

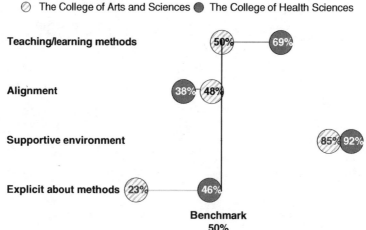

The College of Health Sciences has a higher percentage of learning-centered faculty than the College of Arts and Sciences

The College of Arts and Sciences ● The College of Health Sciences

Teaching/learning methods   50%   69%

Alignment   38% 48%

Supportive environment   85% 92%

Explicit about methods   23%   46%

Benchmark
50%

shown in Figure 12.2. As Figure 12.3 shows, dumbbell charts are useful for comparing two populations. The vertical line in this figure indicates the 50% benchmark that the deans set as the standard they wanted their faculty to reach. You can predetermine benchmarks as the deans did in this study or they can be set as aspirations using baseline data from before-teaching changes (as discussed in chapter 11).

Closing the Assessment Loop by Using the Data

Complete data sets identify faculty who are learning centered teaching leaders and those who are slow to embrace it. The faculty who consistently fall below their peers on their implementation of learning-centered teaching might be good candidates for faculty development efforts. Their chairs might ask them to consider using more learning-centered teaching and ask them to observe their peers who are using learning-centered teaching. Chairs can frame these development efforts to improve teaching and not as criticism.

For faculty development and improvement purposes, I considered the least used and the least understood actions as noted from my faculty interviews (Blumberg, 2016a, 2016b). Then I developed programs that showed faculty how to use these actions in a learning-centered teaching manner. The instructors who had implemented these actions using learning-centered teaching discussed what they did and how it worked. For example, I orchestrated a faculty development session for the College of Arts and Sciences where a few faculty from the College of Health Sciences led a short panel discussion about how they are explicit in explaining their learning-centered teaching. This took place at a college council meeting, so faculty attendance was good.

If the data indicate actions that were rarely used across departments or colleges, then these actions are bottlenecks to the implementation of learning-centered teaching (Blumberg, 2018). Consider whether policies that inhibit learning-centered teaching implementation on this action might be a reason (Von der Heidt & Quazi, 2013). For example, if a college has strict policies for attendance and how students are graded, instructors may not be able to be flexible on course policies, assessment methods, learning methods, and deadlines or how students earn grades, an action on the Balance of Power construct.

Reporting Programmatic Assessment Data

Assessment reports are supposed to tell a story and foster improvements. Begin your report with the model

FIGURE 12.4. **Chapter summary.**

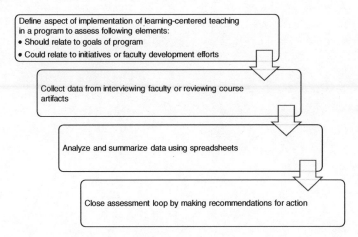

and how you collected and summarized the results. You will need to convey the results so that others can derive meaning from the data. Therefore, the way the data are reported matters. People have trouble seeing the overall message when presented with data tables. However, visualizations convey much information in an easy-to-assimilate manner. Figures 12.1, 12.2, and 12.3 display data clearly, so that most people would be able to interpret the information. Figures such as Figure 12.3 are good at showing whether a population reached a benchmark target, as I did here, or progress over time, as I did in chapter 11. Depending on the changes you want to propose, you may highlight specific data. Add short statements or quotes to the numerical summary data, as they add richness and meaning to the numbers. For example, many faculty were not familiar with the concept of course alignment and I had to explain it to them during the interviews. Once they heard about the concept, it made sense and some said they would try to align their courses.

Share your assessment results and interpretations with all the relevant stakeholders and advocate for further changes. This is a great opportunity to begin a discussion with diverse audiences on the value of learning-centered teaching. If the program is demonstrating learning-centered teaching, this is very good news that should be shared with top administrators, including the cabinet, admissions officers, and even publicly with the media and social media. From the data given here, my university is proud that most faculty create a supportive environment for their students. This could also be used in our marketing material to prospective students and their parents.

Chapter Summary

Figure 12.4 gives a flowchart of the process for program and institutional assessment of learning.

Taking Stock: How You Can Conduct a Program-Wide Assessment of Learning-Centered Teaching

Consider how you can conduct program-wide assessment.

1. Review the goals or strategic plan of your educational program to help you determine what to assess at the program level. What aspects of learning-centered teaching could you assess in your program?

2. Who would be good collaborators on this program assessment? Consider the director of the Teaching and Learning Center, staff within the Office of Institutional Effectiveness or Institutional Research, administrators from the college to be studied, or the chair of the University Assessment Committee.

3. How can you collect programmatic data to determine if these goals are being met? Remember to get Institutional Review Board (IRB) approval before you collect data.

4. What actions within which constructs do you want to assess?

5. How can you use Excel or Google Sheets to analyze and summarize your data?

6. Once you report the data in an easy-to-use way, how might you or others use the information to foster continuous improvement?

Appendix A: Examples of Learning-Centered Teaching Techniques or Practices in Different Types of Courses—A Review of the Literature

For discussions of learning-centered teaching techniques or practices that are especially useful within specific disciplines, see Table P.1 (in the Preface) that lists where to find information on STEM; foreign language learners; and underprepared, unmotivated, or first-year college students. This table also lists where to find information on research and design courses, helping students to succeed, and helping students to engage successfully in group activities

Table A.1 lists learning-centered techniques or teaching/learning practices that transcend disciplines.

Thus, all instructors can use them regardless of discipline. Many of the actions within the five constructs are learning-centered techniques or practices. The list given in Table A.1 does not include these specific actions as described in chapters 3 through 7.

Table A.2 lists learning-centered techniques or teaching/learning practices that use online or electronic educational technologies. You can use these practices for online, hybrid, or face-to-face courses.

TABLE A.1. Learning-Centered Techniques or Teaching/Learning Practices That Transcend Disciplines

Instructional or Pedagogical Technique	Brief Description	Recommended For What Type of Class or Population	Where Discussed in This Book
Backward course design	Start planning course with desired outcomes or endpoints, not content	All	Box 3.3
Collaborative note taking	Students share their class notes for peer correction	Foreign language learning STEM Beginning students	Box 5.4
Concept map	Student represent hierarchical relations to integrate content	STEM Social sciences	Box 3.8
Engage with reading assignments	Answering questions before class, in class; students compare their answers to these questions, first in pairs and then in trios; students correct their written answers Reading notes that form the basis of class discussion	All	Boxes 3.6 and 5.1

(Continues)

TABLE A.1. (Continued)

Instructional or Pedagogical Technique	Brief Description	Recommended For What Type of Class or Population	Where Discussed in This Book
Flipped classroom	Content disseminated outside of class time; students apply content to solve problems or complete tasks during class time	Content-rich courses where students are expected to apply material or solve problems	Boxes 1.2 and 6.4
Instructional design framework	Having students set personal learning goals Supporting students through scaffolding Using peer review	All	Box 4.2
Jigsaw	Reviewing one major aspect of the content in small groups, then going into groups where members have reviewed all aspects and solve new problem	Content-rich courses Business Literature courses Theory courses	Box 4.8
Nonindividualized, standard feedback	Giving students detailed grading rubrics specifying criteria with unacceptable to excellent standards defined	Wherever students need to hand in essays, projects, etc.	Box 6.5
Paired in-depth discussions on content	Students, after reading the material, in pairs debating their perspectives, synthesizing material	Where close reading is important and text is open to different interpretations	Box 4.7
Problem-based learning (PBL)	Students discussing real problems and identifying what they need to learn to solve the problem; students dividing the learning tasks and coming back together to synthesize and solve the problem	Health sciences, STEM, social sciences, business	Box 3.5
Repeated testing as an effective study technique	Students taking several practice exams spaced over the time where the class is working on the content	All	Box 6.3
Small groups working on problem-solving or projects or tasks	Students getting explicit directions on their tasks in the small group work; students held individually accountable for their work	All	Boxes 1.1, 3.5, 4.8, 5.4, 7.6, and 8.1
Using popular culture to make unfamiliar or abstract content understandable and relevant	Music, media, film, popular culture or literature used as analogies helping students understand the content	Humanities, social sciences classes	Boxes 5.2 and 7.7

TABLE A.2. Learning-Centered Techniques or Teaching/Learning Practices That Use Online or Electronic Educational Technologies

Online Instructional or Pedagogical Technique	Brief Description of How It Is Used	Where Discussed in This Book
Blog	Assign prompts for students to respond to. Students need to respond to other students' posts. Students can also post on new topics.	Box 3.4
Discussion board or online or forums	Students responding to questions about content helps them formulate well thought out and quality responses. Students can continue in-class discussions out of class.	Box 3.7
Disseminate information outside of class; flipped course	Readings, videos, websites can be posted on the course's learning management system website. Students are responsible for learning these materials.	Boxes 1.2 and 6.4
Electronic portfolio	Students select samples of their work and reflect on their learning and progress toward meeting learning goals.	Box 5.8
Nonindividualized, standard feedback	Instructor gives students detailed grading rubrics specifying criteria with unacceptable to excellent standards defined.	Box 6.5
Peer review	Students provide detailed feedback on drafts completed by their peers.	Box 6.6 and 7.8
Repeated testing as an effective study technique	Students take several practice exams spaced over the time where the class is working on the content.	Box 6.3

Appendix B: Learning-Centered Teaching Rubrics for All of the Actions Within the Five Constructs

Table B1.1 contains the rubrics for each of the five learning-centered constructs (Role of Instructor, Developing Student Responsibility for Learning, Function of Content, Purposes and Processes of Student Assessment, and Balance of Power).

Each construct has six actions that define the construct, with a corresponding rubric part for each action.

Each rubric part has the following quality levels that describe instructor behaviors:

- Uses instructor-centered approaches
- Minimally uses learning-centered approaches
- Mostly uses learning-centered approaches
- Extensively uses learning-centered approaches

The leaves in Illustration B.1 represent the four levels characterizing each action.

How to Rate Teaching on the Learning-Centered Teaching Rubrics

Use the following methods to rate teaching on the rubrics:

- Indicate by highlighting or underlining all the descriptions that best reflect your actual practices.
- Frequency and use of occurrence is more important to consider than how long the

activity takes in a whole class. For example, if you use clickers frequently and discuss the correct answers, even though these clicker questions may take five minutes in a class, you would indicate that you are at the *mostly uses learning-centered* level for the action "the instructor integrates assessment and learning in the assessment construct."

- Not all items may apply to all courses. If there is no evidence of an action, rate as NA.
- If you do not use this action, rate it as instructor-centered.
- If a level lists more than one description or definition, you can indicate different levels within the same action.
- If the teaching practices fall on two different levels because of different descriptors, indicate all that apply even though they may be on different levels.
- You can also highlight any improvement suggestions that you might adapt as you read through the rubrics. Use the descriptors at the higher learning-centered teaching levels to direct your next areas of impro-vement.
- An instructor or a course can be at all levels on the rubrics, reflecting varying amounts of implementation of learning-centered teaching. Each action's rating is independent.
- If you indicated behaviors at two or more levels because of multiple descriptors, pick the level with a majority of the answers.
- If there is a tie, use a number between the two levels, such as 3.5.

ILLUSTRATION B.1. The Four Levels of Characteristics for Each Action

Instructor-centered
Minimally learning-centered
Mostly learning-centered
Extensively learning-centered

Visit the Stylus Publishing website at https://styluspub.presswarehouse.com/browse/book/9781620368954/Making-Learning-Centered-Teaching-Work to download a PDF of Appendix B.

TABLE B.1. Rubrics for the Actions of the Five Constructs

Construct I: Role of Instructor

Action

The instructor develops and uses challenging, reasonable, and measurable learning outcomes that foster the acquisition of appropriate knowledge, skills, or values. These learning outcomes should be consistent with the goals of the educational program.

Rubric Quality Levels

Uses instructor-centered approaches. Instructor:

- ° Does not develop or not use learning outcomes **OR**
- ° Articulates vague or inappropriate learning outcomes that
  - ▪ Are not consistent with the goals of the educational program **OR**
  - ▪ Do not foster the acquisition of appropriate knowledge, skills, or values **OR**
  - ▪ Are not challenging, reasonable, or measurable

Minimally uses learning- centered approaches. Instructor:

- ° Develops challenging, reasonable, and measurable learning outcomes but these outcomes
  - ▪ Are not consistent with the goals of the educational program **OR**
  - ▪ Do not foster the acquisition of appropriate knowledge, skills, or values

Mostly uses learning-centered approaches. Instructor:

- ° Develops challenging, reasonable, and measurable learning outcomes that are consistent with the goals of the educational program and foster the acquisition of appropriate knowledge, skills, or values **AND**
- ° Places these outcomes in the syllabus, but does not refer to them during the course

Extensively uses learning-centered approaches. Instructor:

- ° Places in the syllabus challenging, reasonable, and measurable learning outcomes that are consistent with the goals of the educational program and foster the acquisition of appropriate knowledge, skills, or values **AND**
- ° Regularly refers to them throughout the course

(Continues)

TABLE B.1. (Continued)

Construct I: Role of Instructor

Action
The instructor uses teaching/learning methods and educational technologies that promote the achievement of student learning outcomes such as knowledge acquisition, application, critical thinking, or solving problems related to the content.

Rubric Quality Levels

Uses instructor-centered approaches. Instructor:

- Uses teaching/learning methods or educational technologies that impede student learning **OR**
- Uses teaching/learning methods or educational technologies that conflict with learning outcomes **OR**
- Uses instructor-centered teaching methods that allow students to be passive and memorize material

Minimally uses learning-centered approaches. Instructor:

- Uses teaching/learning methods or educational technologies without regard for student learning outcomes **OR**
- Uses active-learning approaches during less than half of the course

Mostly uses learning-centered approaches. Instructor:

- Selects teaching/learning methods or educational technologies that should help students achieve learning outcomes **AND**
- Uses active teaching-learning methods in more than half of the course. Such active learning can occur in class, online, or as out-of-class assignments **OR**
- Uses activities where students interact with each other and the instructor about the course content in more than half of the course. Such interactions can occur in-class, online, or as out-of-class assignments as in group projects

Extensively uses learning-centered approaches. Instructor:

- Intentionally uses various pedagogical techniques and/or educational technologies that promote the achievement of student learning outcomes **AND**
- Uses active-learning approaches in at least 90% of the course **AND**
- Explains to students how these methods or technologies promote the achievement of student learning outcomes

(Continues)

TABLE B.1. (Continued)

Construct I: Role of Instructor

Action

The instructor aligns the three essential components of a course (learning outcomes, teaching/learning methods, and assessment measures) in terms of content and consistent verbs representing the same cognitive processing/intellectual skill demands placed on the students.

Rubric Quality Levels

Uses instructor-centered approaches. Instructor:

- Does not align objectives/learning outcomes, teaching/learning methods, and assessment methods **OR**
- Does not understand the concept **OR**
- Does not think about course alignment

Minimally uses learning-centered approaches. Instructor:

- Aligns two out of the three course actions **OR**
- Does not indicate such alignment on the course syllabus

Mostly uses learning-centered approaches. Instructor:

- Aligns objectives/learning outcomes, teaching/learning methods, and assessment methods **AND**
- Shows the alignment on a course document but does not explain the alignment to the students or why it is important

Extensively uses learning-centered approaches. Instructor:

- Explicitly, coherently, and consistently aligns objectives/learning outcomes, teaching/learning methods, and assessment methods **AND**
- Clearly explains and uses this alignment in the course materials

(Continues)

TABLE B.1. (Continued)

Construct I: Role of Instructor

Action

The instructor creates a supportive and success-oriented environment for learning and accomplishment for all students through proactive clear and overt course-specific success techniques.

Rubric Quality Levels

Uses instructor-centered approaches. Instructor:

- Acts, or has an attitude, or uses instructional methods that do not create a supportive environment for all **OR**
- Receives feedback that the environment is not supportive of learning and success for all students because of instructor actions or attitude **AND**
- Does not attempt to improve the environment

Minimally uses learning-centered approaches. Instructor:

- Is available to help students to answer questions or offer clarification **OR**
- Encourages or invites weaker students to come for one-on-one help or extra sessions or tutoring **OR**
- Suggests campus resources where students can get additional help to succeed

Mostly uses learning-centered approaches. Instructor:

- Intentionally strives to create a supportive and success-oriented environment for all students **AND**
- Gives clear and overt specific techniques to help students to succeed (not just generic advice) in one-on-one situations or when students ask for help

Extensively uses learning-centered approaches. Instructor:

- Explicitly addresses clear and overt specific techniques to help students to succeed (not just generic advice). Advice should be given to all students **AND**
- Explains to students how these methods promote student success for all

(Continues)

TABLE B.1. (Continued)

Construct I: Role of Instructor

Action

The instructor creates an inclusive and welcoming environment for learning and success for all students by acknowledging and accepting diversity and differences in background.

Rubric Quality Levels

Uses instructor-centered approaches. Instructor:

- Receives feedback that the class's or institution's environment is not inclusive of all diverse and different backgrounds **AND**
- Does not make changes to be more inclusive

Minimally uses learning-centered approaches. Instructor:

- Does not focus on creating an inclusive or welcoming learning environment **OR**
- Teaches without regard to diversity or differences in background

Mostly uses learning-centered approaches. Instructor:

- Intentionally and consistently includes examples that relate to diversity and differences in background **AND**
- Intentionally considers diversity while promoting inclusion when requiring students to work in groups or to interact with each other

Extensively uses learning-centered approaches. Instructor:

- Creates an inclusive and welcoming environment that responds to and benefits from differences to foster the development and learning of all students. This environment is characterized by mutual reciprocity and respect **AND**
- Promotes discussion of diversity and differences in background and abilities in an inclusive and welcoming environment

(Continues)

TABLE B.1. (Continued)

Construct I: Role of Instructor

Action

The instructor explicitly states the chosen teaching/learning methods and explains why they promote deep student learning and foster future use of learning.

Rubric Quality Levels

Uses instructor-centered approaches. Instructor:

- Does not mention anything about teaching and learning methods to students **OR**
- Does not explain how the chosen teaching/learning methods promote deep student learning and foster future use of learning

Minimally uses learning-centered approaches. Instructor:

- Identifies the teaching and learning methods used on the syllabus without further explanation **OR**
- Explains choice of teaching and learning methods without being clear that they promote deep student learning and foster future use of learning

Mostly uses learning-centered approaches. Instructor:

- Describes the teaching and learning methods used in the course on the syllabus, course site on the learning management system, and through interactions with students **OR**
- Explains how the chosen teaching/learning methods promote deep student learning and foster future use of learning

Extensively uses learning-centered approaches. Instructor:

- Explicitly addresses how the students should use the teaching and learning methods employed in the course and explains why they are used to further learning throughout the course **AND**
- Models ideal student behaviors to achieve deep learning such as the following:
  - How they should work in groups
  - Expectations for participation

(Continues)

TABLE B.1. (Continued)

Construct II: Development of Student Responsibility for Learning

Action

The instructor sets student expectations, which enable the responsibility for learning to be shared between the instructor and the students with a greater amount assumed by the students.

Rubric Quality Levels

Uses instructor-centered approaches. Instructor:

- ○ Assumes responsibility for student learning by any of the following:
  - ▪ Does not set student expectations or does not inform students of these expectations
  - ▪ Provides detailed notes, complete presentations, extensive reading guides
  - ▪ Tells students exactly what will be on examinations
  - ▪ Constantly reminds students of assignments, deadlines, or test dates
  - ▪ Provides students with missing papers, syllabi, or another course material **OR**
- ○ Receives feedback that instructor micromanages students which allows them to not accept responsibility for their learning and does not change behaviors

Minimally uses learning-centered approaches. Instructor:

- ○ States on the syllabus that students and instructors should share responsibility for learning without further explanation **OR**
- ○ States expectations for learning, assignments, time commitment **OR**
- ○ Encourages students to know where to find information about assignments, deadlines, and so on without telling them the answer

Mostly uses learning-centered approaches. Instructor's actions illustrate that students should assume the responsibility for learning:

- ○ Explains on the syllabus and in class what taking responsibility for learning means **AND**
- ○ Provides opportunities for students to assume responsibility for their own learning and explains the rationale **OR**
- ○ Informally explains how students should take responsibility for their learning, when requested by students. This explanation may be in one-on-one interactions or in an out-of-class experience

Extensively uses learning-centered approaches. Instructor actively fosters students to take responsibility for their learning:

- ○ Explains what taking responsibility for learning means through repeated, concrete examples **AND**
- ○ Provides opportunities for students to assume responsibility for their own learning throughout the course **AND**
- ○ Explicitly and intentionally explains how students assume responsibility and how to take responsibility actively, using explanations and teaching systematically done with everyone and not just those who seek extra help

(Continues)

TABLE B.1. (Continued)

Construct II: Development of Student Responsibility for Learning

Action

The instructor helps students to develop responsibility for learning by providing scaffolding support. At the beginning the instructor provides more support and feedback, and as the semester progresses the instructor expects increasing student independence.

Rubric Quality Levels

Uses instructor-centered approaches. Instructor:

- Does not provide scaffolding support **OR**
- Does not increase expectations for student independence

Minimally uses learning-centered approaches. Instructor:

- Provides the same amount and type of scaffolding support throughout the semester **OR**
- Provides the same scaffolding to all students without recognizing that some students might need more or less support

Mostly uses learning-centered approaches. Instructor:

- Informally models how to do things independently, when requested by students; this modeling may be in one-on-one interactions or in an out-of-class experience **OR**
- Provides additional scaffolding support to some students when they request it and may provide different types of scaffolding to these students, as needed **OR**
- Removes scaffolding support as the semester progresses

Extensively uses learning-centered approaches. Instructor:

- Explicitly, intentionally models responsibility, teaching how to take responsibility actively; this modeling or teaching must be systematically done with everyone and not just those who seek extra help **AND**
- Provides different types of scaffolding support as needed: procedural for process, conceptual for content organization, and/or metacognitive for goal setting, planning, organizing, self-monitoring, and self-evaluation **AND**
- Removes scaffolding support in an intentional manner, thus allowing students to take more responsibility as the course progresses **AND**
- Recognizes when students are not yet ready to take such responsibility **AND**
- Responds to individual students' needs for scaffolding support throughout the course

(Continues)

TABLE B.1. (Continued)

Construct II: Development of Student Responsibility for Learning

Action

The instructor fosters development of learning or learning to learn skills that are directed toward school success. Examples of these learning skills include the following:

- *Time management*
- *Self-monitoring*
- *Goal setting*
- *How to read independently*

Rubric Quality Levels

Uses instructor-centered approaches. Instructor:

- Allows students to meet course objectives without developing further learning skills **OR**
- Assumes students will develop learning skills without assistance **OR**
- Does not consider learning skills **OR**
- Considers learning skills irrelevant

Minimally uses learning-centered approaches. Instructor:

- Does not teach the development of any learning or learning to learn skills to foster school success **OR**
- Provides three or fewer opportunities for students to practice at least one of these learning skills due to the nature of the course requirements; instructor does not pay much attention to these learning skills

Mostly uses learning-centered approaches. Instructor:

- Intentionally teaches appropriate learning or learning to learn skills to foster school success **AND**
- Provides opportunities throughout the course for students to practice at least two learning skills

Extensively uses learning-centered approaches. Instructor must meet criteria for mostly uses learning-centered approaches **AND**

- Explicitly facilitates students to develop various and appropriate skills for further learning **AND**
- Provides formative feedback to all students on their development **AND**
- Assesses these learning skills and not just the product of the use of these skills

(Continues)

TABLE B.1. (Continued)

Construct II: Development of Student Responsibility for Learning

Action

The instructor fosters the development of self-directed, lifelong learning skills. Examples of these lifelong learning skills include the following:

- *Determining a personal need to know more on a regular basis, or possessing an inquiring mind*
- *Having information literacy skills of finding, evaluating, and using information ethically*
- *Acquiring a range of strategies for learning in diverse contexts*
- *Determining when need to know about a topic is met*
- *Fostering a growth mind-set attitude*

Rubric Quality Levels

Uses instructor-centered approaches. Instructor:

- ○ Allows students to meet course objectives without developing deep, self-directed, lifelong learning skills **OR**
- ○ Assumes students will develop self-directed learning skills without assistance **OR**
- ○ Does not consider self-directed learning skills **OR**
- ○ Considers self-directed learning skills irrelevant to the course **OR**
- ○ Does not foster a growth mind-set attitude

Minimally uses learning-centered approaches. Instructor:

- ○ Does not teach how to develop any of the self-directed or lifelong learning skills **OR**
- ○ Does not foster the development of a growth mind-set attitude **OR**
- ○ Provides three or fewer opportunities for students to practice at least one of these self-directed, lifelong learning skills due to the nature of the course requirements. The instructor does not pay much attention to these learning skills

Mostly uses learning-centered approaches. Instructor:

- ○ Intentionally teaches many of the appropriate self-directed, lifelong learning skills **AND**
- ○ Provides opportunities throughout the course for students to practice at least two self-directed, lifelong learning skills **AND**
- ○ Intentionally fosters a growth mind-set attitude

Extensively uses learning-centered approaches. Instructor must meet criteria for mostly uses learning-centered approaches **AND**

- ○ Explicitly facilitates student development of various and appropriate lifelong learning skills and growth mind-set attitude **AND**
- ○ Provides formative feedback to all students on their development **AND**
- ○ Assesses these learning skills and not just the product of the use of these skills

(Continues)

Construct II: Development of Student Responsibility for Learning

Action

The instructor fosters students' engagement in reflection and critical review of their learning through well-structured activities. Reflection and critical review should include self-assessment of learning abilities, one's mastery of objectives, and strengths and weaknesses.

Rubric Quality Levels

Uses instructor-centered approaches. Instructor:

- Provides no or very occasional opportunities for student reflection, critical review, and self-assessment of their learning **OR**
- Receives feedback from students that the reflection critical review and self-assessment activities are too unstructured to foster learning and the instructor does not try to improve these activities

Minimally uses learning-centered approaches. Instructor:

- Does not teach how to do reflection, critical review, or self-assessment of their learning **AND**
- Provides three or fewer opportunities for student reflection, critical review, and self-assessment of their learning

Mostly uses learning-centered approaches. Instructor:

- Intentionally teaches how to do reflection, critical review, and self-assessment of learning **AND**
- Provides opportunities throughout the course for student reflection, critical review, and self-assessment of their learning, using activities that are structured and specific enough to allow students to learn from them

Extensively uses learning-centered approaches. Instructor must meet criteria for mostly uses learning-centered approaches **AND**

- Explicitly facilitates student development of reflection, critical review, and self-assessment skills of their learning **AND**
- Provides formative feedback to all students on their ability to reflect and conduct critical review and self-assessment of their learning **AND**
- Assesses reflection, critical review, and self-assessment skills of learning and not just the product of the use of these skills **AND**
- Explains how and why these periodic opportunities for student reflection, critical review, and self-assessment result in greater student understanding

(Continues)

TABLE B.1. (Continued)

Construct II: Development of Student Responsibility for Learning

Action

The instructor fosters the students' use of metacognitive skills and habits of the mind to assist students to solve real-life problems and to gain a positive outcome. Examples of these metacognitive skills include the following:

- *Planning*
- *Monitoring*
- *Evaluating*

Frequently cited examples of habits of the mind include the following:

- *Ability to postpone judgment/managing impulsivity*
- *Creativity/creating, imagining, innovating*
- *Curiosity/questioning and posing problems*
- *Flexibility*
- *Interdependent learning and working*
- *Openness/listening with understanding and empathy*
- *Persistence*
- *Responsible risk-taking*
- *Striving for accuracy, clarity, and precision*
- *Transfer of learning/applying past knowledge to new situations*

Rubric Quality Levels

Uses instructor-centered approaches. Instructor:

- Allows students to meet course objectives without fostering the use of metacognitive skills and habits of the mind **OR**
- Does not consider metacognitive skills and habits of the mind **OR**
- Considers metacognitive skills and habits of the mind irrelevant

Minimally uses learning-centered approaches. Instructor:

- Does not teach how to develop any of the metacognitive skills and habits of the mind to solve real-life problems and to gain a positive outcome **AND**
- Provides three or fewer opportunities for students to practice at least one of these metacognitive skills and habits of the mind; instructor does not pay much attention to these metacognitive skills and habits of the mind

Mostly uses learning-centered approaches. Instructor:

- Must model or teach intentionally five or more metacognitive skills and habits of the mind **AND**
- Provides students opportunities throughout the course for student to practice five or more metacognitive skills and habits of the mind to solve real-life problems and to gain a positive outcome

(Continues)

Action

The instructor fosters students' use of metacognitive skills and habits of the mind (continued).

Extensively uses learning-centered approaches. Instructor must meet criteria for mostly uses learning-centered approaches **AND**

- ° Explicitly facilitates student development of various and appropriate metacognitive skills and habits of the mind to solve real-life problems and to gain a positive outcome **AND**
- ° Teaches individual or groups of students how to use metacognitive skills when deficiencies are detected **AND**
- ° Provides formative feedback to all students on their development **AND**
- ° Explains how and why using metacognitive skills and habits of the mind assist students to solve real-life problems and to gain a positive outcome **AND**
- ° Assesses these metacognitive skills and habits of the mind and not just the product of the use of these skills and habits

(Continues)

TABLE B.1. (Continued)

Construct III: Function of Content

Action

The instructor uses organizing schemes that are discipline-specific conceptual frameworks to integrate material and provide a context for further learning. Organizing schemes are discipline-specific conceptual frameworks that help experts integrate much of the material and to learn new material. Novices have not organized the content well enough to use them unless they are explicitly taught. Examples include the following:

- *The periodic table of chemical elements is an organizing scheme in chemistry.*
- *Homeostasis is an organizing theme in physiology.*
- *Moving toward modernity is an organizing theme in history.*
- *Dewey decimal system or the Library of Congress system for organizing books for librarians.*

Rubric Quality Levels

Uses instructor-centered approaches. Instructor:

- Does not use organizing schemes in teaching

Minimally uses learning-centered approaches. Instructor:

- Uses organizing schemes to plan the overall scope and sequence of the course **BUT**
- Does not convey these organizing schemes to the students **OR**
- Informally models how to use organizing schemes in one-on-one interactions or in an out-of-class experience

Mostly uses learning-centered approaches. Instructor:

- Uses organizing schemes to formulate student learning outcomes and states them on the syllabus **AND**
- Teaches students how to learn using organizing schemes. This teaching is done systematically with everyone and not just those who seek extra help **AND**
- Provides students 10 or more opportunities to use organizing schemes

Extensively uses learning-centered approaches. Instructor must meet criteria for mostly uses learning-centered approaches **AND**

- Explicitly uses organizing schemes throughout the course to create student learning outcomes, teaching/learning activities, and assessment activities **AND**
- Frequently discusses these organizing schemes to help students learn content **AND**
- Provides formative feedback to all students on their use of organizing schemes **AND**
- Uses assessments that require students to demonstrate that they integrate content into organizing schemes

(Continues)

Construct III: Function of Content

Action

The instructor promotes meaningful student engagement with the content. This engagement of content occurs through personal meaning-making to facilitate mastery.

Rubric Quality Levels

Uses instructor-centered approaches. Instructor:

- Allows students to memorize content as it was given to them without requiring understanding or without placing into a context **OR**
- Uses assessments in which student can succeed without knowing the material (e.g., open-book factual exams)

Minimally uses learning-centered approaches. Instructor:

- Requires minimal transformation or creation of their own meaning of the content **OR**
- Assesses students such that they can succeed without really understanding or reflecting on the content

Mostly uses learning-centered approaches. Instructor:

- Requires students to articulate concepts in their own words and to develop associations with the content **OR**
- Requires students to transform and reflect on the content to make their own meaning **AND**
- Uses some assessments that require students to demonstrate meaning of concepts

Extensively uses learning-centered approaches. Instructor:

- Requires students to transform and reflect on all the content to create their own meaning **OR**
- Requires students to do something integrative using material from the course in a large assignment or activity **AND**
- Uses assessments consistently that require students to demonstrate that they have created meaning of the content

---

(Continues)

TABLE B.1. (Continued)

Construct III: Function of Content

Action

The instructor fosters the development and use of discipline-specific methodologies. Examples of these discipline-specific methodologies include the following:

- *Reading articles written by scholars in the discipline*
- *Reading primary source material in the discipline*
- *Evaluating evidence*
- *Communicating using the conventions of the discipline (e.g., proper citations, use of equations)*
- *Conducting research that is appropriate for the level of the course*
- *Acquiring laboratory skills*

Rubric Quality Levels

Uses instructor-centered approaches. Instructor:

○ Does not help students acquire discipline-specific methodologies that they need in the course

Minimally uses learning-centered approaches. Instructor:

○ Provides three or fewer opportunities to practice at least one of these methodologies **OR**
○ Encourages or invites weaker students to come for one-on-one help on these discipline-specific methodologies **OR**
○ Informally models how to use discipline-specific methodologies when requested by students; modeling may be in one-on-one interactions or in an out-of-class experience

Mostly uses learning-centered approaches. Instructor:

○ Teaches appropriate discipline-specific methodologies with some intent. This teaching is done systematically with everyone and not just those who seek extra help **OR**
○ Provides repeated opportunities to learn and practice at least two of these methodologies, using activities that are structured and specific enough to allow students to learn from them
○ Provides assistance when students are practicing discipline-specific methodologies

Extensively uses learning-centered approaches. Instructor must meet criteria for mostly uses learning-centered approaches **AND**

○ Explicitly facilitates students to develop appropriate discipline-specific methodologies **AND**
○ Provides formative feedback to all students on their ability to use discipline-specific methodologies **AND**
○ Assesses these discipline-specific methodologies and not just the product of the use of these methodologies

(Continues)

Construct III: Function of Content

Action
In addition to building a knowledge base, the instructor helps students understand why they need to learn the content for use in their careers or personal growth.

Rubric Quality Levels

Uses instructor-centered approaches. Instructor:

- Only uses content to build a knowledge base **OR**
- Does not help students understand why they need to learn the content for use in their careers or personal growth

Minimally uses learning-centered approaches. Instructor:

- Helps students recognize why they need to learn the content **OR**
- Provides very limited (e.g., fewer than three) opportunities to help students understand why they need to learn the content

Mostly uses learning-centered approaches. Instructor:

- Provides 10 or more opportunities to help students understand why they need to learn the content for use in their careers or personal growth **OR**
- Gives students five or more opportunities to discuss the relevance to their careers or their personal growth **OR**
- Gives students five or more opportunities to practice using the content for their careers or personal growth **OR**
- With 50% or more of the assignments, students are required to explain why or to show how they can use content in other contexts that relate to their careers or their personal growth

Extensively uses learning-centered approaches. Instructor must meet the criteria for mostly uses learning-centered approaches **AND**

- Provides formative feedback to all students on their ability to explain why or show how they use content in other contexts that relate to their careers or their personal growth **AND**
- Student work on applications to their careers or their lives is graded and counts in their final grade

(Continues)

TABLE B.1. (Continued)

Construct III: Function of Content

Action

The instructor provides practice using inquiry or ways of thinking in the discipline to solve discipline-specific, real-world problems that are appropriate for the level of the course.

Uses instructor-centered approaches. Instructor:

- Does not use content to help students practice using inquiry or ways of thinking in the discipline to solve discipline-specific or real-world problems **OR**
- Does not teach inquiry or ways of thinking in the discipline to solve discipline-specific or real-world problems **OR**
- Assesses students ability to use inquiry or ways of thinking in the discipline to solve discipline-specific or real-world problems, without previously providing instruction or practice

Minimally uses learning-centered approaches. Instructor:

- Helps students recognize how why and how inquiry or ways of thinking in the discipline can solve discipline-specific or real-world problems **OR**
- Provides very limited opportunities (e.g., three or fewer) to help students practice using inquiry or ways of thinking in the discipline to solve discipline-specific or real-world problems **OR**
- Informally models how to use inquiry or ways of thinking in the discipline to solve discipline-specific or real-world problems, when requested by students; modeling may be in one-on-one interactions or in an out-of-class experience

Mostly uses learning-centered approaches. Instructor:

- Teaches inquiry or ways of thinking in the discipline to solve discipline-specific or real-world problems with some intent. This teaching is done systematically with everyone and not just those who seek extra help **AND**
- Provides students 10 or more opportunities to practice using inquiry or ways of thinking in the discipline to solve discipline-specific or real-world problems **OR**
- With 50% or more of the assignments, students are required to use inquiry or ways of thinking in the discipline to solve discipline-specific or real-world problems

Extensively uses learning-centered approaches. Instructor must meet the criteria for mostly uses learning-centered approaches **AND**

- Explicitly facilitates students' ability to develop ways of thinking in the discipline to solve discipline-specific or real-world problems independently **AND**
- Provides repeated (at least weekly) student practice using inquiry or ways of thinking in the discipline to solve discipline-specific or real-world problems **AND**
- Provides formative feedback to all students on their ability to use inquiry or ways of thinking in the discipline to solve discipline-specific or real-world problems **AND**
- Requires students to use inquiry or ways of thinking in the discipline to solve discipline-specific or real-world problems. This work is graded and counts enough in their final grade for it to matter to the students

(Continues)

TABLE B.1. (Continued)

Construct III: Function of Content

Action

The instructor helps students acquire in-depth conceptual understanding of the content to facilitate deep and future learning and develop transferable skills.

Rubric Quality Levels

Uses instructor-centered approaches. Instructor:

- Allows students to learn superficially **OR**
- Does not provide opportunities for students to apply knowledge to new content or contexts **OR**
- Does not encourage the development of transferable skills

Minimally uses learning-centered approaches. Instructor:

- Provides content so the best students can acquire conceptual understanding of the content to facilitate deep learning, but does not actively teach how to do this **OR**
- Provides students with limited (five or fewer) opportunities to apply knowledge to new content **OR**
- Provides students with limited (five or fewer) opportunities to gain and practice transferable skills **OR**
- Informally models how to acquire in-depth conceptual understanding of the content to facilitate deep and future learning and develop transferable skills, when requested by students; modeling may be in one-on-one interactions or in an out-of-class experience

Mostly uses learning-centered approaches. Instructor:

- Frames content so all students can see how it can be applied in the future **OR**
- Teaches how to acquire in-depth conceptual understanding of the content to facilitate deep and future learning and develop transferable skills, with some intent. This teaching is done systematically with everyone and not just those who seek extra help **AND**
- Requires all students to use content in other contexts

Extensively uses learning-centered approaches. Instructor must meet the criteria for mostly uses learning-centered approaches **AND**:

- Frames and organizes content so students can and do learn additional content that is not taught **AND**
- Provides repeated (at least weekly) student practice acquiring in-depth conceptual understanding of the content to facilitate deep and future learning and develop transferable skills **AND**
- Provides formative feedback to all students on their ability to acquire in-depth conceptual understanding of the content to facilitate deep and future learning and develop transferable skills **AND**
- Requires students to demonstrate deep learning and further learning on their own in a large paper or project, in an assignment that counts enough toward the grade that students take it seriously

(Continues)

TABLE B.1. (Continued)

Construct IV: Purposes and Processes of Student Assessment

Action
The instructor integrates assessment and learning.

Rubric Quality Levels

Uses instructor-centered approaches. Instructor:

- Does not integrate assessment and learning **OR**
- Does not provide students an indication of how well they are doing in time to make change or improve

Minimally uses learning-centered approaches. Instructor:

- Returns student work in a timely manner with comments that could help students learn from their previous mistakes **OR**
- Briefly answers student questions once graded work is returned

Mostly uses learning-centered approaches. Instructor:

- Integrates learning with assessment and assessment with learning **AND**
- Spends time going over answers to exams, explaining what constitutes an excellent answer **OR**
- Helps students to see assessment as part of the learning process **OR**
- Allows students to justify their answers

Extensively uses learning-centered approaches. Instructor meets the criteria for mostly uses learning-centered approach **AND**:

- Continuously integrates assessment within the learning process through regular formal and informal assessments **AND**
- Provides students with standards of what constitutes outstanding, good, and average work

(Continues)

Construct IV: Purposes and Processes of Student Assessment

Action

The instructor uses fair, objective, and consistent policies and standards to assess all students.

Rubric Quality Levels

Uses instructor-centered approaches. Instructor:

- ° Does not establish assessment policies and standards **OR**
- ° Does not consistently enforce fair and objective assessment policies and standards **OR**
- ° Provides final grades without a rationale for the grade

Minimally uses learning-centered approaches. Instructor:

- ° Develops fair, objective, and consistent policies and standards to assess all students **OR**
- ° Consistently uses specified grading standards such as grading rubrics or specified weights for projects and assignments

Mostly uses learning-centered approaches. Instructor:

- ° Maintains consistency, fairness, and equity in applying all policies and standards to assess all students, using policies and standards that are listed on the syllabus, but not discussed further **AND**
- ° Consistently uses specified grading standards such as grading rubrics or specified weights for projects and assignments, using standards about which students are informed in advance of due dates

Extensively uses learning-centered approaches. Instructor:

- ° Maintains consistency, fairness, and equity in applying all policies and standards to assess all students, using standards and policies that are explained to the students throughout the course **AND**
- ° Consistently uses specified grading standards such as grading rubrics or specified weights for projects and assignments, using standards about which students are informed in advance of due dates and about which they can ask questions **AND**
- ° Maintains a policy that allows students to know how they can improve upon previous efforts and have assessments graded prior to the handing in of the next assessment

(Continues)

Construct IV: Purposes and Processes of Student Assessment

Action

The instructor provides students with frequent, useful, and timely formative feedback to foster learning gains.

Rubric Quality Levels

Uses instructor-centered approaches. Instructor:

- Grades assignments without offering recommendations for improvement **OR**
- Overwhelms students with too much feedback, especially on repeated mistakes, spelling, and grammar **OR**
- Provides students with no constructive feedback **OR**
- Does not return student work in a timely way **OR**
- Is aware of complaints that the students have no idea what grade they are getting or how they earned their final grade and does not attempt to remediate the situation

Minimally uses learning-centered approaches. Instructor:

- Provides students with limited or not useful constructive feedback **AND**
- Makes positive comments only or never makes positive comments **OR**
- Helps clarify what good performance is in terms of goals, criteria, and expected standards **OR**
- Provides formative feedback only to students who seek it and not to the entire class

Mostly uses learning-centered approaches. Instructor:

- Delivers high-quality and information-rich feedback to students about their progress toward meeting the learning outcomes **AND**
- Makes recommendations for improvement without grading or praising **OR**
- Gives all students formative feedback that provides insights into how to improve **OR**
- Provides all students with constructive feedback following assignments **AND**
- Provides constructive feedback in a timely and beneficial manner

Extensively uses learning-centered approaches. Instructor must meet the criteria for the mostly uses learning-centered approaches **AND**:

- Discloses the gap between current and desired level of performance and provides opportunities for students to work to reduce the gap between these two levels **AND**
- Encourages a dialogue around learning between the feedback giver and receiver **AND**
- Integrates formative feedback and constructive feedback to all students consistently **AND**
- Grades recent student performance considering if students incorporate previous formative feedback

(Continues)

TABLE B.1. (Continued)

Construct IV: Purposes and Processes of Student Assessment

Action
The instructor promotes the use of student peer and self-assessment.

Rubric Quality Levels

Uses instructor-centered approaches. Instructor:

- ° Does not consider peer and self-assessment relevant **OR**
- ° Does not provide students opportunities for peer and self-assessment **OR**
- ° Allows students to determine their own or their peer's grade without the instructor's oversight

Minimally uses learning-centered approaches. Instructor:

- ° Requires students to use peer and self-assessments once or twice **OR**
- ° Does not factor peer and self-assessments into final grade

Mostly uses learning-centered approaches. Instructor:

- ° Teaches students how to meaningfully conduct peer and self-assessments **AND**
- ° Requires students to use peer and self-assessments five or more times during a course **AND**
- ° Counts peer and self-assessment in the final grade guided by the instructor's oversight

Extensively uses learning-centered approaches. Instructor meets the criterion for uses mostly learning-centered approaches **AND**:
- ° Models how to conduct meaningful peer and self-assessments **AND**
- ° Routinely requires students to use peer and self-assessments **AND**
- ° Provides feedback to students on how well they conduct peer and self-assessments **AND**
- ° Counts peer and self-assessment enough that they are taken seriously, and instructor provides oversight on accuracy of feedback

(Continues)

TABLE B.1. (Continued)

Construct IV: Purposes and Processes of Student Assessment

Action
The instructor allows the students to demonstrate mastery of the objectives and ability to learn from mistakes.

Rubric Quality Levels

Uses instructor-centered approaches. Instructor:

- Does not provide any opportunities for students to demonstrate that they learned from mistakes **OR**
- Does not provide any opportunities for students to show mastery beyond the first attempt

Minimally uses a learning-centered approach. Instructor:

- Provides one opportunity for students to demonstrate that they have mastered the material after the first attempt **OR**
- Gives all students the opportunity to seek feedback on one major assignment before it is graded

Mostly uses learning-centered approaches. Instructor:

- Allows all students opportunities to demonstrate that they have learned from mistakes **AND**
- Provides practice quizzes with the correct answers given after each quiz **OR**
- Allows students to find the correct answers in materials created by the instructor or required course materials, write the answer in their own words, and receive partial credit for this redone assignment **OR**
- Encourages all students to seek feedback on one major assignment before it is graded

Extensively uses learning-centered approaches. Instructor:

- Provides regular opportunities for students to demonstrate that they have mastered the objectives. Such opportunities might include the following:
  - Provides practice quizzes with feedback on why answers are incorrect and where to seek more information
  - Allows students to take online quizzes repeatedly, where the best grade counts, using questions that come from a pool of items, so students get different questions on each attempt
  - Provides students opportunity to retake an exam or redo an assignment at least three times during the semester **AND**
- Allows students two or more opportunities to demonstrate mastery of content in an alternative way **AND**
- Allows students to redo graded products or assignments after feedback **AND**
- Allows students to retake exams or exam sections by discussing the content and handing in a group answer

(Continues)

TABLE B.1. (Continued)

Construct IV: Purposes and Processes of Student Assessment

Action
The instructor uses authentic assessment (what practitioners/professionals do).

Rubric Quality Levels

Uses instructor-centered approaches. Instructor:

- Rarely or never uses authentic assessment

Minimally uses learning-centered approaches. Instructor:

- Uses one authentic assessment that is weighted less than 20% of the final grade **OR**
- Uses assessment that have authentic elements that count less than 20% of the final grade

Mostly uses learning-centered approaches. Instructor:

- Uses authentic assessments that are weighted 50% or more of the final grade **OR**
- Uses assessments that have authentic elements that count 50% or more of the final grade **AND**
- Explains to students how these assessments simulate real situations if done in non-real-life situations

Extensively uses learning-centered approaches. Instructor:

- Uses authentic assessments throughout the course that count 80% or more of the final grade **AND**
- Asks practitioners to review these authentic assessments and provide feedback

---

(Continues)

TABLE B.1. (Continued)

Construct V: Balance of Power

Action
The instructor establishes a safe, moral, and ethical environment that empowers all students.

Rubric Quality Levels

Uses instructor-centered approaches. Instructor:

- Uses inappropriate behaviors or expresses inappropriate attitudes **OR**
- Has received feedback that the class or institution is not a safe, moral, and ethical environment for all students **AND**
- Does not make changes to correct these inappropriate behaviors and attitudes

Minimally uses learning-centered approaches. Instructor:

- Abides by ethical and moral standards and laws **AND**
- Provides accommodation for students with disabilities

Mostly uses learning-centered approaches. Instructor meets the criteria for minimally uses learning-centered approaches **AND**:

- Maintains consistency, fairness, and equity in applying all policies and standards to all students **AND**
- Maintains privacy of student records **AND**
- Maintains proper relationships with all students, including on social media

Extensively uses learning-centered approaches. Instructor meets the criteria for mostly uses learning-centered approaches **AND**:

- Encourages and abides by ethical and moral standards and laws **AND**
- Encourages ethical behaviors in academic student conduct **AND**
- Prevents or responds appropriately to violations of harassment or ethical standards **AND**
- Models appropriate ethical and moral behaviors and teaches their importance to students

(Continues)

TABLE B.1. (Continued)

Construct V: Balance of Power

Action
The instructor provides syllabi and other course artifacts demonstrating that students and instructors share power to promote learning.

Rubric Quality Levels

Uses instructor-centered approaches. Instructor:

- Does not mention learning in the syllabus **OR**
- States policies, expectations, and assignments as demands, directives, or ironclad rules **OR**
- Uses tone that sets up adversarial relationship

Minimally uses learning-centered approaches. Instructor:

- States reasons why subject/content are worth learning, important, or interesting **OR**
- States that students and instructor engage in learning together **OR**
- Invites students to learn and grow **OR**
- Discusses personal excitement about learning or about this content **OR**
- Uses an inviting and less controlling tone

Mostly uses learning-centered approaches. Instructor meets the criteria for minimally uses learning-centered approaches **AND**:

- States clearly defined and measurable learning outcomes **AND**
- States what students must do to meet the learning outcomes and how they can earn their grades **AND**
- Explains how and why course will be conducted, what students will do in class or online, and how they will prepare for class **OR**
- Explains how students can succeed **OR**
- Seeks feedback on the tone of the syllabus

Extensively uses learning-centered approaches. Instructor meets the criteria for mostly uses learning-centered approaches **AND**:

- Uses a welcoming tone that shows that the instructor is approachable and a human being **AND**
- Makes all of the following types of statements:
  - Clearly defined and measurable learning outcomes and how they fit with the larger educational program's outcomes
  - How students will get useable feedback on how they are doing throughout the course
  - How the instructor will know if teaching is helping students reach learning objectives **OR**
- Makes an explicit statement about sharing power **OR**
- Gives motivational messages that set lofty yet achievable goals

(Continues)

TABLE B.1. (Continued)

Construct V: Balance of Power

Action
The instructor allows for some flexibility on course policies, assessment methods, learning methods, deadlines, or how students earn grades. Instructor informs students of decisions.

Rubric Quality Levels

Uses instructor-centered approaches. Instructor:

- Mandates all policies, learning and assessment methods, and deadlines **OR**
- Does not adhere to stated policies **OR**
- Allows some students flexibility in deadlines or how they earn grades but does not let other students know about these possibilities

Minimally uses learning-centered approaches. Instructor:

- Informs students of policies, methods, deadlines, and how student earn grades **AND**
- Consistently maintains and enforces all of the preceding **AND**
- Is flexible on one of the following: course policies, learning processes, assessment methods, deadlines, or how students earn grades **AND**
- Allows all students the same flexibility

Mostly uses learning-centered approaches. Instructor:

- Is flexible on at least two of the following: course policies, learning processes, assessment methods, deadlines, and how students earn grades **AND**
- Always adheres to what has been agreed upon **OR**
- Provides participation options for some activities (e.g., allowing students to participate in class discussions or using online discussion boards after the class) **AND**
- Seeks feedback on policies, methods, and deadlines

Extensively uses learning-centered approaches. Instructor meets criteria for uses mostly learning-centered approaches **AND**:

- Is flexible on at least four aspects of the following: course policies, learning processes, assessment methods, deadlines, and how students earn grades **AND**
- Actively seeks student feedback on policies, processes, methods, attendance options, and deadlines and responds to their feedback with appropriate and considered changes

(Continues)

TABLE B.1. (Continued)

Construct V: Balance of Power

Action
The instructor provides students opportunities to learn and helps students to recognize when they have missed opportunities to learn.

Rubric Quality Levels

Uses instructor-centered approaches. Instructor:

- Does not allow opportunities to learn beyond what the instructor does or required reading **OR**
- Frames all learning as required for grades

Minimally uses learning-centered approaches. Instructor:

- Provides alternative learning opportunities beyond instructor and required reading **AND**
- Provides opportunities to learn, such as discussions, peer feedback, or out-of-class experiences that count 5% to 10% of the final grade

Mostly uses learning-centered approaches. Instructor meets the criteria for minimally uses learning-centered approaches **AND**:

- Explains how varied activities are learning opportunities **AND**
- Encourages learning for life in addition to learning for school **OR**
- Creates high impact learning activities that may extend beyond the classroom, which count 25% or more of the final grade

Extensively uses learning-centered approaches. Instructor meets the criteria for mostly uses learning-centered approaches **AND**

- Helps students to take advantage of opportunities to learn even if they are not graded **AND**
- Fosters understanding of consequences of not taking advantage of learning opportunities **AND**
- Empowers students to recognize why they should learn even if it is not required **AND**
- Fosters learning to occur beyond the course or learning for life, not just learning for school

(Continues)

TABLE B.1. (Continued)

Construct V: Balance of Power

Action

The instructor empowers students learning through appropriate freedom of expression, for example by encouraging alternative perspectives, open-ended assignments, or the ability to determine some course content.

Rubric Quality Levels

Uses instructor-centered approaches. Instructor:

- Does not allow freedom of expression in any form **OR**
- Demonstrates that the instructor's perspective is the only acceptable one **OR**
- Entirely determines course content, including assigning topics to students for large papers, presentations, or projects

Minimally uses learning-centered approaches. Instructor:

- Allows freedom of expression in any form during less than 20% of the course **OR**
- Allows students to select their own topics for large papers, presentations, or projects

Mostly uses learning-centered approaches. Instructor:

- Allows students freedom of expression by encouraging alternative perspectives, when appropriate, open-ended assignments, or the ability to determine some course content they want to learn about 50% of the time **AND**
- Listens to students' perspectives and does not indicate that they are wrong even if they do not agree with the instructor

Extensively uses learning-centered approaches. Instructor meets the criteria for mostly uses learning-centered approaches **AND**:

- Encourages and empowers students to express alternative perspectives, when appropriate, even when instructor disagrees **AND**
- Facilitates students having a voice in determining optional or additional content to be learned **OR**
- Evaluates students through assignments that are open-ended or allows alternative paths, using assessments that count 80% of the total grade

(Continues)

TABLE B.1. (Continued)

Construct V: Balance of Power

Action
The instructor responds to feedback from students to improve teaching and learning.

Rubric Quality Levels

Uses instructor-centered approaches. Instructor:

- Does not solicit feedback from students **OR**
- Does not use feedback provided by students

Minimally uses learning-centered approaches. Instructor:

- Considers all student feedback offered through standard course evaluation forms **AND**
- Reflects on all feedback received, but does not make an action plan to improve **OR**
- Makes small changes because of feedback

Mostly uses learning-centered approaches. Instructor:

- Asks for feedback on at least three aspects of the course, including teaching approach, content, assessment methods, schedule of assignments, readings, policies, or workload; feedback may be solicited beyond the standard course evaluations **AND**
- Uses student feedback to develop an action plan **AND**
- Continues to seek student feedback to refine action plan

Extensively uses learning-centered approaches. Instructor meets the criteria for mostly learning-centered approaches **AND:**

- Seeks feedback early enough in the course to make changes for the current students, when possible **OR**
- Makes changes to teaching approach, schedule, policies, or assessment methods, because of student feedback **AND**
- Tells students about changes made as result of feedback

Determining the Appropriate Score
Use the following methods to arrive at an appropriate score and record the appropriate rubrics score and documentation on Table B.2:

- If you sometimes (more than minimally, but less than mostly) use a learning-centered teaching approach, you can score it a 2. This may occur with the rubrics that indicate percentage of use, such as the action "the instructor uses authentic assessment."
- If your actions do not quite meet the criteria for extensively using learning-centered teaching, but exceed mostly, you can score it 3.5.

- Indicate your rationale and support for these choices in the last section of Table B.2 titled "Evidence to Support this Rating." Because you may be using these rubrics over time or sharing them with others, it is essential that you document how you have reached your ratings. Therefore, each rubric asks you to provide evidence to support a rating.
- List any suggestions for improvement that come from the rubric descriptions

Use the template Table C.1 in Appendix C to aggregate all of these scores.

TABLE B.2. Rubric Score Summary and Documentation for Each Action for the Five Constructs

Construct I: Role of Instructor

Action

The instructor develops and uses challenging, reasonable, and measurable learning outcomes that foster the acquisition of appropriate knowledge, skills, or values. These learning outcomes should be consistent with the goals of the educational program.

Rubric Scoring

☐ Uses instructor-centered approaches = 0

☐ Minimally uses learning-centered approaches = 1

☐ Mostly uses learning-centered approaches = 3

☐ Extensively uses learning-centered approaches = 4

☐ No evidence to support rating = NA

Evidence to support this rating: Briefly summarize.

Document location of evidence (i.e., syllabus, assignment). Attach and notate.

Suggestions for improvement:

Action

The instructor uses teaching/learning methods and educational technologies that promote the achievement of student learning outcomes such as knowledge acquisition, application, critical thinking, or solving problems related to the content.

Rubric Scoring

☐ Uses instructor-centered approaches =0

☐ Minimally uses learning-centered approaches = 1

☐ Mostly uses learning-centered approaches = 3

☐ Extensively uses learning-centered approaches = 4

☐ No evidence to support rating = NA

Evidence to support this rating: Briefly summarize.

(Continues)

TABLE B.2. (Continued)

Document location of evidence (i.e., syllabus, assignment). Attach and notate.

Suggestions for improvement:

Action
The instructor aligns the three essential components of a course (learning outcomes, teaching/learning methods and assessment measures) in terms of content and consistent verbs representing the same cognitive processing/intellectual skill demands placed on the students.

Rubric Scoring

☐ Uses instructor-centered approaches = 0
☐ Minimally uses learning-centered approaches = 1
☐ Mostly uses learning-centered approaches = 3
☐ Extensively uses learning-centered approaches = 4
☐ No evidence to support rating = NA

Evidence to support this rating: Briefly summarize.

Document location of evidence (i.e., syllabus, assignment). Attach and notate.

Suggestions for improvement:

Action
The instructor creates a supportive and success-oriented environment for learning and accomplishment for all students through proactive clear and overt course-specific success techniques.

Rubric Scoring

☐ Uses instructor-centered approaches = 0
☐ Minimally uses learning-centered approaches = 1
☐ Mostly uses learning-centered approaches = 3
☐ Extensively uses learning-centered approaches = 4
☐ No evidence to support rating = NA
Evidence to support this rating: Briefly summarize.

Document location of evidence (i.e., syllabus, assignment). Attach and notate.

Suggestions for improvement:

Action

The instructor creates an inclusive and welcoming environment for learning and success for all students by acknowledging and accepting diversity and differences in background.

Rubric Scoring

☐ Uses instructor-centered approaches = 0
☐ Minimally uses learning-centered approaches = 1
☐ Mostly uses learning-centered approaches = 3
☐ Extensively uses learning-centered approaches = 4
☐ No evidence to support rating = NA

Evidence to support this rating: Briefly summarize.

Document location of evidence (i.e., syllabus, assignment). Attach and notate.

Suggestions for improvement:

Action

The instructor is explicit about the chosen teaching/learning methods and explains why they promote deep student learning and foster future use of learning.

Rubric Scoring

☐ Uses instructor-centered approaches = 0
☐ Minimally uses learning-centered approaches = 1
☐ Mostly uses learning-centered approaches = 3
☐ Extensively uses learning-centered approaches = 4
☐ No evidence to support rating = NA

Evidence to support this rating: Briefly summarize.

Document location of evidence (i.e., syllabus, assignment). Attach and notate.

Suggestions for improvement:

TABLE B.2. (Continued)

Construct II: Development of Student Responsibility for Learning

Action

The instructor sets student expectations, which enable the responsibility for learning to be shared between the instructor and the students with a greater amount assumed by the students.

Rubric Scoring

☐ Uses instructor-centered approaches = 0
☐ Minimally uses learning-centered approaches = 1
☐ Mostly uses learning-centered approaches = 3
☐ Extensively uses learning-centered approaches = 4
☐ No evidence to support rating = NA

Evidence to support this rating: Briefly summarize.

Document location of evidence (i.e., syllabus, assignment). Attach and notate.

Suggestions for improvement:

Action

The instructor helps students to develop responsibility for learning by providing scaffolding support. At the beginning the instructor provides more support and feedback, and as the semester progresses the instructor expects increasing student independence.

Rubric Scoring

☐ Uses instructor-centered approaches = 0
☐ Minimally uses learning-centered approaches = 1
☐ Mostly uses learning-centered approaches = 3
☐ Extensively uses learning-centered approaches = 4
☐ No evidence to support rating = NA
Evidence to support this rating: Briefly summarize.

Document location of evidence (i.e., syllabus, assignment). Attach and notate.

Suggestions for improvement:

Action
The instructor fosters development of learning or learning to learn skills that are directed toward school success.

Rubric Scoring

- ☐ Uses instructor-centered approaches = 0
- ☐ Minimally uses learning-centered approaches = 1
- ☐ Mostly uses learning-centered approaches = 3
- ☐ Extensively uses learning-centered approaches = 4
- ☐ No evidence to support rating = NA

Evidence to support this rating: Briefly summarize.

Document location of evidence (i.e., syllabus, assignment). Attach and notate.

Suggestions for improvement:

Action
The instructor fosters the development of self-directed, lifelong learning skills.

Rubric Scoring

- ☐ Uses instructor-centered approaches = 0
- ☐ Minimally uses learning-centered approaches = 1
- ☐ Mostly uses learning-centered approaches = 3
- ☐ Extensively uses learning-centered approaches = 4
- ☐ No evidence to support rating = NA

Evidence to support this rating: Briefly summarize.

(Continues)

TABLE B.2. (Continued)

Document location of evidence (i.e., syllabus, assignment). Attach and notate.

Suggestions for improvement:

Action

The instructor fosters students' engagement in reflection and critical review of their learning through well-structured activities.

Rubric Scoring

☐ Uses instructor-centered approaches = 0
☐ Minimally uses learning-centered approaches = 1
☐ Mostly uses learning-centered approaches = 3
☐ Extensively uses learning-centered approaches = 4
☐ No evidence to support rating = NA

Evidence to support this rating: Briefly summarize.

Document location of evidence (i.e., syllabus, assignment). Attach and notate.

Suggestions for improvement:

Action

The instructor fosters the students' use of metacognitive skills and habits of the mind to assist students to solve real-life problems and to gain a positive outcome.

Rubric Scoring

☐ Uses instructor-centered approaches = 0
☐ Minimally uses a learning-centered approach = 1
☐ Mostly uses learning-centered approaches = 3
☐ Extensively uses learning-centered approaches = 4
☐ No evidence to support rating = NA

Evidence to support this rating: List the metacognitive skills and habits of the mind that you teach, provide student opportunities to practice and/or assess.

Briefly summarize the evidence.

Document location of evidence (i.e., syllabus, assignment). Attach and notate.

Suggestions for improvement:

Construct III: Function of Content

Action

The instructor uses organizing schemes that are discipline-specific conceptual frameworks to integrate material and provide a context for further learning.

Rubric Scoring

☐ Uses instructor-centered approaches = 0
☐ Minimally uses learning-centered approaches = 1
☐ Mostly uses learning-centered approaches = 3
☐ Extensively uses learning-centered approaches = 4
☐ No evidence to support rating = NA

Evidence to support this rating: List the organizing schemes used:

Briefly summarize the evidence.

Document location of evidence (i.e., syllabus, assignment). Attach and notate.

Suggestions for improvement:

Action

The instructor promotes meaningful student engagement with the content.

(Continues)

TABLE B.2. (Continued)

Rubric Scoring

☐ Uses instructor-centered approaches = 0
☐ Minimally uses learning-centered approaches = 1
☐ Mostly uses learning-centered approaches = 3
☐ Extensively uses learning-centered approaches = 4
☐ No evidence to support rating = NA

Evidence to support this rating: Briefly summarize.

Document location of evidence (i.e., syllabus, assignment). Attach and notate.

Suggestions for improvement:

Action
The instructor fosters the development and use of discipline-specific methodologies

Rubric Scoring

☐ Uses instructor-centered approaches = 0
☐ Minimally uses learning-centered approaches = 1
☐ Mostly uses learning-centered approaches = 3
☐ Extensively uses learning-centered approaches = 4
☐ No evidence to support rating = NA

Evidence to support this rating: Briefly summarize.

Document location of evidence (i.e., syllabus, assignment). Attach and notate.

Suggestions for improvement:

Action
In addition to building a knowledge base, the instructor helps students understand why they need to learn the content for use in their careers or personal growth.

Rubric Scoring

☐ Uses instructor-centered approaches = 0
☐ Minimally uses learning-centered approaches = 1

☐ Mostly uses learning-centered approaches = 3
☐ Extensively uses learning-centered approaches = 4
☐ No evidence to support rating = NA

Evidence to support this rating: Briefly summarize.

Document location of evidence (i.e., syllabus, assignment). Attach and notate.

Suggestions for improvement:

Action

The instructor provides practice using inquiry or ways of thinking in the discipline to solve discipline-specific, real-world problems that are appropriate for the level of the course.

Rubric Scoring

☐ Uses instructor-centered approaches = 0
☐ Minimally uses learning-centered approaches = 1
☐ Mostly uses learning-centered approaches = 3
☐ Extensively uses learning-centered approaches = 4
☐ No evidence to support rating = NA

Evidence to support this rating: Briefly summarize.

Document location of evidence (i.e., syllabus, assignment). Attach and notate.

Suggestions for improvement:

(Continues)

TABLE B.2. (Continued)

Action

The instructor helps students acquire in-depth conceptual understanding of the content to facilitate deep and future learning and develop transferable skills.

Rubric Scoring

☐ Uses instructor-centered approaches = 0
☐ Minimally uses learning-centered approaches = 1
☐ Mostly uses learning-centered approaches = 3
☐ Extensively uses learning-centered approaches = 4
☐ No evidence to support rating = NA

Evidence to support this rating: Briefly summarize.

Document location of evidence (i.e., syllabus, assignment). Attach and notate.

Suggestions for improvement:

Construct IV: Purposes and Processes of Student Assessment

Action

The instructor integrates assessment and learning.

Rubric Scoring

☐ Uses instructor-centered approaches = 0
☐ Minimally uses learning-centered approaches = 1
☐ Mostly uses learning-centered approaches = 3
☐ Extensively uses learning-centered approaches = 4
☐ No evidence to support rating = NA

Evidence to support this rating: Briefly summarize.

Document location of evidence (i.e., syllabus, assignment). Attach and notate.

Suggestions for improvement:

Action

The instructor uses fair, objective, and consistent policies and standards to assess all students.

Rubric Scoring

☐ Uses instructor-centered approaches = 0
☐ Minimally uses learning-centered approaches = 1
☐ Mostly uses learning-centered approaches = 3
☐ Extensively uses learning-centered approaches = 4
☐ No evidence to support rating = NA

Evidence to support this rating: Briefly summarize.

Document location of evidence (i.e., syllabus, assignment). Attach and notate.

Suggestions for improvement:

Action

The instructor provides students with frequent, useful, and timely formative feedback to foster learning gains.

Rubric Scoring

☐ Uses instructor-centered approaches = 0
☐ Minimally uses learning-centered approaches = 1
☐ Mostly uses learning-centered approaches = 3
☐ Extensively uses learning-centered approaches = 4
☐ No evidence to support rating = NA

Evidence to support this rating: Briefly summarize.

Document location of evidence (i.e., syllabus, assignment). Attach and notate.

Suggestions for improvement:

(Continues)

TABLE B.2. (Continued)

Action

The instructor promotes the use of student peer and self-assessment.

Rubric Scoring

☐ Uses instructor-centered approaches = 0
☐ Minimally uses learning-centered approaches = 1
☐ Mostly uses learning-centered approaches = 3
☐ Extensively uses learning-centered approaches = 4
☐ No evidence to support rating = NA

Evidence to support this rating: Briefly summarize.

Document location of evidence (i.e., syllabus, assignment). Attach and notate.

Suggestions for improvement:

Action

The instructor allows the students to demonstrate mastery of the objectives and ability to learn from mistakes.

Rubric Scoring

☐ Uses instructor-centered approaches = 0
☐ Minimally uses learning-centered approaches = 1
☐ Mostly uses learning-centered approaches = 3
☐ Extensively uses learning-centered approaches = 4
☐ No evidence to support rating = NA

Evidence to support this rating: Briefly summarize.

Document location of evidence (i.e., syllabus, assignment). Attach and notate.

Suggestions for improvement:

Action

The instructor uses authentic assessment.

Rubric Scoring

☐ Uses instructor-centered approaches = 0
☐ Minimally uses learning-centered approaches = 1
☐ Mostly uses learning-centered approaches = 3
☐ Extensively uses learning-centered approaches = 4
☐ No evidence to support rating = NA

Evidence to support this rating: Briefly summarize.

Document location of evidence (i.e., syllabus, assignment). Attach and notate.

Suggestions for improvement:

Construct V: Balance of Power

Action

The instructor establishes a safe, moral, and ethical environment that empowers all students.

Rubric Scoring

☐ Uses instructor-centered approaches = 0
☐ Minimally uses learning-centered approaches = 1
☐ Mostly uses learning-centered approaches = 3
☐ Extensively uses learning-centered approaches = 4
☐ No evidence to support rating = NA

Evidence to support this rating: Briefly summarize.

Document location of evidence (i.e., syllabus, assignment). Attach and notate.

(Continues)

TABLE B.2. (Continued)

Suggestions for improvement:

Action

The instructor provides syllabi and other course artifacts demonstrating that students and instructors share power to promote learning.

Rubric Scoring

☐ Uses instructor-centered approaches = 0
☐ Minimally uses learning-centered approaches = 1
☐ Mostly uses learning-centered approaches = 3
☐ Extensively uses learning-centered approaches = 4
☐ No evidence to support rating = NA

Evidence to support this rating: Briefly summarize.

Document location of evidence (i.e., syllabus, assignment). Attach and notate.

Suggestions for improvement:

Action

The instructor allows for some flexibility on course policies, assessment methods, learning methods, deadlines, or how students earn grades. Instructor informs students of decisions.

Rubric Scoring

☐ Uses instructor-centered approaches = 0
☐ Minimally uses learning-centered approaches = 1
☐ Mostly uses learning-centered approaches = 3
☐ Extensively uses learning-centered approaches = 4
☐ No evidence to support rating = NA

Evidence to support this rating: Briefly summarize.

Document location of evidence (i.e., syllabus, assignment). Attach and notate.

Suggestions for improvement:

Action

The instructor provides students opportunities to learn and helps students to recognize when they have missed opportunities to learn.

Rubric Scoring

☐ Uses instructor-centered approaches = 0
☐ Minimally uses learning-centered approaches = 1
☐ Mostly uses learning-centered approaches = 3
☐ Extensively uses learning-centered approaches = 4
☐ No evidence to support rating = NA

Evidence to support this rating: Briefly summarize.

Document location of evidence (i.e., syllabus, assignment). Attach and notate.

Suggestions for improvement:

Action

The instructor empowers students learning through appropriate freedom of expression.

Rubric Scoring

☐ Uses instructor-centered approaches = 0
☐ Minimally uses learning-centered approaches = 1
☐ Mostly uses learning-centered approaches = 3
☐ Extensively uses learning-centered approaches = 4
☐ No evidence to support rating = NA

Evidence to support this rating: Briefly summarize.

Document location of evidence (i.e., syllabus, assignment). Attach and notate.

Suggestions for improvement:

(Continues)

TABLE B.2. (Continued)

Action
The instructor responds to feedback from students to improve teaching and learning.

Rubric Scoring

☐ Uses instructor-centered approaches = 0
☐ Minimally uses learning-centered approaches = 1
☐ Mostly uses learning-centered approaches = 3
☐ Extensively uses learning-centered approaches = 4
☐ No evidence to support rating = NA

Evidence to support this rating: Briefly summarize.

Document location of evidence (i.e., syllabus, assignment). Attach and notate.

Suggestions for improvement:

Aggregate all of these individual scores onto Table C.1 in Appendix C.

Appendix C: Template for Summary of Rubric Scores on All Actions by Construct

Table C.1 is a template to record all rubric scores. This aggregates all the individual rubric scores recorded on Table B.2 in Appendix B.

You can use this template to look at your changes over time.

This template can be shared with others to document teaching effectiveness and how you changed your teaching over time.

You also can copy this template onto a computer spreadsheet.

TABLE C.1 Learning-Centered Teaching Summary of Rubric Scores on All Actions by Construct

Instructor_____

Date _____ Course(s) reviewed_____

Teaching materials reviewed_____

_____

	Constructs				
Action	*Role of Instructor*	*Responsibility for Learning*	*Function of Content*	*Student Assessment*	*Balance of Power*
Action 1 *Score (0, 1, 3, or 4 for each action)*	Learning outcomes	Set expectations	Organizing schemes	Integrate assessment and learning	Moral and ethical environment
Action 2 *Score (0, 1, 3, or 4 for each action)*	Teaching/learning activities	Scaffolding	Engagement with content	Assessment policies and standards	Welcoming syllabus
Action 3 *Score (0, 1, 3, or 4 for each action)*	Course alignment	Learning skills	Discipline specific methods	Timely formative feedback	Flexibility
Action 4 *Score (0, 1, 3, or 4 for each action)*	Environment for success	Self-directed learning	Understand why learn	Peer and self-assessment	Opportunities to learn

(Continues)

Vist the Stylus Publishing website at https://styluspub.presswarehouse.com/browse/book/9781620368954/Making-Learning-Centered-Teaching-Work to download a PDF of Appendix C.

TABLE B.2. (Continued)

Action 5 Score (0, 1, 3, or 4 for each action)	Inclusive, welcoming environment	Reflection, review	Inquiry in discipline	Demonstrate mastery	Freedom of expression
Action 6 Score (0, 1, 3, or 4 for each action)	Explicit about methods	Metacognitive skills	Fosters future learning	Authentic assessment	Responds to student feedback

Construct (Column) Summaries					
Action	*Role of Instructor*	*Responsibility for Learning*	*Function of Content*	*Student Assessment*	*Balance of Power*
Percent instructor-centered (scored as 0)					
Percent minimally learning-centered (scored as 1)					
Percent mostly learning-centered (scored as 3)					
Percent extensively learning-centered (scored as 4)					
Dichotomous Summary of Scores					
Total percentage not learning-centered (scored as 0–1)					
Total percentage learning-centered (scored as 3–4)					
Range					
Mode (most frequent score)					

Type of Assessment:

☐ Baseline (Pre-intervention)　☐ Post-intervention 1　☐　Post-intervention 2

Key:

0 = Uses instructor-centered approaches

1 = Minimally uses learning-centered approaches

3 = Mostly uses learning-centered approaches

4 = Extensively uses learning-centered approaches

Notes:

1. Because instructors or courses can indicate behaviors at more than one level for each action, additional scores such as 2 or 3.5 are possible. Therefore, you can modify the column summaries to reflect these scores.
2. Since this is intentionally an ordinal and not an interval scale, do not report the means and standard deviations.

References

Abdelmalak, M., & Trespalacios, J. (2013). Using a learner-centered approach to develop an educational technology course. *International Journal of Teaching & Learning in Higher Education, 25*(3), 324–332.

Alexander, P. A., & Murphy, P. K. (1998). The research base for APA's learner-centered psychological principles. In N. M. Lambert & B. L. McCombs (Eds.), *How students learn* (pp. 25–60). Washington DC: American Psychological Association.

Altman, W., & Miller, R. (2017). What to do when students bomb the exam. In R. Obeid, A. Schwartz, C. Shane-Simpson, & P. J. Brooks (Eds.), *How we teach now: The GSTA guide to student-centered teaching* (pp 153–163). Washington DC: Society for the Teaching of Psychology. Retrieved from https://teachpsych.org/ebooks/howweteachnow

Al-Zu'be, M. F. A. (2013). The difference between the learner-centred approach and the teacher-centred approach in teaching English as a foreign language. *Educational Research International, 2*(2), 24–31. Retrieved from http://www.erint.savap.org.pk/PDF/Vol.2(2)/ERInt.2013(2.2-04).pdf

Ambrose, S. A., Bridges, M. W., DiPietro, M., Lovett, M. C., & Norman, M. K. (2010). *How learning works.* San Francisco, CA: Jossey-Bass.

American Council on Education. (2018). *ACE research outlines best practices to support effective teaching and improve student learning.* Retrieved from https://www.acenet.edu/news-room/Pages/ACE-Research-Outlines-Best-Practices-to-Support-Teachers-and-Improve-Student-Learning.aspx

American Psychological Association. (1997). *Learner-centered psychological principles: A framework for school reform and redesign.* Retrieved from http://www.apa.org/ed/governance/bea/learner-centered.pdf

American Society for Quality. (2016). *Strengths, opportunities, aspirations, results (SOAR) analysis.* Retrieved from http://asqservicequality.org/glossary/strengths-opportunities-aspirations-results-soar-analysis/

Anderson, L. W., Krathwohl, D. R., Airasian, P. W., Cruikshank, K. A., Mayer, R. E., Pintrich, P. R., . . . Wittrock, M. C. (2001). *A taxonomy for learning, teaching, and assessing.* New York, NY: Longman.

Angelo, T. A., & Cross, K. P. (1993). *Classroom assessment techniques* (2nd ed.). San Francisco, CA: Jossey-Bass.

Arceo, F. D. B. (2016). Learner-centred curriculum revisited. *European Journal of Curriculum Studies, 3*(2), 505–519.

Arum, R., & Roksa, J. (2011). *Academically adrift.* Chicago, IL: University of Chicago Press.

Association of College and Research Libraries (ACRL). (2016). *Guidelines, standards, and frameworks, American Library Association, July 24, 2006.* Retrieved from http://www.ala.org/acrl/standards (Document ID: fdbf8f68-a665-9144-41f6-b4f1abc82f4a)

Austin, A., & McDaniels, M. (2006). Preparing the professoriate of the future: Graduate student socialization for faculty roles. In J. C. Smart (Ed.), *Higher Education: Handbook of Theory and Research* (Vol. 21, pp. 397–456). Dordrecht, Netherlands: Springer Netherlands.

Bach, D. J., Wei, P., Inkelas, K. K., & Riewerts, K. (2016). Introducing and assessing learning-focused course design at the University of Virginia, USA and at Bielefeld University, Germany. *Die Hochschullehre Zitiervorschlag.* Retrieved from http://www.hochschullehre.org/wp-content/files/diehochschullehre_2016_bach_et_al.pdf

Baepler, P., Walker, J. D., Brooks, D. C., Saichaie, K., Petersen, C., & Cohen, B. A. (2016). *A guide to teaching in the active learning classroom: History, research, and practice.* Sterling, VA: Stylus.

Bain, K. (2004). *What the best college teachers do.* Cambridge, MA: Harvard University Press.

Barr, R. B., & Tagg, J. (1995). From teaching to learning: A new paradigm for undergraduate education. *Change, 27*, 12–25.

Barrett, B. (2013). Strategies for enhancing HRM courses: Transforming theory into hands-on applications. In V. Ribiere & L Worasinchai (Eds.), *Proceedings of the International Conference on Management, Leadership and Governance: ICMLG 2013* (pp. 18–24). Retrieved from https://books.google.com/books?id=KkIBAAAQBAJ&dq=Barrett%2C+B.+%282013%29.+Strategies+for+enhancing+HRM+courses%3A+Transforming+theory+into+hands-on+applications.+Management%2C+Leadership+and+Governance%2C&q=

Bean, J. C. (2011). *Engaging ideas* (2nd ed.). San Francisco, CA: Jossey-Bass.

Beichner, B., & Isern, S. (2017). *Scale-up.* Pedagogy in Action. Retrieved from https://serc.carleton.edu/sp/library/scaleup/index.html

Beichner, R. J., Saul, J. M., Abbott, D. S., Morse, J. J., Deardorff, D., Allain, R. J. . . . Risley, J. S. (2007). The student-centered activities for large enrollment undergraduate programs (SCALE-UP) project. *Research-Based Reform of University Physics, 1*(1), 2–39.

Bekkers, R., & Bombaerts, G. (2017). Introducing broad skills in higher engineering education: The patents and standards courses at Eindhoven University of Technology. *Technology & Innovation, 19*(2), 493–507.

Benninga, J. S. (2003). Moral and ethical issues in teacher education. *ERIC Digest.* ED482699 2003-10-00

Biggs, J. (1999). *Teaching for quality learning at university.* Buckingham, UK: Open University Press.

Blackburn, R., & Lawrence, J. (1995*). Faculty at work: Motivation, expectation and satisfaction.* Baltimore, MD: Johns Hopkins Press.

Blomgren, O. (2015). Group project: Turning students into teachers. In J. Fletcher, A. Najarro, & H. Yelland (Eds.), *Fostering habits of mind in today's students: A new approach to developmental education* (pp. 181–187). Sterling, VA: Stylus.

Bloom, B. S. (Ed.). (1956). *Taxonomy of educational objectives: The classification of educational goals—Handbook I: Cognitive domain.* New York, NY: McKay.

Blumberg, P. (2009). *Developing learner-centered teaching: A practical guide for faculty.* San Francisco, CA: Jossey-Bass.

Blumberg, P. (2014). *Assessing and improving your teaching: Strategies and rubrics for faculty growth and student learning.* San Francisco, CA: Jossey-Bass.

Blumberg, P. (2015). How critical reflection benefits faculty as they implement learner-centered teaching. *New Directions for Teaching and Learning, 144,* 87–97.

Blumberg, P. (2016a). Assessing implementation of learner-centered teaching while providing faculty development. *College Teaching, 64*(4), 194–203.

Blumberg, P. (2016b). Factors that influence faculty adoption of learning-centered approaches. *Innovative Higher Education, 41*(4), 303–315.

Blumberg, P. (2017a). Academic program assessment: A new expertise for faculty to develop. *The Journal of Faculty Development, 31*(3), 31–37. Retrieved from https://search.proquest.com/docview/2036983217

Blumberg, P. (2017b). Educational development efforts aligned with the assessment cycle. *To Improve the Academy, 36*(1), 50–60.

Blumberg, P. (2018). Two underused, best practices for improvement-focused assessments. *Research & Practice in Assessment, 13*(Summer/Fall), 77–83.

Blumberg, P. (2019). Designing for effective group process in PBL using a learner-centered teaching approach. In M. Moallem, W. Hung, & N. Dabbagh (Eds.), *The Wiley handbook of problem-based learning* (pp. 343–365). New York, NY: Wiley.

Blumberg, P., & Pontiggia, L. (2011). Benchmarking the learner-centered status of courses. *Innovative Higher Education, 46*(3), 189–202.

Board on Science Education, Division on Behavioral and Social Sciences and Education, National Research Council. (2015). *Reaching students: What research says about effective instruction in undergraduate science and engineering.* Washington DC: National Academies Press.

Bok, D. (2015). *Higher education in America* (revised ed.). Princeton, NJ: Princeton University Press. Retrieved from http://www.fachportal-paedagogik.de/fis_bildung/suche/fis_set.html?FId=1028485

Boud, D. (2012). *Developing student autonomy in learning.* New York, NY: Routledge.

Bransford, J. D., Brown, A. L., & Cocking, R. R. (2000). *How people learn: Brain, mind, experiences and school.* Washington DC: National Academies Press.

Brookfield, S. (1985). Self-directed learning: A critical review of research. *New Directions for Adult and Continuing Education, 25,* 5–16.

Brosowsky, N. P., & Parshina, O. (2017). Using the QALMRI method to scaffold reading of primary sources. In R. Obeid, A. Schwartz, C. Shane-Simpson, & P. J. Brooks (Eds.), *How we teach now: The GSTA guide to student-centered teaching* (pp. 297–299). Washington DC: Society for the Teaching of Psychology. Retrieved from https://teachpsych.org/ebooks/howweteachnow

Brown, J. (2007). Feedback: The student perspective. *Research in Post-Compulsory Education, 12*(1), 33–51.

Burchfield, C. M., & Sappington, J. (2000). Compliance with required reading assignments. *Teaching of Psychology.* Retrieved from http://psycnet.apa.org/record/2000-07173-017

Butler, L. (2013). Effective teaching methods to engage human services students: A closer look at learner-centered teaching. *2012 NOHS National Conference Proceedings* (p. 23). Retrieved from https://www.nationalhumanservices.org/assets/documents/2012-nohs-conference-proceedings.pdf#page=24

Byrne, L. B. (2016). *Learner-centered teaching activities for environmental and sustainability studies* (ed.). New York, NY: Springer.

Cañas, A. J., & Novak, J. D. (2010). The theory underlying concept maps and how to construct and use them. *Práxis Educativa, 5*(1), 9–29. Retrieved from https://doaj.org/article/400f40862ec049fd9496936f41766236

Candy, P. C., Crebert, G., & O'Leary, J. (1994). *Developing lifelong learners through undergraduate education.* Canberra, Australia: Australian Government Publishing Service (AGPS).

Carr, N. G. (2010). *The shallows: What the Internet is doing to our brains.* New York, NY: Norton.

Center for Educational Innovation, University of Minnesota. (2016). *Teaching in active learning classrooms (ALC).* Retrieved from https://cei.umn.edu/teaching-active-learning-classroom-alc

Chen, X. (2013). *STEM attrition: College students' paths into and out of STEM fields* (NCES 2014-001). Washington DC: National Center for Education Statistics, U.S. Department of Education.

Colbeck, C. L., Campbell, S. E., &. Bjorklund, S. A. (2000). Grouping in the dark: What college students learn from group projects. *The Journal of Higher Education, 71*(1), 60–83.

Collier, P. J., & Morgan, D. L. (2008). "Is that paper really due today?" Differences in first-generation and traditional college students' understandings of faculty expectations. *Higher Education, 55*(4), 425–446.

Cornelius-White, J. (2007). Learner-centered teacher-student relationships are effective: A meta-analysis. *Review of Educational Research, 77*(1), 113–143.

Costa, A. L., & Kallick, B. (2008). *Learning and leading with habits of mind: 16 essential characteristics for success.* Retrieved from http://www.chsvt.org/wdp/Habits_of_Mind.pdf

Davis, T. A. (2013). Connecting students to content: Student-generated questions. *Bioscene: Journal of College Biology Teaching, 39*(2), 32–34.

Divoll, K., & Browning, S. (2013). "Read the text, as if!" The reading retention strategy. *International Journal for the Scholarship of Teaching and Learning, 7*(1), article 8.

Dolan, J., Kain, K., Reilly, J., & Bansal, G. (2017). How do you build community and foster engagement in online courses? *New Directions for Teaching and Learning, 151,* 45–60.

Doyle, T. (2008). *Helping students learn in a learner-centered environment.* Sterling, VA: Stylus.

Doyle, T. (2011). *Learner-centered teaching: Putting the research on learning into practice.* Sterling, VA: Stylus.

Dunlosky, J., Rawson, K. A., Marsh, E. J., Nathan, M. J., & Willingham, D. T. (2013). Improving students' learning with effective learning techniques: Promising directions from cognitive and educational psychology. *Psychological Science in the Public Interest, 14*(1), 4–58.

Dweck, C. S. (2008). *Mindset: The new psychology of success.* New York, NY: Random House Digital.

Elder, V. K. (2014). *Benchmarking the use of learner-centered teaching practices in Missouri community colleges* (Doctoral dissertation, Lindenwood University). Retrieved from https://search.proquest.com/docview/1530298464

Eliason, S., & Holmes, C. L. (2012). A course redesign project to change faculty; orientation toward teaching. *Journal of the Scholarship of Teaching and Learning, 12*(1), 36–48.

Ellis, D. E. (2013). *Students' responses to innovative instructional methods: Exploring learning-centred methods and barriers to change* (Doctoral dissertation, University of Waterloo, Waterloo, Canada). Retrieved from https://uwspace.uwaterloo.ca/bitstream/handle/10012/7414/Ellis_Donna.pdf?sequence=1

Ellis, D. E. (2015). What discourages students from engaging with innovative instructional methods: Creating a barrier framework. *Innovative Higher Education, 40*(2), 111.

Ellis, D. M. (2015). The role of nurse educators' self-perception and beliefs in the use of learner-centered teaching in the classroom. *Nurse Education in Practice, 16*(1), 66–70.

European Association for Quality Assurance in Higher Education. (2009). *Standards and guidelines for quality assurance in the European Higher Education Area* (3rd ed.). Helsinki, Finland: ENQA. Retrieved from http://www.enqa.eu/wp-content/uploads/2013/06/ESG_3edition-2.pdf

Evergreen, S. (2017). *Effective data visualizations: The right chart for the right data.* Thousand Oaks, CA: Sage.

Federe, M., & Leishman, C. (2014). Developing a learner-centered Pashto curriculum for specific purposes: A case study. *Proceedings of the 1st Conference on Central Asian Languages and Linguistics* (pp. 143–153). Retrieved from http://citeseerx.ist.psu.edu/viewdoc/download?doi=10.1.1.901.1180&rep=rep1&type=pdf

Felder, R. M., & Brent, R. (2016). *Teaching and learning STEM.* San Francisco, CA: Jossey-Bass.

Ficek, A. (2015). Visualizing descriptive statistics with dot plots. *AEA365: A tip-a-day by and for evaluators* (American Evaluation Association). Retrieved from https://aea365.org/blog/angie-ficek-on-visualizing-descriptive-statistics-with-dot-plots/

Fink, L. D. (2013). *Creating significant learning experiences* (2nd ed.). San Francisco, CA: Jossey-Bass.

Fletcher, J., Najarro, A., & Yelland, H. (2015). *Fostering habits of mind in today's students: A new approach to developmental education.* Sterling, VA: Stylus.

Fox, R. (2001). Constructivism examined. *Oxford Review of Education, 27*(1), 23–35.

Freeman, S., Eddy, S. L., McDonough, M., Smith, M. K., Okoroafor, N., Jordt, H., & Wenderoth, M. P. (2014). Active learning boosts performance in STEM courses. *Proceedings of the National Academy of Sciences, 111*(23), 8410–8415.

Gray, C. M. (2013). Informal peer critique and the negotiation of habitus in a design studio. *Art, Design & Communication in Higher Education, 12*(2), 195–209.

Gronlund, N. E., & Brookhart, S. M. (2009). *Gronlund's writing instructional objectives* (8th ed.). Upper Saddle River, NJ: Pearson Education.

Haras, C., Taylor, S. C., Sorcinelli, M. D., & von Hoene, L. (2017). *Institutional commitment to teaching excellence.* Washington DC: American Council on Education (ACE).

Harris, M., & Cullen, R. (2010). *Leading the learner-centered campus: An administrator's framework for improving student learning outcomes.* San Francisco, CA: Jossey-Bass.

Hoy, A. W., & Hoy, W. K. (2009). *Instructional leadership: A research based guide to learning in schools.* Boston, MA: Pearson.

Huba, M. E., & Freed, J. E. (2000). *Learner-centered assessment on college campuses: Shifting the focus from teaching to learning.* Needham Heights, MA: Allyn & Bacon.

Ikenberry, S. O., & Kuh, G. D. (2015). From compliance to ownership: Why and how colleges and universities assess student learning. In G. Kun, S. Ikenberry, N. Jankowski, T. Cain, P. Ewell, P. Hutchings, & J. Kinzue (Eds.), *Using evidence of student learning to improve student learning* (pp. 1–23). San Francisco, CA: Jossey-Bass.

James, A., & Brookfield, S. D. (2014). *Engaging imagination.* San Francisco, CA: Jossey-Bass.

Jansson, S., Soderstrom, H., Andersson, P. L., & Nording, M. L. (2015). Implementation of problem-based learning in environmental chemistry. *Journal of Chemical Education, 92*(12), 2080. Retrieved from https://search.proquest.com/docview/1750054201

Johnson, M. L. (2013). Faculty perception and use of learning-centered strategies to assess student performance. *Social Science Premium Collection.* Retrieved from https://search.proquest.com/docview/1437014373

Kaplan, M., Silver, N., LaVaque-Manty, D., & Meizlish, D. (2013). *Using reflection and metacognition to improve student learning: Across the disciplines, across the academy.* Sterling, VA: Stylus.

Keamy, R. L., Nicholas, H. R., Mahar, S., & Herrick, C. (2007). *Personalising education: From research to policy and practice.* Melbourne, Australia: Office for Education Policy and Innovation, Department of Education and Early Childhood Development.

Keeney-Kennicutt, W., Gunersel, B., A., & Simpson, N. (2008). Overcoming student resistance to a teaching innovation. *International Journal for the Scholarship of Teaching and Learning, 2*(1), article 5. Retrieved from https://files.eric.ed.gov/fulltext/EJ1136783.pdf

Kernahan, C., & Chick, N. L. (2017). How do you listen to your students to help them learn about race and racism? *New Directions for Teaching and Learning, 151,* 17–30.

Knouse, S. M., Gupton, T., & Abreu, L. (2015). *Teaching Hispanic linguistics: Strategies to engage learners. Hispania 98*(2), 319–332. American Association of Teachers of Spanish and Portuguese.

Kolb, D. A. (1984). *Experiential learning: Experience as a source of learning and development.* Englewood Cliffs, NJ: Prentice-Hall.

Kreniske, P., & Todorova, R. (2017). Using blogs to engage first-generation college students. In R. Obeid, A. Schwartz, C. Shane-Simpson, & P. J. Brooks (Eds.), *How we teach now: The GSTA guide to student-centered teaching,* (pp. 283–296). Washington DC: Society for the Teaching of Psychology. Retrieved from https://teachpsych.org/ebooks/howweteachnow

Kuh, G. D. (2008). *High-impact educational practices.* Washington DC: Association of American Colleges and Universities.

Kuh, G. D. (2009). *The national survey of student engagement: Conceptual and empirical foundations.* San Francisco, CA: Jossey-Bass.

Kuh, G., Ikenberry, S., Jankowski, N., Cain, T., Ewell, P., Hutchings, P., & Kinzie, J. (Eds.). (2015). *Using evidence of student learning to improve higher education.* San Francisco, CA: Jossey-Bass.

Kuh, G. D., Kinzie, J., Schuh, J. H., & Whitt, E. J. (2010). *Student success in college.* San Francisco, CA: Jossey-Bass.

Kuh, G. D., Kinzie, J., Schuh, J. H., & Whitt, E. J. (2011). Fostering student success in hard times. *Change: The Magazine of Higher Learning, 43*(4), 13–19.

Kuit, T., & Fildes, K. (2014). *Changing curriculum design to engage students to develop lifelong learning skills in biology.* Sydney, Australia: University of Sydney. Retrieved from http://openjournals.library.usyd.edu.au/index.php/CAL/article/view/8253

Laird, T. F. N., Shoup, R., Kuh, G. D., & Schwarz, M. J. (2008). The effects of discipline on deep approaches to student learning and college outcomes. *Research in Higher Education, 49*(6), 469–494.

Lange, D. R., & Simkins, B. J. (2013). *Employee benefit and retirement planning: A learner-centered teaching approach.* Retrieved from https://academyfinancial.org/resources/Documents/Proceedings/2013/G1_Lange_Simkins.pdf

Lee, E., & Hannafin, M. (2016). A design framework for enhancing engagement in student-centered learning: Own it, learn it, and share it. *Educational Technology Research and Development, 64*(4), 707–734.

Lewandowski, G. W. Jr., Ciarocco, N. J., & Strohmetz, D. B. (2017). Research methods 2.0: A new approach for today's students. In R. Obeid, A. Schwartz, C. Shane-Simpson, & P. J. Brooks (Eds.), *How we teach now: The GSTA guide to student-centered teaching* (pp. 311–327). Washington DC: Society for the Teaching of Psychology. Retrieved from https://teachpsych.org/ebooks/howweteachnow

Lipnevich, A. A., McCallen, L. N., Miles, K. P., & Smith, J. K. (2014). Mind the gap! Students' use of exemplars and detailed rubrics as formative assessment. *Instructional Science, 42*(4), 539–559.

Lobasz, J., & Valeriano, B. (2015). Teaching international relations with film and literature: Using non-traditional texts in the classroom. *Handbook on Teaching and Learning in Political Science and International Relations, 33,* 399.

Ludwig, M. A., Bentz, A. E., & Fynewever, H. (2011). Your syllabus should set the stage for assessment for learning. *Journal of College Science Teaching, 40*(4), 20–23. Retrieved from https://www.jstor.org/stable/42992873

Lueddeke, G. R. (2003). Professionalising teaching practice in higher education: A study of disciplinary variation and "teaching-scholarship." *Studies in Higher Education, 28*(2), 213–228.

Lund, T. J., Pilarz, M., Velasco, J. B., Chakraverty, D., Rosploch, K., Undersander, M., & Stains, M. (2015). The best of both worlds: Building on the COPUS and RTOP observation protocols to easily and reliably measure various levels of reformed instructional practice. *CBE Life Sciences Education, 14*(2). Retrieved from http://www.ncbi-nlm-nih-gov.db.usciences.edu/pubmed/25976654

Mahalingam, M., & Fasella, E. (2017). Effective use of technology for asynchronous learning to elevate students' knowledge and problem solving ability. In S. P. Ferris & H. A. Wilder (Eds.), *Unplugging from the classroom* (pp 149–158). Cambridge, MA: Chandos.

Mahalingam, M., Schaefer, F., & Morlino, E. (2008). Promoting student learning through group problem solving in general chemistry recitations. *Journal of Chemical Education, 85*(11), 1577–1581.

Mahmoud, A. (2016). Learner-centered group work in multi-level EFL classes. *Arab World English Journal, 7*(2), 7. Retrieved from http://gateway.proquest.com/openurl?ctx_ver=Z39.88-2003&xri:pqil:res_ver=0.2&res_id=xri:ilcs-us&rft_id=xri:ilcs:rec:abell:R05516319

Mazur, E. (1997). *Peer instruction: A user's manual.* Upper Saddle River, NJ: Prentice Hall.

McCombs, B. (2015). Learner-centered online instruction. *New Directions for Teaching and Learning, 2015*(144), 57–71.

McFarland, J., Hussar, B., de Brey, C., Snyder, T., Wang, X., Wilkinson-Flicker, S. . . . Bullock Mann, F. (2017). *The condition of education 2017* (NCES 2017-144). Washington DC: National Center for Education Statistics, U.S. Department of Education.

McGuire, S. Y., & McGuire, S. (2015). *Teach students how to learn: Strategies you can incorporate into any course to improve student metacognition, study skills, and motivation.* Sterling, VA: Stylus.

McKeachie, W. J. (2007). Good teaching makes a difference—and we know what it is. In R. P. Perry & J. C.

Smart (Eds.), *The scholarship of teaching and learning in higher education: An evidence-based perspective* (pp. 457–474). Dordrecht, Netherlands: Springer.

Michael, J. (2007). Faculty perceptions about barriers to active learning. *College Teaching, 55*(2), 42–47.

Miller, C. W. (2010). "Psalms are not interesting": Learner-centered approaches to teaching biblical poetry and the psalms. In F. R. Ames & C. W. Miller (Eds.), *Foster biblical scholarship: Essays in honor of Kent Harold Richards* (pp. 189–214). Atlanta, GA: Society of Biblical Literature.

Millis, B. J. (2010). *Cooperative learning in higher education.* Sterling, VA: Stylus.

Moog, R. (n.d.). The POGIL Project team. *POGIL.* Retrieved from https://www.pogil.org/educators/become-a-pogil-practitioner/curricular-materials

Moon, J. A. (2006). *Learning journals: A handbook for reflective practice and professional development* (2nd ed.). New York, NY: Routledge.

Mostrom, A., & Blumberg, P. (2012). Does learning-centered teaching promote grade improvement? *Innovative Higher Education, 37*(5), 397–405.

Myers, C. B., & Myers, S. M. (2015). The use of learner-centered assessment practices in the United States: The influence of individual and institutional contexts. *Studies in Higher Education, 40*(10), 1904–1918.

Naruemon, D. (2013). *Thai pre-service teachers' beliefs about the learner-centered approach and their classroom practices* (Doctoral dissertation, University of Newcastle, Callaghan, Australia). Retrieved from https://search.proquest.com/docview/1810881087

National Academies of Sciences, Engineering, and Medicine. (2018). *How people learn II: Learners, contexts, and cultures.* Washington D.C: The National Academies Press.

Nicol, D., Thomson, A., & Breslin, C. (2014). Rethinking feedback practices in higher education: A peer review perspective. *Assessment & Evaluation in Higher Education, 39*(1), 102–122.

Nilson, L. B. (2010). *Teaching at its best* (3rd ed.). Bolton, MA: Anker.

Nilson, L. B. (2012). Time to raise questions about student ratings. *To Improve the Academy, 31*(1), 213–228.

Nilson, L., & Stanny, C. J. (2015). Specifications grading: Restoring rigor, motivating students, and saving faculty time. Sterling, VA: Stylus.

Njoku, A., Wakeel, F., Reger, M., Jadhav, E., & Rowan, J. (2017). Developing a learner-centered curriculum for a rural public health program. *International Journal of Teaching and Learning in Higher Education, 29*(3), 560–570.

Oakley, B., Felder, R. M., Brent, R., & Elhajj, I. (2004). Turning student groups into effective teams. *Journal of Student Centered Learning, 2*(1), 9–23.

Obeid, R., Schwartz, A., Shane-Simpson, C., & Brooks, P. J. (Eds.). (2017). *How we teach now, A GSTA guide to student-centered teaching.* Washington DC: Society for the Teaching of Psychology. Retrieved from https://teachpsych.org/ebooks/howweteachnow

Palmer, M. S., Bach, D. J., & Streifer, A. C. (2014). Measuring the promise: A Learning-Focused syllabus rubric. *To Improve the Academy, 33*(1), 14–36.

Pape-Zambito, D., & Mostrom, A. (2014). *A formal active mentoring program for teachers and its implementation.* Retrieved from lillyconferences.com/bethesda/presenters(2014)

Paquette, K., & Trudel, P. (2018). Learner-centered coach education: Practical recommendations for coach development administrators. *International Sport Coaching Journal, 5*(2), 1–7.

Pascarella, E. T., & Terenzini, P. T. (2005). *How college affects students: Vol. 2. A third decade of research.* San Francisco, CA: Jossey-Bass.

Pashler, H., McDaniel, M., Rohrer, D., & Bjork, R. (2008). Learning styles concepts and evidence. *Psychological Science in the Public Interest, 9*(3), 105–119.

Pereira, D. A. R. (2016). *Assessment in higher education and quality of learning: Perceptions, practices and implications* (Unpublished doctoral dissertation). Universidade do Minho, Braga, Portugal.

Piskadlo, K. S. (2016). *A case study on the influence of organizational structures and policies on faculty implementation of learner-centered teaching* (Doctoral dissertation, University of Massachusetts). Retrieved from https://search.proquest.com/docview/1803936469

Polich, S. (2007). Assessment of a faculty learning community program: Do faculty members really change? *To Improve the Academy, 26*(1), 106–118.

Prochaska, J. O., Redding, C. A., & Evers, K. (2002). The trans-theoretical model and stages of change. In K. Glanz, B. K. Rimer, & F. M. Lewis (Eds.), *Health behavior and health education: Theory, research, and practice* (3rd ed., p. 8). San Francisco, CA: Jossey-Bass.

Ramsden, P. (2003). *Learning to teach in higher education* (2nd ed.). London, UK: RoutledgeFalmer.

Revkin, A. (2014, January 23). Ursula King, Andrew Revkin, and David Sloan Wilson—Teilhard de Chardin's "planetary mind" and our spiritual evolution [Radio show]. From Krista Tippett, *On Being* (NPR). Retrieved from http://www.onbeing.org/program/teilhard-de-chardin-on-the-planetary-mind-and-our-spiritual-evolution/transcript/6112#main_content

Rice, L. L. (2015). *Teaching beliefs and instructional practices of award-winning faculty at two agricultural universities* (Doctoral dissertation, Pennsylvania State University). Retrieved from https://search.proquest.com/docview/1734868184

Richmond, A. S., Boysen, G. A., Regan, A. R. G., Tazeau, Y. N., Meyers, S. A., & Sciutto, M. J. (2014). Aspirational model teaching criteria for psychology. *Teaching of Psychology, 41*(4), 281–295.

Roediger, H. L. III, & Karpicke, J. D. (2006). Test-enhanced learning: Taking memory tests improves long-term retention. *Psychological Science, 17*(3), 249–255.

Rogers, E. (2003). *Diffusion of innovations* (5th ed.). Delran, NJ: Simon & Schuster.

SALG. (2013). *Student Assessment of their Learning Gains* [Survey]. Retrieved from http://www.salgsite.org.

Sawatsky, A., Ratelle, J., Bonnes, S., Egginton, J., & Beckman, T. (2017). Faculty support for self-directed learning in internal medicine residency: A qualitative study using grounded theory. *Academic Medicine, 93*(6), 943–951.

Schon, D. (1987). *Educating the reflective practitioner.* San Francisco, CA: Jossey-Bass.

Schroeder, S. J. (2012). Infusing learner-centered strategies into the classroom. *Occupational Therapy in Health Care, 26*(4), 218–223.

Schunk, D. H. (2016). *Learning theories: An educational perspective* (7th ed.). Boston, MA: Pearson.

Schuster, J. H., & Finkelstein, M. J. (2008). *The American faculty: The restructuring of academic work and careers.* Baltimore, MD: Johns Hopkins University Press.

Schwenn, J. O., & Codjoe, H. (2013). *Quality enhancement plan. Improving the academic performance of high-risk students through learning support English* (Getting on the "Write" Path, Dalton State College). Retrieved from https://www.daltonstate.edu/skins/userfiles/files/institutional-research-and-planning/sacs-accreditation-reports/pdf/dsc-quality-enhancement-plan-sept-2012.pdf

Shulman, L. S. (2004). *Teaching as community property.* San Francisco, CA: Jossey-Bass.

Simon, E. (2014). Teaching political science research methods in Hungary: Transferring student-centred teaching practices into a subject-focused academic culture. *European Political Science, 13*(1), 78–95.

Sohn, B. K. (2016). *The student experience of other students.* Sterling, VA: Stylus.

Stains, M., Pilarz, M., & Chakraverty, D. (2015). Short and long-term impacts of the Cottrell scholars' collaborative new faculty workshop. *Journal of Chemical Education, 92*(9), 1466. Retrieved from https://search-proquest.com.db.usciences.edu/docview/1712851557

Stevens, D. D., & Cooper, J. E. (2009). *Journal keeping: How to use reflective writing for learning, teaching, professional insight and positive change.* Sterling, VA: Stylus.

Strashnaya, R., & Dow, E. (2017). Purposeful pedagogy through backward course design. In R. Obeid, A. Schwartz, A. Shane Simpson, & P. J. Brooks (Eds.), *How we teach now: The GSTA guide to student-centered teaching* (pp. 82–92). Washington DC: Society for the Teaching of Psychology. Retrieved from https://teachpsych .org/ebooks/howweteachnow

Sursock, A., & Smidt, H. (2010). *Trends 2010: A decade of change in European higher education.* Brussels, Belgium: European University Association.

Suskie, L. (2009). *Assessing student learning* (2nd ed.). San Francisco, CA: Josscy-Bass.

Swan, K. (2003). Learning effectiveness online: What the research tells us. In J. Bourne & J. Moore (Eds.), *Elements of quality online education: Practice and direction* (pp. 13–45). Needham, MA: Sloan Center for Online Education.

Tinto, V. (2010). From theory to action: Exploring the institutional conditions for student retention. In J. C. Smith (Ed.), *Higher education: Handbook of theory and research* (pp. 51–89) New York, NY: Springer.

U.S. Department of Education, Office of Policy, Evaluation, and Policy Development. (2010). *Evaluation of evidence-based practices in online learning: A meta-analysis and review of online learning studies.* Retrieved from http://www.ed.gov/rschstat/eval/tech/evidence-based-practices/finalreport.pdf

Vaughn, S. M. (2014). *Reshaping adjunct faculty training by employing an andragogical approach: An action research study* (Doctoral dissertation, Capella University). Retrieved from https://search.proquest.com/ docview/1620832238

Verst, A. L. (2010). *Outstanding teachers and learner-centered teaching practices at a private liberal arts institution* (Doctoral dissertation, University of Arizona). Retrieved from https://search.proquest.com/docview/500027359?pq-origsite=gscholar

Von der Heidt, T. (2015). Concept maps for assessing change in learning: A study of undergraduate business students in first-year marketing in China. *Assessment & Evaluation in Higher Education, 40*(2), 286–308.

Von der Heidt, T., & Quazi, A. (2013). Enhancing learning-centeredness in marketing principles curriculum. *Australasian Marketing Journal, 21*(4), 250–258.

Vygotsky, L. S. (1978). *Mind in society: The development of higher mental process.* Cambridge, MA: Harvard University Press.

Walvoord, B. E. (1998). *Effective grading.* San Francisco, CA: Jossey-Bass.

Wanner, T., & Palmer, E. (2015). Personalizing learning: Exploring student and teacher perceptions about flexible learning and assessment in a flipped university course. *Computers & Education, 88,* 354–369.

Weiman, C. (2015). A better way to evaluate undergraduate teaching. *Change Magazine, 47,* 6–15.

Weimer, M. (2002). *Learner-centered teaching: Five key changes to practice.* San Francisco, CA: Jossey-Bass.

Weimer, M. (2010). *Inspired college teaching.* San Francisco, CA: Jossey-Bass.

Weimer, M. (2013). *Learner-centered teaching: Five key changes to practice* (2nd ed.). San Francisco, CA: Jossey-Bass.

Wiggins, G. P., & McTighe, J. (2005). *Understanding by design.* Alexandria, VA: Association for Supervision and Curriculum Development.

Williams, B. (2018). "Who's drivin' this bus?" The learner-centered string class. *American String Teacher, 68*(2), 26–31.

Wood, K. H. (2017). Curative pedagogy in the undergraduate theatre historiography classroom. *Theatre Topics, 27*(3), 187–196.

Wright, M. C., Bernstein, J. L., & Williams, R. (2013). The stairs of the ladder keep going up: A case study of hevruta as reflective pedagogy in two universities. In M. Kaplan, N. Silver, D. Iavaque-Manty, & D. Meizlish (Eds.), *Using reflection and metacognition to improve student learning* (pp. 104–121). Sterling, VA: Stylus.

Yuan, H. (2014). *A follow-up study to determine the effectiveness of a faculty development program designed to transition to a student-centered approach at Xi'an Eurasia University in China* (Doctoral dissertation, Duquesne University). Retrieved from https://search-proquest .com.db.usciences.edu/docview/1524022557

About the Author

Phyllis Blumberg is a consultant and presenter focusing on the teaching/learning process, assessment of student learning outcomes, and effective teaching in higher education. From 1999 until 2019, she was the director of the Teaching and Learning Center at the University of the Sciences in Philadelphia, where she was also assistant provost for faculty development, as well as research professor in education and professor of psychology. Blumberg has taught first-year college students through graduate and medical students. She has been working with instructors in the health sciences and the sciences as a faculty developer for over 40 years to help them change their teaching so that their students will learn more.

Blumberg is an internationally recognized educator, presenter, writer, and consultant on teaching effectiveness, promoting deep and lasting learning, as well as assessment of teaching and learning. Blumberg is the author of more than 70 articles on active learning, learning-centered teaching, problem-based learning, and program assessment. Her books include a guidebook on how to implement learner-centered teaching, *Developing Learner-Centered Teaching: A Practical Guide for Faculty* (Jossey-Bass, 2009), which is the foundation for this book, and a book that describes a new way to self-assess and improve teaching, *Assessing and Improving Your Teaching Strategies and Rubrics for Faculty Growth and Student Learning* (Jossey-Bass, 2014).

Blumberg earned her master's degree and doctorate in educational and developmental psychology from the University of Pittsburgh Learning Research and Development Center and her bachelor's degree in psychology from Washington College in Chestertown, Maryland.

Index

Creating Engaging Discussions

Strategies for "Avoiding Crickets" in Any Size Classroom and Online

Jennifer H. Herman and Linda B. Nilson

Foreword by Stephen D. Brookfield

"I've stolen a lot from this book. I regard myself as an avid collector of new pedagogic baubles and love it when I stumble across a new way to engage my students, which I have done many times by reading Herman and Nilson's work. I have no doubt that as you read this book your own collection of discussion-based teaching strategies will be significantly enlarged."—***Stephen D. Brookfield***, *University of St. Thomas, Minneapolis-St. Paul*

"*Creating Engaging Discussions* encourages instructors to have high expectations for, and give serious attention to, discussions. This insightful, practical book not only summarizes best practices, explains common problems, and suggests possible solutions but also helps us to diagnose and frame problems with discussions in the larger context of overall course design, challenging us to think carefully about and make explicit the exact purposes for discussions, vis-a-vis well-conceived course learning goals and assessments."—***Alan Bender***, *Associate Professor, Biology; Indiana University, Bloomington*

Teaching as the Art of Staging

A Scenario-Based College Pedagogy in Action

Anthony Weston

Foreword by Peter Felten

"Do you want to be a truly creative and inspiring instructor? Then you must read Weston's *Teaching as the Art of Staging*. Taking 'student-centered' and 'experiential learning' to whole new levels, this innovative pedagogy relies on staging learning situations and letting your students run with them. Weston deftly demonstrates how you can become an impresario with scenarios, whatever your discipline, by drawing on his broad teaching experience in the sciences, social sciences, and humanities."—***Linda B. Nilson***, *Director Emerita, Office of Teaching Effectiveness and Innovation, Clemson University*

"For those who believe that higher education is stuck in a rut, Anthony Weston's far-ranging and provocative book offers a way out: Instructors can move beyond being energized performers ('sage on the stage') or wise facilitators ('guide on the side') and instead become 'impresarios with scenarios' who educate students by staging powerful active-learning experiences. Weston surveys scores of different 'staging' techniques and supplements them with many ingenious examples from his own classroom."—***Mark C. Carnes***, *Professor of History, Barnard College/ Columbia University, and Executive Director, Reacting Consortium*

22883 Quicksilver Drive
Sterling, VA 20166-2019

Subscribe to our e-mail alerts: www.Styluspub.com

Making Learning-Centered Teaching Work Course Design Institutes and Workshops

Phyllis Blumberg offers *Making Learning-Centered Teaching Work* Course Design Institutes and a variety of related workshops.

Course Design Institutes

A three-day concentrated Course Design Institute provides guidance to instructors in a process that culminates in the design or significant redesign of a course.

Groups of faculty members who teach in a given educational program can design or align a curriculum.

During a Course Design Institute, faculty members will use the practical how-to guidance developed in *Making Learning-Centered Teaching Work* to design a course to improve student learning. Participants will discuss the application of learning-centered teaching to their disciplines and their classes. They will learn how to spend their time facilitating learning and teaching students how to take responsibility for their learning. The newly designed course will incorporate better-designed learning outcomes and engage students.

Registration is open to individual faculty members or groups, or a Course Design Institute can be given on your campus.

In addition, Phyllis offers programs on pedagogy and effective teaching techniques. She shows faculty members how to assess students, student learning outcomes, and educational programs.

Workshops

Workshop topics are customized to serve the needs of an institution or interested faculty members. Given your needs or budget, events can range from a standalone workshop that lasts a few hours to a series of modules on different topics that span several days.

Sample workshops to help faculty implement learning-centered teaching include:

- Course planning: Developing significant and measurable learning outcomes, developing objectives
- Creating an inviting, learning-centered syllabus and course
- Developing student responsibility for learning
- Evidence-based, learning-centered instructional models: Problem-based learning, team-based learning, the flipped classroom
- Fostering success for all students
- Student engagement techniques

For more information or questions contact Blumbergphyllis@gmail.com or visit IntegrateEd.com